FRENCH
PAINTING

CHARLES F. STUCKEY

FRENCH PAINTING

Hugh Lauter Levin Associates, Inc.

Distributed by Macmillan Publishing Company, New York

I dedicate this volume to our baby,

Douglas Leitgen Stuckey, who fills me with wonder

for what his brand-new eyes can see.

CHARLES F. STUCKEY

Copyright © 1991, Hugh Lauter Levin Associates, Inc.

Design by Nai Chang

Editorial production by Harkavy Publishing Service, New York

Photo research by Catherine Stofko

Typeset by U.S. Lithograph, typographers, New York

Printed in Singapore

ISBN 0-88363-973-4

Jacket illustration:

CLAUDE MONET
Garden at Sainte-Adresse, 1867
Oil on canvas, 38⅝ × 51⅛″ (98.1 × 129.9 cm)
The Metropolitan Museum of Art, New York
Purchased with Special Contributions and Purchase Funds
Given or Bequeathed by Friends of the Museum, 1967

Frontispiece:

HENRI MATISSE
Goldfish, 1912
Oil on canvas, 57⅞ × 38⅝″ (147 × 98 cm)
Pushkin Museum of Art, Moscow

Contents

Foreword

SINCE PREHISTORIC TIMES, MANY OF THE MOST WONDERFUL PAINTINGS HAVE BEEN MADE WITHIN the geographical borders of present-day France or by artists who were born within those borders. Although their cave paintings remained undiscovered until 1940, the initiators of the French tradition were the shaman artists who rendered awesome bulls and horses in the main cavern and galleries at Lascaux, datable to around 15,000 B.C. Judging from similar, if less dramatic, discoveries made at other sites beginning in the late nineteenth century, the region between the Rhone River and the Atlantic Ocean was an important zone of prehistoric culture. With so little surviving cave art to study, however, this earliest phase of painting in what would become France is more mystery than history.

It comes as a surprise, but there was a similar near-total loss of the paintings that were made, whatever they may have been, during the course of the next sixteen millennia, until the late Middle Ages. Constant warfare, vandalism, fire, neglect, and disintegration over time share the blame. As a result, the surviving works by almost any one artist active after 1600 outnumber those by all the French painters before 1500 combined. It was only in the mid-nineteenth century that scholars and collectors began to appreciate and search out so-called primitive fifteenth-century French paintings or those done in the next century. Works by members of the Le Nain family were likewise not rediscovered until the mid-nineteenth century, and those by La Tour went unrecognized until just before World War I. It is important to realize from the outset that history is shaped as much by what we cannot or do not yet know as it is by the available facts.

An especially thorough history of French painting, written by Mrs. Clara Harrison Stranahan (1831–1905) for publication in 1888, contains only seven pages covering fifteenth-century works and eight pages for those of the sixteenth-century, compared to fifty-seven and fifty-three pages devoted to painting in the seventeenth and eighteenth centuries, respectively, and 136 pages for nineteenth-century painting. Of course, the need to devote more coverage to recent art is predicated on an explosion in the number of artists, the number of paintings each has produced, the number of collectors and museums, and so on. History as we write it today seems to stress the modern periods simply because advances in record-making and record-keeping make recent history so much "bigger" than earlier history, and contemporary art history is getting bigger still with every new decade. Painters, dealers, and collectors alike now associate historical documentation with artistic achievement; consequently, they generate, distribute, and preserve materials for historians. Burdened by advertising in the guise of criticism, the history of recent art is swelling to the bursting point. Contributing to a false sense of intellectual security, the abundance of information can often be as blinding as a scarcity.

There has been some aggravation for me in having to exclude works of painters worthy of consideration in this brief history of French painting. Too often, exclusions had to be based on the rationale of nationality, which has to do with politics, not art. In a historically organized museum collection, works by Whistler, to my mind, ought to hang with works by Manet and Monet. Because Whistler was an American citizen, however, this rarely happens. There is no one satisfactory way to define "French," and for this book inconsistency has been the rule. Since several of the greatest French painters have been Italian-, Dutch-, or Spanish-born, many nonFrench artists working in France are included. Other foreign-born masters (like Whistler, Man Ray, and Magritte) had to be left out. Conversely, the activities of French-born artists working abroad, from Poussin to Duchamp, have been included on the grounds of birthright.

In truth, French painting has usually been a manifestation of some international visual consciousness. Sixteenth- and seventeenth-century French painting is, arguably, a branch of Italian art history. Although some painters, like Renoir, sought to paint in an essentially French spirit, many more, including David, Manet, and Duchamp, tried to develop universal visual languages incorporating conventions of representation developed by nonFrench artists, including artisans of ancient Greece, of eighteenth-century Japan, or of modern factories. Paris grew as an international art center, and Parisian painting gained global popularity, thanks in large part to a centuries-old dedication by artists working in France — classicists, realists, surrealists, and abstractionists alike — to transcend nationalism in art.

Finally, the term "painting" is as difficult to define as "French." Category-minded seventeenth-century artists (for whom egg tempura, gold leaf, and other medieval techniques were outmoded crafts) defined modern painting in terms of fresco, oil, and canvas, the most popular Italian Renaissance materials. Paper was still a rarity, and before the eighteenth century drawing was considered just a tool with which painters developed their most elementary ideas. However, during the Enlightenment creativity came to be associated with disregard for conventional academic categories and with pioneering experiments in new materials. For example, eighteenth-century masters like Maurice-Quentin de la Tour (1704–1788) and Swiss-born Jean-Etienne Liotard (1702–1789) made "paintings" with pastels, often on paper supports instead of canvas. Considering how later painters like Degas and Toulouse-Lautrec emulated these artists' range of colors and textures in more complex mediums, can masters of pastel fairly be excluded from a history of French painting?

For many artists the greatest challenge was to use materials in unconventional ways — to work oil paints with the speed inherent in drawing or watercolor, for instance. By the end of the nineteenth century, some drawings and prints were conceived as elaborately as large paintings, while some paintings were so slight and sketchy that they seemed hardly more than what was once termed drawing. Hybridization became the norm during the course of the twentieth century, as artists started to incorporate real objects into paintings or to paint on three-dimensional elements, confusing categories of art and nonart as well as of painting, sculpture, and architecture, all in the name of artistic freedom and progress.

Determined to liberate painting from the control of a wealthy, academy-educated oligarchy, the artists of the Dada movement stressed the crucial, underlying conceptual value of truly great art and found ways to make "paintings" without paint at all. Guided by the dubious assumption that the most significant paintings are unique objects that fit in frames, some collectors and museums have still not learned to cope with the liberating changes. Innovation no longer seems possible in certain sorts of abstract or realist painting: it has become as hard to conceive of an original approach to landscape painting as it has to find an original way to make an abstract grid. Too often, painting sidesteps this problem by addressing its own history with humor or irony, but such art about art is most often academic-minded art merchandise for an elite art-oriented audience. For some critics, new media like video seem more promising than painting, but 150 years ago, with the introduction of photography, painting already appeared to some to be dead. In fact, it was very alive to change. Thus, while excluding some fine conventional paintings because of space limitations, this survey includes some works that readers might not accept as paintings. Yet, the extended notion of painting in no sense precludes conventional materials and formats. Evidence of evolutionary progress, or innovation, in painting was once an important criterion for art-historical importance; today it is less compelling in the determination of quality. History has already changed — for the better, in my opinion — as a result.

Writing this book has been a lot of fun, especially when my ignorance forced me to turn for help to countless colleagues and friends. While the errors and misconceptions are mine alone, the good parts would not be nearly as good without the generous advice I have received. In particular, I wish to thank Ziva Amishai-Maisels, Timothy Baum, Neal Benezra, Mel Bochner, Walter Hopps, Alain Kirili, Robert Knott, Albert Kostenevich, Charlotta Kotik, John Neff, Gerald Nordland, John Richardson, Anne Rorimer, Robert Rosenblum, Daniel Templon, Edward Thorp, John Vinci, and Martha Wolff. Kate Stofko did a superb job of getting the illustrations together and coordinating everyone's efforts, and did so cheerfully. For the concept and the support to carry it out on my terms, I owe my usual special debt to Hugh Levin, who knows how to make books a pleasure. Most of all, of course, I thank my wife, Elizabeth Leitgen Stuckey, who can make me look at things in ways that never occurred to me before and who patiently tolerated a project that I promised to finish much sooner than I actually did.

CHARLES F. STUCKEY

PALEOLITHIC 15,000–10,000 B.C.
  Portion of Cave Painting
  Lascaux, France
  Courtesy Caisse Nationale des Monuments
  Historiqueset des Sites, Paris

I.

An Age of War and Faith

FRANCE EVOLVED INTO A NATION SLOWLY, VIOLENTLY, ABSURDLY, AND GLORIOUSLY AS THE Holy Roman Empire splintered among Charlemagne's heirs. Although a line of Capetian monarchs was in existence by the end of the tenth century, the long struggle to establish a strong and lasting central government had only just begun.

As late as 1415, when Jean, the Duke of Berry, commissioned Pol de Limburg and his brothers to illustrate a prayer book of incomparable elegance, English invaders led by Henry V humiliated the French Army at Agincourt and installed the Duke of Bedford as regent to the court in Paris. The victory extended English control over nearly all of the western and northern regions of modern France. Had it not been for Joan of Arc and Charles VII, who turned the tide by the middle of the fifteenth century, American tourists today would not experience an embarrassing language barrier.

Like all the emerging nations of Europe during the Middle Ages, France inherited the arts of the Catholic Church of Rome. While the dark, thick-walled churches and precious libraries of hand-illustrated sacred books made during these Romanesque centuries have survived, the mural-scale fresco paintings have weathered into ruin. Changing tastes and destructive wars apparently took an even larger toll on the secular arts, at least until around 1100, when the University of Paris became a powerful cultural center apart from the Church, adding its prestige to the French "illuminated" book workshops that were world-famous for producing art in miniature. It was apparently during the thirteenth century that the great tapestry workshops at Paris and Arras geared up to provide insulating art for the damp northern walls of knights and ladies.

By that time, in response to the vigorous and visionary Abbot Suger, who remodeled his church at Saint-Denis just outside Paris in a daring new Gothic style with tall vaults, lancet windows, and spires, France had become the art center of Europe. Engineers, architects, and sculptors from all over the Continent were drawn to Paris and the surrounding region to work on ambitious Church building projects. Painting was relatively unimportant, however, unless the magnificent stained-glass windows of these Gothic cathedrals are thought of as a monumental new form of painting. Certainly the brilliant luminosity of these windows set a challenge for French painters ever since to express the worldly and otherworldly powers of light in their art.

The artistic preeminence of France, centered in Gothic Paris, expanded when a French Pope was elected and the southern city of Avignon became a Rome away from Rome for spiritual politics with their extensive cultural trimmings. Despite the auspicious start, however, the fourteenth century was a disaster for France. Helped by the English, Flanders broke away from French control, and English forces won overwhelming victories at Crécy and Poitiers, creating rival factions among the French. Civil wars followed before national power could be reconsolidated, and during these political tempests artists sought work and safety outside of France, sometimes in England.

How to categorize (that is, as French or English) key surviving works from the period, such as King Richard II's private altarpiece, known as the Wilton Diptych, still bothers scholars. Could an English king commission a French artist or an artist with a predilection for the French variation of the courtly International Style? There seems to be no other explanation for the delicacy of drawing and the rich simplicity of color used here to render a host of tall blond Gothic angels who watch Richard kneel before a serious Parisian type of infant Christ. The painter's nationality notwithstanding, the Wilton Diptych shows God on the side of the English

LIMBURG BROTHERS (15th century)

Les Trés Riches Heures de Jean Duc de Berry, 1413–1416
Calendar page for January, approx. 8½ × 5½"
(21.6 × 14 cm)
Musée Condé, Chantilly

king, and as a rule Gothic and early Renaissance paintings portray would-be alliances between church and state.

One of the dispersed panels from a large altarpiece executed in Paris a century later is a glorious culmination to this tradition of devotional art obsessed with secular history. Known as the Master of St. Giles, the painter of this altarpiece was well aware that fifteenth-century painters like himself had revolutionized art. Using the new science of perspective to suggest the sculptural fullness of space, the Renaissance-minded Master of St. Giles posed models to recreate a ninth-century drama in the twelfth-century Church of Saint-Denis, a setting resplendent with the sorts of iconic art that had been put aside as old-fashioned by realist fifteenth-century painters.

The great strides in fifteenth-century painting were made in Ghent by Jan van Eyck and in Florence by Masaccio while France was at war. The few painters at work in France during the fifteenth century were in a difficult, if potentially rich, situation. The heirs to a defunct Gothic heritage, they apparently felt obliged to celebrate French artistic traditions even as they promptly assimilated foreign innovations. The resulting hybrid appearance of fifteenth-century French painting in effect begins another, more lasting tradition of synthesis that extends through the "Japoniste" impressionists to the melting pot spirit of Montparnasse in the 1920s.

Like the miniatures by Limburg, the stately portrait in profile of a woman dressed in high Gothic fashion is often considered by specialists to exemplify the so-called International Style of around 1400. With only slight variations for local costume and facial type, the same portrait formula was used by up-to-date Florentine painters close to the Medici court in Florence.

By around 1415 Pol de Limburg had displayed this adventuresome synoptic spirit in his master illustrations for the Duke of Berry, whose portrait at table dominates the January page of the so-called *Très Riches Heures*. Limburg's elongated figures bend and twist like Gothic statues come to life in a world that is almost as close to Persian miniature painting as it is to Italian murals. As if to stress the traditional nature of his style here, however, the artist incorporated a typically French picture within his picture: a tapestry of battling knights used as both background and backdrop.

Respect for Gothic tradition can be seen everywhere in French Renaissance painting, which is filled with conceits about the interaction of old art and modern life. Portrayed as a "real" person in van Eyck fashion, the Virgin in the Annunciation altarpiece painted in Aix around 1445 wears a robe with a floral design in the spirit of Gothic manuscript border decorations. Meanwhile, more thoroughly modern, albeit tiny, figures celebrate mass in the background of the Gothic church, meditating on the sort of miraculous apparitions conjured up in the same physical space by the master painter. Modern with regard to the elongated, agonized figures with their Eyckian facial types, the monumental lamentation scene by Enguerrand Quarton lacks the same sort of realistic interior or landscape background that might be expected in an up-to-date painting from the Netherlands done around the middle of the century. Instead, Quarton's figures are silhouetted against an archly medieval gold background stamped with halos for the figures. The contrast between the old and new modes of religious drama heightens the impact of this magnificent altarpiece commissioned by a priest in Avignon.

A few years later, in 1454, another priest commissioned Quarton to attempt a far more complex scene celebrating the coronation of the Virgin. The landscape background here, which includes a narrow horizontal zone near the bottom, is a thoroughly modern panoramic portrait of the southern countryside, culminating in the silhouette of Mont Sainte-Victoire in the distance. For the mountain's much later admirer, Cézanne, the entire remainder of this visionary scene would seem superficially unrelated. However, the way in which Quarton stressed the hypnotic beauty of twisted folds of drapery anticipates the visual idiom that the painter from Aix perfected more than four centuries later. Quarton's coronation is, of course, to be understood on its own terms, which are those of the waning medieval world hierarchy, ranked on each side in five rows, archangels and biblical figures highest up, king, Pope, and emperor closer down near earth. The central group of identical figures of God the Father and God the Son placing a crown on the Virgin, levitated here on the wings of the Dove of the Holy Spirit, are depicted with remarkable realism of gesture and facial expression. The convincing weight of their draperies makes their apparition here seem all the more miraculous. Meanwhile, the changing scale from the tiny hellbound figures in the lower border to the slightly larger hosts of the blessed in the margins and finally to the large central group, apparently observed in close-up through a telescope, establishes a spiritual perspective between heaven and earth that is extraordinary.

Perhaps no work better exemplifies the superficially contrary need to become modern and pragmatic while remaining faithful to an earlier visionary Gothic age than the two-panel altarpiece commissioned by Charles VII's royal treasurer, Etienne Chevalier. Arguably the masterpiece of France's first painter to the king, Jean Fouquet, this work is at once ultramodern and ultranostalgic. There is nothing Gothic about Chevalier's costume or the modern church interior setting in the left-hand panel, but in the right-hand panel the pale white Virgin and

Child with their retinue of naked red and blue angels are extraterrestrial. It is hard to imagine that the realist Fouquet would choose to render the Virgin's exposed nursing breast so awkwardly unless he intended to stress the old-fashioned Gothic naiveté of this visionary realm.

Charles VII's brother-in-law, King René of Anjou, was an artist and writer contemporary with Jacques Villon and Fouquet. Apart from Fouquet's works, the illustrations by an unidentified master for René's romantic allegory *The Lovesick Heart* (*Le Coeur d'Amour Epris*) are probably the most astonishing French paintings of the fifteenth century. It is fitting that these hand-painted book illustrations done in the 1460s should have such importance, since with the invention of mechanical printing in Haarlem in 1446 this sort of French art specialty had come to an end. Painted on pages decorated with floral borders in the spirit of bygone times, these vignettes are especially impressive as early modern landscapes observed with distinct light conditions.

Indeed, the same sensitivity to, but not an equal talent for, landscape characterizes the masterpiece of Nicolas Froment, the altarpiece for the Cathedral of Aix also commissioned by King René. These fantastical poetic works, one in miniature and one at mural scale, foreshadow what would become a prevailing spirit in French art from Claude Lorrain to Cézanne — the close observation of nature as a meditation to awaken the mind to the transforming power of light. Light is represented in a medieval, abstract fashion in the most magnificent late fifteenth-century French painting, the central panel of a triptych altarpiece in the Cathedral of Moulins. The Virgin and Child, painted with the easy naturalism that is closely associated with such Italian masters as Perugino, levitate on a throne that blocks the sun from view, except for its rainbow aureoles, and the Virgin uses the crescent moon as a footrest. Wonderfully real angels encircle this seemingly royal family. The same model evidently posed for all the angels, with the result that this heavenly realm has an unreal consistency of beauty. Moreover, the painter evidently used just one set of drawings for the angel groups, reversing them on the right to mirror the figures on the left. The identity of this artist with such sure grace of execution and clarity of design is still open to question, but Jean Hey, celebrated by the Renaissance poet Jean Lemaire as the equal of Leonardo, Gentile Bellini, and Perugino, must be the right name for the remarkable Italian-minded artist responsible for this fifteenth-century French masterpiece.

ANONYMOUS

Notre Dame de la Belle Vernière, Center, 12th
century; sides, 13th century; first window in
the aisle of the choir, south side, 192 × 92½"
(487.6 × 235 cm)
Musée des Beaux Arts, Chartres
Chartres Cathedral

ANONYMOUS (Franco-Flemish, Brussels workshop)

*The Hunt of the Unicorn, VII: The Unicorn in
Captivity*, ca. 1500
Silk, wool, silver and silver-gilt threads,
145 × 99" (368.3 × 251.5 cm)
The Metropolitan Museum of Art, New York
Gift of John D. Rockefeller, Jr., The Cloisters
Collection, 1937

SCHOOL OF PARIS

Wilton Diptych, ca. 1395–1399
Oil on panel, 45 × 27″ (114.3 × 68.6 cm)
Reproduced by courtesy of the Trustees,
The National Gallery, London

MASTER OF ST. GILES (Franco-Flemish, active ca. 1500)

The Mass of St. Giles, ca. 1500
Oil on panel, 24¼ × 18″ (61.6 × 45.7 cm)
Reproduced by courtesy of the Trustees,
The National Gallery, London

MASTER OF THE AIX ANNUNCIATION (15th century)

Annunciation Triptych, central panel, 1445
Oil on panel, 61 × 69¼″ (155 × 176 cm)
Eglise Sainte Marie-Madeleine, Aix-en-Provence

ANONYMOUS (Franco-Flemish, early 15th century)

Profile Portrait of a Lady, ca. 1415
Oil on panel, painted surface, 20⅜ × 14³/₁₆″
(53 × 37.6 cm)
The National Gallery of Art, Washington, D.C.
Andrew W. Mellon Collection

ENGUERRAND QUARTON (b. ca. 1410, Laon–d. 1466)

Lamentation of Christ, with Donor (The *Pietà* of
Villeneuve-les-Avignon), ca. 1455
Oil on panel, 64 × 86¼″ (163 × 219 cm)
Musée du Louvre, Paris

ENGUERRAND QUARTON

Coronation of the Virgin, 1453
Oil on panel, 72 × 86⅝" (182.8 × 220 cm)
Musée de l'Hospice, Villeneuve-les-Avignon

JEAN FOUQUET (b. ca. 1420, Tours–d. ca. 1484)

Saint Stephen Presenting Etienne Chevalier, from left half of
Melun Diptych, ca. 1450
Oil on panel, 93 × 85″ (236.2 × 215.9 cm)
Gemäldegalerie, Staatliche Museen, Berlin

JEAN FOUQUET

Virgin and Child, right half of Melun Diptych
Oil on panel, 37¼ × 33¹¹⁄₁₆″ (94.5 × 85.5 cm)
Koninklijk Museum voor Schone Kunsten, Antwerp

HEC · EST · ILLA · DEQVA · SACRA · CANVNT · EVLOGIA · SOLE · AMICTA
LVNAM · HABENS · SVB · PEDIBZ · STELIS · MERVIT · CORONARI · DVODENIS

MASTER OF MOULINS, probably Jean Hey
(active last quarter 15th century)

Moulin Altarpiece, central panel, ca. 1498
Oil on panel, 11½ × 61⅞″ (283 × 157 cm)
Cathédrale de Moulins, Moulins

NICOLAS FROMENT (b. Uzès, Languedoc–d. after 1483)

Moses and the Burning Bush, 1476
Oil on panel, 120 × 88½″ (305 × 225 cm)
Cathédrale Saint-Sauveur, Aix-en-Provence

II.

Courtly Art from Italy

KING RENÉ OF ANJOU, WITH A FAMILY CLAIM TO THE THRONE OF NAPLES, INAUGURATED A HALF century of military adventurism in Italy, carried out with at best mixed political results by the French monarchs. These policies had an enormous impact on French art.

As a result of marriages and alliances, when Charles I of Spain was elected Holy Roman Emperor in 1519, France was in effect surrounded by Hapsburg powers. This constant threat increased the resolution of the French kings to centralize their authority at home and increase their influence in the Italian states, which also were threatened by Hapsburg ambitions.

Indeed, Francis I, who had summoned Leonardo da Vinci to France in 1516 (where he died three years later), consolidated what would become a crucial alliance with the Medici family, who ruled Tuscany and whose members were elected to the papacy (and thus to power in Rome) in 1513 and again in 1523. French fifteenth-century rulers seldom commissioned portraits of themselves, except in the marginal role of donor for altarpieces. Following the Medici fashion of asserting the significance of the secular individual, however, Francis I initiated a taste for portraiture that would busy several generations of master royal painters, beginning with Jean Clouet (?1485–?1545). Born in Flanders, Clouet would become the French rival of Holbein and Titian. His portrait of the king (circa 1520), with broad shoulders draped in gold-embroidered silken splendor, epitomizes what would become a pervasive taste for Tuscan art. The painter's son, François (d. 1572), who became painter to the king in 1540, was thoroughly familiar with Medici portraits by Pontormo (1494–1557) and Bronzino (d. 1572), judging from his masterful likeness of the Renaissance man Pierre Quthe (1562), a Paris druggist with a famous garden of medicinal plants.

Francis I's unsuccessful invasion of northern Italy, however, backfired for Medici interests, resulting in the sack of Rome by unpaid Hapsburg troops. Under the circumstances, the great Italian artists who had come to Rome to take advantage of Vatican commissions dispersed after 1527.

Many of them took advantage of Francis I's domestic ambition (now that he had married a Hapsburg for the sake of peace) to transform the royal hunting lodge at Fontainebleau outside of Paris into a magnificent palace. With their experience in fresco technique, painters such as Rosso Fiorentino (1494–1540), Francesco Primaticcio (1504–1570), and Niccolo dell'Abbate (?1512–1571) came to France to oversee the extensive decorations for the palace. Not only in terms of technique and style but also in terms of subject matter, these decorative programs followed the Italian taste for pagan mythology personified by idealized nudes to celebrate the superhuman ancestors of contemporary secular powers. Most of the frescoes undertaken for Francis I and his successors have fallen into irreparable ruin, but Rosso's Galerie Francis I, after cleaning and restoration, gives a good idea of the opulent Renaissance murals at Fontainebleau in its heyday. The even more extensive cycle for the Ulysses Room, however, was completely destroyed. Only an oil painting by Primaticcio, evidently a copy of an especially popular scene from the cycle in which Ulysses and Penelope are reunited, suggests the ultimate accomplishment of Fontainebleau art with its emphasis on sculptural nudes in the spirit of Michelangelo, posed expressively with theatrical gestures. A very closely related oil on canvas by Niccolo dell'Abbate showing Cupid and Psyche in place of the Homeric lovers not only underlines this admiration for Primaticcio's composition but suggests the same sort of Italian workshop dynamics, with students closely following the teacher's example, that would become institutionalized into an academy in the next century.

Of special interest with regard to these two paintings is the treatment of nudity at Fontainebleau. Apparently, full-length female nudity was unpopular, or perhaps it was considered improper for artists to work from life models. As a result, most female nudes in this period are half-length figures with only the breasts exposed, as in the case of Penelope and Psyche, both largely hidden behind their male counterparts by Primaticcio and Niccolo as if to avoid controversy. As a result, these works are intimately related to perhaps the most recurrent type of nude in sixteenth-century French painting, the half-length woman seated in her bath. The type was apparently introduced by François Clouet to portray Henry II's mistress, Diane de Poitiers (1499–1566), with a sort of ultramodest paganism seldom encountered in the Italy of Titian. In a variant of this type by an unknown painter, the nipples are rendered with as little attention to correct anatomy as Fouquet paid when he fashioned breasts for the Virgin of his Melun altarpiece a century earlier. Ironically, this woman in her bath owns the sort of elaborate mirror usually associated with the great Florentine goldsmith Benvenuto Cellini (1500–1571), who came to Fontainebleau in 1540 and spent five years there. Cellini and his assistants were far better informed about female nudity, and so the presence of the mirror with its nudes for supports merely stresses the peculiar modesty of the woman in the bath. For a full-length portrait of the same Diane de Poitiers in the role of her mythological namesake, Diana the huntress, the artist apparently used a male model, adding a breast and the sitter's head in an inadvertently comic masquerade.

Perhaps this full-length allegorical nude was done by a French student artist in Primaticcio's workshop. Archival documents have preserved the names of many of the French and Flemish artists who came to Fontainebleau to work during the mid-sixteenth century, but unfortunately, it is no longer possible to attach these names to surviving works of art. Among the few known French artists, a standout is Jean Cousin (d. 1560 or 1561), known as the French Michelangelo. His nearly life-size reclining femme fatale composite of Eve and Pandora is perhaps the most advanced nude of the century. Presumably, Cousin based it on an engraving after an Italian painting.

Increasingly familiar with Italian Neoplatonic culture after the arrival of Catherine de Medici as Henry II's bride in 1533, the court at Fontainebleau often staged entertainments based on mythological themes. *The Funeral of Love*, a large oil painting by an artist from the circle of Antoine Caron, seems to represent this type of semilicentious pageant. Indeed, Henry and Catherine's features can be identified in the faces of Jupiter and Juno in certain frescoes, and their son, Charles IX, commissioned the poet Pierre de Ronsard (1524–1585) to write *The Franciade*, a tedious nationalistic epic stressing the descent of the French monarchs from the heroes of antiquity.

Even if it began in response to Italian court culture, this fascination with erudite, witty paganism at Fontainebleau — and later in Shakespearean England — might also be understood as a form of escape from the unpleasant realities outside the court. The spread of Calvinism in France ultimately factionalized the country along religious lines; it would take Henry IV, the first Bourbon monarch, to impose the sort of tolerance mandated by the Edict of Nantes (1598) that France would need to strengthen and eventually reassert its national culture in the seventeenth century.

NICCOLO DELL' ABBATE (b. 1512, Moderna, Italy–d. 1571)

Venus and Cupid, n.d.
Oil on canvas, 39⅛ × 36⅝″ (100 × 93 cm)
Detroit Institute of Arts, Founders Society, Detroit
Purchase, Robert H. Tannahill Fund

FRANCESCO PRIMATICCIO (b. 1504, Bologne–d. 1570)

Ulysses and Penelope, ca. 1560
Oil on canvas, 44¼ × 48¼″ (113.6 × 123.8 cm)
The Toledo Museum of Art, Toledo, Ohio
Gift of Edward Drummond Libbey

JEAN CLOUET (b. ca. 1485, Paris–d. 1540)

Portrait of François I, King of France, ca. 1520–1525
Oil on panel, 37¼ × 29⅛″ (96 × 74 cm)
Musée du Louvre, Paris

TOP:
JEAN COUSIN THE ELDER (b. ca. 1490, Sens–d. ca. 1560)

Eva Prima Pandora, before 1538
Oil on panel, 38⅛₆ × 59″ (97 × 150 cm)
Musée du Louvre, Paris

BOTTOM:
ROSSO FIORENTINO, born Giovanni Battista di Jacopo
(b. 1494, Florence–d. 1540)

The Fountain of Youth, 1534–1537
Fresco
Galerie François I, Chateau de Fontainebleau

SCHOOL OF FONTAINEBLEAU

> *Lady at Her Toilet*, mid-16th century
> Oil on canvas, 41⅜ × 27⅞″ (105 × 70.8 cm)
> Musée des Beaux-Arts, Dijon

SCHOOL OF FONTAINEBLEAU

> *Diana the Huntress*, ca. 1550
> Oil on canvas, 75⅝ × 52⅜″ (192 × 133 cm)
> Musée du Louvre, Paris

ANTOINE CARON (b. 1521, Beauvais–d. 1599)

Allegory: The Funeral of Love, n.d.
Oil on canvas, 65½ × 82¼″ (164 × 209 cm)
Musée du Louvre, Paris

III.

French Artists in Caravaggio's Shadow

HENRY IV'S CORONATION IN 1589 HERALDED A GREAT NEW AGE OF FRENCH CULTURE THAT HAS been virtually uninterrupted ever since. A convert to Catholicism, Henry advocated religious tolerance for the sake of political strength. Within the first decade of his reign a galaxy of new talents was born, including not only writers such as Descartes (1596–1650), but the artists Simon Vouet (1590–1649), Valentin de Boulogne (1591–1632), Jacques Callot (1592–1635), Georges de La Tour (1593–1652), and Nicolas Poussin (1594–1665). The new century began auspiciously for the arts when in 1600 Henry married Marie de Medici, whose patronage helped Paris to eclipse Fontainebleau and once again become the cultural center of France and eventually of the world. The sort of economic expansion that would make France's golden age a reality began in earnest under Henry, during whose reign faraway trading outposts such as Nova Scotia and Quebec were founded.

Whereas sixteenth-century French art was limited to a single imported taste from Italy, seventeenth-century French culture developed in several different directions at once. Culture came to be understood not only as a political symbol of peace and prosperity but as a potentially valuable export, and with the founding of a national art academy in 1648, the promotion of French art became an affair of state. Whereas Italian and Spanish were the international court languages of the sixteenth century, an awareness of the need to elevate French language, thought, and art to this status fostered such rich talents as Racine (1639–1699), Molière (1622–1673), and Jean de La Fontaine (1621–1695). The obligation to attain cultural primacy in Europe is clearly reflected in the nearly twenty-five-fold growth of the royal art collections at the Louvre palace during this century.

While Marie de Medici invited foreign talents such as Rubens (1577–1640) to provide monumental allegories for her new Luxembourg Palace in Paris, French artists almost without exception headed for Rome, the best place to study firsthand the history of art back to its sources in antiquity. There they fell under the spell of Caravaggio (1565–1609), a controversial master whose decorations for a chapel in the French church in Rome at the end of the sixteenth century inaugurated a new form of down-to-earth, Counter-Reformation piety. Caravaggio's contempt for idealized figures and settings evocative of a pagan golden age was tonic to young artists bored with the elite allegories of mannerist classicism practiced at Fontainebleau. His everyday characters, emerging dramatically from the shadows of drab rooms, inhabited a palpable new sort of space defined by tides of light and dark — chiaroscuro — rather than by the even, mathematical progression of perspective.

Valentin de Boulogne, who arrived in Rome in 1608 and stayed there until his death, even adopted Caravaggio's bohemian life-style by associating with underworld toughs. Disrespectfully lounging on a stone decorated with a classical relief carving, such unwashed characters apparently served as models for his gloomy concert scene. By midcentury Valentin's stylistically up-to-date paintings were avidly collected in Paris, and Louis XIV hung five of these works in his bedroom at Versailles. Valentin's example or that of one of the many other so-called French *Caravaggisti* presumably guided the Le Nain brothers from Normandy to pioneer their unique portraits of rural French families huddled together silently, straight-backed, in working clothes, returning the

viewer's curiosity as if they were no less audience than spectacle. Contrasting more than light and shadow, Louis Le Nain (d. 1648) traded on an implied contrast between the monumental commoners in his paintings and the courtiers at Versailles.

Although Louis XIII, who annexed the duchy of Lorraine to France, was impressed by its great provincial master, Georges de La Tour, this highly individualistic painter fell into oblivion until the early twentieth century. Recent scholarship has indicated that he too made the art pilgrimage to Rome around 1610–1615 and there encountered the example of Caravaggio. In La Tour's hands, however, darkness becomes something frozen and flesh is as waxy and unblemished as porcelain. His crisp observation of costume detail seems peculiarly old-fashioned in a Gothic way, but his understanding of simplicity, as seen in the easy gesture of the hand to still the air for the candlelight or in the neat silhouettes of a haloless Virgin and Child, foreshadows the sort of so-called primitive perfection sought as an especially modern quality by Gauguin and Picasso at the turn of our own century. Among his greatest masterpieces are works that transcend formula, such as the *Blind Beggar Playing a Hurdy Gurdy*, which portrays an antihero as dilapidated as the rubble he sits upon, the unwitting spectacle for eyes that have the equivalent of perfect pitch.

rubble he sits upon, the unwitting spectacle for eyes that have the equivalent of perfect pitch.

La Tour treats his figures with the stiffness of objects in still lifes, and it is not surprising that some of the greatest masters of this genre came from the easternmost provinces, close to the Low Countries, where still life had its greatest vogue during the seventeenth century. Anticipated by such fantastical decorations as the parliament of fowls now in the museum in Strasbourg, the collection of glasses and goblets rendered by Sebastian Stosskopff (1597–1657) is probably the most elegant Caravaggesque still life ever painted. Reflecting and refracting the light like a chorus of bells, the inanimate vessels shimmer and flicker mysteriously with something like Gothic spirituality. Working in Paris, Jacques Linard (d. 1645) also sought to elevate still-life painting to a new height of prestige, anticipating Chardin. Early in his career, Linard won patronage from Cardinal Richelieu for *The Five Senses*, a collection of disparate objects that would be called "encyclopedic" by eighteenth-century standards. Demonstrating the painter's ability to render light as it invades shadow and plays off lustrous wood, metal, and mirrored glass, this carefully tiered display of flowers, vegetables, and household objects is a compelling lesson about the bounty of essential sensory values in seventeenth-century French life.

GEORGES DE LA TOUR

> *The Newborn*, 1644
> Oil on canvas, 29⅞ × 35⅞" (75.8 × 91 cm)
> Musée des Beaux-Arts, Rennes

OPPOSITE, TOP:
LE VALENTIN, born Valentin de Boulogne
  (b. 1594, Coulommiers–d. 1632)

> *The Concert*, ca. 1622–1625
> Oil on canvas, 68⅛ × 84¼" (173 × 214 cm)
> Musée du Louvre, Paris

OPPOSITE, BOTTOM:
LOUIS LE NAIN (b. 1593, Laon–d. 1648)

> *Peasant Family in an Interior*, ca. 1640–1645
> Oil on canvas, 44½ × 62⅝" (113 × 159 cm)
> Musée du Louvre, Paris

OPPOSITE:
Anonymous, French

Birds, 1619
Oil on canvas,
55½ × 37¾″ (141 × 96 cm)
Musée des Beaux-Arts,
Ville de Strasbourg, Strasbourg

RIGHT:
Sebastian Stosskopff
(b. 1597, Strasbourg–d. 1657)

Still Life with Basket of Glasses, 1644
Oil on canvas, 20 × 24⅛″
(51 × 62 cm)
Musée de l'Oeuvre Notre Dame,
Strasbourg

BOTTOM:
Jacques Linard (b. 1600, Paris–d. 1645)

The Five Senses, 1627
Oil on panel, 21⅝ × 27³⁄₁₆″
(55 × 68 cm)
Musée des Beaux-Arts,
Alger, Algeria

IV.
French Classicism and the Academy

THE ECUMENICAL SCOPE OF FRENCH SEVENTEENTH-CENTURY PAINTING WAS ENCOURAGED BY Cardinal Richelieu (1585–1642), who was able to mediate between the queen mother, Marie de Medici, and Louis XIII, whose prime minister he became in 1629. Richelieu advocated support for French culture and in 1635 instituted the French Academy of Letters and Sciences, a prototype for the Fine Arts Academy founded a decade later. However, his taste was not limited by nationalistic sentiment. In 1621 he commissioned a copy after one of Caravaggio's paintings, and his private art collection, installed in his city residence (today part of the Palais Royal) across the street from the Louvre, included paintings by such Italian masters as Mantegna and Perugino. Part of this collection was a gallery of portraits of illustrious men commissioned from emerging painters such as Vouet.

It was Philippe de Champaigne (1602–1674), born in Brussels but naturalized as a French citizen in 1629, whom Richelieu chose to paint his own portrait, thus setting a tone of sober virtuosity that would dominate French portraiture for the next two hundred years. Champaigne was an associate of the ultraconservative Jansenists, and his austere Catholicism is classical in its simplicity rather than in its erudition. Perhaps his most memorable work is a devotional double portrait painted to commemorate the recovery of his daughter, a nun, from an illness, thanks to the prayers of Mother Agnes. Their stark, colorless world has weighty dignity and a commanding grace designed to show French piety as the most devout in Europe.

Not a favorite of Richelieu, Vouet had had the monetary support of the young Louis since 1617, and a decade later the monarch called him back from Rome to take up residence in the Louvre. Originally a follower of Caravaggio, Vouet, like other members of the foreign colony, was a beneficiary of Pope Urban VIII's ambition to reestablish Rome as the world art center it had been in the days of Raphael and Michelangelo. Their cool sense of color, complex poses, and idealized proportions became touchstones for Vouet when he began to receive Church commissions, including one for St. Peter's. Back in France, Vouet initiated a workshop that served to train a generation of gifted painters in this grand revival style. His own decorative ensembles have mostly been destroyed; it is in the murals of students such as Charles Le Brun (1619–1690), who made ancient and modern history the obligatory backdrop for state rooms of every sort, that Vouet's enormous influence is apparent everywhere today in France.

Vouet's great rival, a special favorite of Richelieu and in many people's opinion the greatest of all French painters, was Nicolas Poussin, who settled in Rome in 1624 and returned only once to France, reluctantly and briefly, from 1640 to 1642 at the request of the king. Like Vouet, Poussin responded to the High Renaissance revival under Urban VIII, but with a passionate concern for the classical premises that had guided Raphael and Michelangelo. Poussin's art, which advocated the stoic and pantheistic principles of antiquity, gained enormous respect among Italian collectors, beginning with Cardinal Barberini, who commissioned *The Death of Germanicus*, a picture that demonstrated how art can embody lessons in virtue. Poussin's rendition of a moving scene from early Roman history in which loyalty took precedence over grief is keyed to the stark architecture, suggesting that the most noble Roman acts reflected the restrained beauty of Roman culture.

As much a philosopher as an artist, Poussin sought to express the abiding fundamentals of self-knowledge that shape life. *Echo and Narcissus*, a canvas that epitomizes the artist's early command of landscape as a vehicle for philosophical meditation, is more than the didactic illustration of a pagan myth about unrequited love. Based on unblinking observations of adolescent behavior, his listless figures are like clinical studies of the enervating depressions that result from obsessive concern for the self. Perhaps Poussin's influential brand of classicism is best expressed in the *Landscape with Diogenes*, a tribute to the philosopher who sought to simplify life to its necessities and here realizes that a bowl is a luxury. An advocate of precise drawing as the foundation of all painting, Poussin made his famous *Self-Portrait* nearly colorless, a dignified rejection of vanity in favor of logic and clarity. Depicting uneducated youths excited to discover a noble classical tomb like those to be found throughout the Roman countryside, *The Shepherds of Arcadia* sums up Poussin's advocacy of antiquity as an elegiac challenge to attain nobility that can inspire future generations.

Claude Lorrain (1600–1682), Poussin's next-door neighbor in Rome, shared his passion for classical archaeology and history and, like Poussin, was as much a realist as a poet, observing the drama of light in landscape as no artist had before. But Claude did not necessarily paint only what he saw in unedited fashion. Instead, he pieced together the gentlest, stateliest, or most elegant elements from an assortment of real-life views to compose diaphanous golden age settings that would herald the rococo world of Watteau, Boucher, and Fragonard. His paintings were influential in a more literal way in England than in France. Indeed, Claude's panoramic views of ancient buildings and ruins disappearing into the roseate or golden vapors of atmospheric perspective so deeply impressed first Wilson and Turner and then Cole and the American Hudson River School painters that after two centuries his extraordinary innovations had come to seem trite from overuse. By teaching himself to render the different moods of light as surely as any aspects of the physical world, Claude reinvented the idea of landscape painting. Properly orchestrated with light, the landscape could reach moments of perfection worthy of the greatest moments in legend or history. Like a visionary Hollywood locations manager, Claude reconstituted the glories of shrines and imaginary palaces to conjure up the sort of timeless world that the Sun King would try with only partial success to construct at Versailles beginning in 1661.

While Poussin and Claude perfected their respective styles of easel painting in Italy, in Paris Vouet, working with Le Brun and his other students, successfully petitioned the queen mother and the ten-year-old heir to the throne, Louis XIV, to establish an Academy of Fine Arts in 1648, modeled on the one in Rome. With this school to train future generations of artists, France thus recognized the economic as well as symbolic importance of becoming an art center. Under Colbert, in 1666 the academy opened a Roman campus for prizewinners. The following year a series of regular exhibitions of contemporary art (later called Salons) held under the auspices of the academy gave French artists and their public in Paris a forum to debate and encourage the direction of art for centuries to come. Requiring mastery of facial expressions and dramatic poses as well as an understanding of great literature, history painting was ranked highest in the academy's hierarchy. Genre paintings recording everyday scenes ranked below history, with landscape and still life considered the least demanding genres.

The status of the French academic artists is demonstrated magnificently by Nicolas de Largillière (1656–1746), who presented a portrait of its president, Le Brun, as his reception piece for membership in the academy. In the informality of his studio Le Brun gestures to an easel-scale version of one of his many allegorical murals for Louis XIV (in this case, Louis conquering the Franche-Comté) while all around are little copies of ancient statues and copies of treatises to signify the principles and teachings of the academy. Together with Hyacinthe Rigaud (1659–1743), Largillière elaborated the sober portrait type of Champaigne, and this new type would be repeated until the middle of the next century as the appropriate manner to honor monarchs, nobles, and celebrities. There is no better example of this grand tradition than Rigaud's official portrait of Louis XIV with all its loving attention to royal attire and props, including the canopy of flying draperies that was a typical mannerism of this kind of icon. This grandiose Louis ruled a far-flung realm reaching to the Mississippi River by the end of the century.

PHILIPPE DE CHAMPAIGNE

*Mother Catherine Agnès Arnauld and Sister Catherine de
Sainte Suzanne, the Artist's Daughter, the Et-Voto of 1622*
Oil on canvas, 64¹⁵⁄₁₆ × 90³⁄₁₆″ (165 × 229 cm)
Musée du Louvre, Paris

PHILIPPE DE CHAMPAIGNE (b. 1602, Brussels–d. 1674)

Cardinal Richelieu, n.d.
Oil on canvas, 100⅛ × 87⅛″ (255 × 222 cm)
Musée du Louvre, Paris

SIMON VOUET (b. 1590, Paris–d. 1649)

> *Wealth*, n.d.
> Oil on canvas, 67 × 48″ (170 × 124 cm)
> Musée du Louvre, Paris

CHARLES LE BRUN (b. 1619, Paris–d. 1690)

> *The Family of Darius at the Feet of Alexander,*
> 1660–1661
> Oil on canvas,
> 120⁷⁄₁₆ × 181¹⁄₁₆″ (306 × 460 cm)
> Château de Fontainebleau, Versailles

NICOLAS POUSSIN

> *Shepherds of Arcadia,,* 1863
> Oil on canvas, 33½ × 47⅝″ (85 × 121 cm)
> Musee du Louvre, Paris

NICOLAS POUSSIN

Self-Portrait, 1650
Oil on canvas, 38⁹⁄₁₆ × 29⅛" (98 × 74 cm)
Musée du Louvre, Paris

OPPOSITE, TOP:
NICOLAS POUSSIN (b. 1594, Les Andelys–d. 1665)

The Death of Germanicus, 1627
Oil on canvas, 58¼ × 78" (147.9 × 198.1 cm)
Minneapolis Institute of Arts, Minneapolis
The William Hood Dunwoody Fund

OPPOSITE, BOTTOM:
NICOLAS POUSSIN

Echo and Narcissus, 1628–1630
Oil on canvas, 29¼ × 39¼" (74 × 100 cm)
Musée du Louvre, Paris

NICOLAS POUSSIN

Landscape with Diogenes, 1648
Oil on canvas, 63 × 87″ (160 × 221 cm)
Musée du Louvre, Paris

Nicolas de Largillière (b. 1656, Paris–d. 1746)

Charles Le Brun, 1686
Oil on canvas, 99⅜ × 73⅝" (232 × 187 cm)
Musée du Louvre, Paris

HYACINTHE RIGAUD (b. 1654, Perpignan–d. 1743)

Louis XIV, King of France, 1701
Oil on canvas, 109 × 76⅜" (277 × 194 cm)
Musée du Louvre, Paris

V.
Opera Sets for Love and Sex: The Rococo

JEAN-ANTOINE WATTEAU

Le Mezzetin, ca. 1718
Oil on canvas, 21¾ × 17″
(55.2 × 43.2 cm)
The Metropolitan Museum of Art,
New York
Munsey Fund, 1934

EVERY ACCOUNT OF FRENCH EIGHTEENTH-CENTURY PAINTING BEGINS AFTER THE DEATH OF Louis XIV in 1715 had ended an era of astounding wealth, accomplishment, and overreaching ambition, during which native artists regained the sort of self-confidence that had characterized Gothic France. Golden Age glories, however, came at a heavy cost, and the burden of debt bequeathed by the Sun King to his heirs transformed the kingdom into a bubble doomed to burst or a house of cards with dangers unapparent to the amused eighteenth-century children chronicled in Chardin's pictures. The inevitable collapse of Louis XIV's realm, however, was accompanied by cultural as well as political revolution, by an Enlightenment investigation of the basic and universal laws of science and society governing nature and the individual, regardless of institutionalized powers such as kings and Popes.

The brief, extraordinary career of Jean Antoine Watteau (1684–1721) both exemplifies and justifies the open-minded, egalitarian Enlightenment spirit. Watteau was deprived of the classical education the academy advised for young artists. Although he never studied in Italy, he was passionate about Italian culture, especially the masquerade theater known as the commedia dell'arte. Immensely popular in France before they were expelled for offensive satire in 1697, these players were allowed back by the regent in 1716. Nostalgia for this world of artifice and illusion inspired Watteau, who initiated a poetic behind-the-scenes treatment of make-believe and costume that would ultimately inspire Degas, Toulouse-Lautrec, and Picasso. Despite Watteau's lack of interest in the grand academic genres of history and portraiture, he was welcomed into the academy on his own terms. Indeed, in order to accept the painting that Watteau presented as a prerequisite for membership, the academy had to bend its rules and create a new category, the *fête galante* (which might be translated as a "lovers' holiday"), which in fact portrayed modern life, albeit as a charade in the form of an elaborate courtly entertainment. Five years in the making, *Pilgrimage to the Island of Cythera* was a monumental culmination of the dozens of paintings in which Watteau had portrayed such fashionable entertainments with young courtiers and ladies at leisure in shady parks, as if France were indeed celebrating a Golden Age, or at least a revival of Gothic pageantry. Cythera, with its shrine to Venus, is one of the Ionian islands, and according to best-sellers of the time, wealthy Europeans made pleasure cruises there.

Watteau's famous painting is thus an imaginary journalistic rendition of modern life, utterly contrary to the academic dogma that art should address the noblest events of ancient history. A fantastical boat escorted by a flock of Cupids is ready for boarding and embarkation toward a theatrical world in the spirit of Claude, tinged with both gold and silver as if the sun and moon were combining their powers supernaturally. Watteau's *fêtes galantes*, like Italianate allegories starring French dandies, were rendered in virtuoso fashion, with flourishes and glistening highlights of caressing brushwork left visible as if to reveal the artifice of painting. This sort of opulent art-for-art's sake technique was a necessity for mural paintings such as the decorations by Rubens that Watteau so admired, but introduced into Watteau's paintings on a smaller scale, such brushwork stressed artifice and informality, as if these were virtues of the human condition.

Once among the treasures collected by Catherine the Great of Russia, Watteau's intimately

scaled *Le Mezzetin* is like a detail removed from the *Pilgrimage*. This fragment is so carefully selected, however, that by itself it conveys a big subject with universal appeal; like so many of Watteau's paintings, it was published immediately as an engraving to meet a growing popular demand. Here the crucial theme of looking at looking comes into its own as a staple in French painting, for Watteau presents an actor in the act of looking at something that we do not see, rolling his eye up to gaze at his secret lover just as he cocks an ear to listen to a melody we cannot hear. His isolation in the painting as a fragment of an activity raises the possibility of rejection, a mood sustained by the statue that faces away in the background. With just these essential details, Watteau obtained the eternal sympathy of all viewers familiar with the sweet pains of love. In *Pierrot*, he intensified even more the viewer's direct interaction with the work of art. Now the gestureless, expressionless actor, isolated from his colleagues in the background, looks out of the picture sphinxlike, as if to question his role there or the spectator's interest in him. The result of detailed observation of a real person whose real job is to suggest an illusion, *Pierrot* is a spellbinding allegory of life. Looking at the picture, it is impossible to determine whether a play is about to begin or has just ended.

Watteau's monumental *Sign-Board for the Shop of the Art Dealer Gersaint*, purchased for the collection of Frederick the Great in Berlin not long after the artist's death, is probably as much wishful thinking as a true-to-life document of the artistic life in early eighteenth-century Paris. The picture purports to represent a commercial gallery on the Pont Notre Dame, with the storefront left out to reveal the rich inventory and active trade inside and with the walls covered floor to ceiling (as was the fashion well into the next century) with the frivolous mythological nudes that were the rage at that time. Unknown a century earlier, this sort of shop remains a fixture in today's art market. Thus, Watteau's painting heralds a modern era for the context of art, now no longer simply at the service of courts and churches but available for collector-connoisseurs whose taste will play a fundamental role in the development of painting.

Surely the greatest collector of Watteau's day was the Duke of Orléans, regent to the future Louis XV, who would add three hundred pictures to the royal collection and who set the crucial precedent of opening the Luxembourg Palace two days a week so that a limited public could see a small part of the collection. Otherwise, aside from engravings published after renowned paintings and aside from shops like Gersaint's, the best chances to see art were provided by the exhibitions of contemporary art held, with few exceptions, under the auspices of the academy. Unfortunately for Watteau, the academy suspended these biennial events during the first quarter of the century, but the tradition resumed in 1725, and "Salons" became extremely popular events that attracted hundreds of visitors each day. Describing the Salon of 1777, Sir Joshua Reynolds, president of the relatively new English Royal Academy wrote, "This mingling of all orders of the state, of all ranks of all sexes, of all ages . . . is for an Englishman an admirable sight. . . . At the Salon, the Savoyard elbows with impunity the 'cordon bleu'; the fisherwoman exchanges her odors of brandy with the perfumes of the woman of rank, who is often obliged to hold her nose; here scholars give lessons to their masters, etc."

Three remarkable painters made their debuts at the Salon of 1737: Boucher (1703–1770), Chardin (1699–1779), and Van Loo (1705–1765). Like Nicolas Lancret (1690–1743), Carle Van Loo sought to extend the modern life idiom, but neither artist possessed Watteau's delicacy of observation or touch, and in their hands Watteau's fetes became boisterous picnics for porcelain figures. Trading on the sort of eroticized mythology Boucher perfected, Van Loo became wealthy by cranking out hundreds of rococo paintings for the booming art market, and three years before his death he was named first painter to the king. Indeed the verb *vanlooter* was coined for his manner of dashed-off, ultracommercial painting.

François Boucher, who would assume the position of first painter upon Van Loo's death, made his fortune and reputation as a book illustrator, copying works by Watteau for publications that began to appear in the 1720s. Capitalizing from the start on the market for erotic art, Boucher adopted the lusty wit of Rubens to create dramatically sensuous paintings such as *Hercules and Omphale*, in which the virtues of classical learning are lost in unchecked voyeurism. With a sense for mock-heroic parody, Boucher revised the premises of Renaissance mythological painting, replacing the heroic nudes of antiquity with realistic, unidealized figures in informal poses. Sprawled languorously, Boucher's nudes are dimpled girls playacting goddesses agreeable to pleasure. What ought to be Olympian settings are transformed into disheveled boudoirs, with sea

foam or clouds spilling everywhere to delight audiences of airborne Cupids.

The extraordinary brio of these settings, rendered with feathery virtuoso brushwork, later made Boucher a hero for impressionists such as Berthe Morisot and Auguste Renoir. In his own lifetime Boucher was a favorite of Madame de Pompadour, who became the king's mistress in 1744, and false rumors spread that the artist had supplied her with a series of erotic pictures to arouse the monarch's waning passions. More reliable sources indicate, however, that the king's appetites increased and that the teenage models who posed for Boucher were among his favorites. One of these may be the young courtesan portrayed ready for pleasure in Boucher's *Blonde Odalisque*, with its smoking censer to evoke the quarters of an exotic harem. Casanova's tattletale memoirs of these licentious times in France are the obvious counterpart to Boucher's behind-the-scenes glimpses into the life-styles of the sex toys of the rich and famous. Beaumarchais, whose spoof of court morals, *The Marriage of Figaro* (1784), was the century's greatest theatrical success, presumably got the material for his text firsthand while employed at Versailles, starting in 1759, to teach Louis XV's four unwed daughters how to play the harp.

JEAN-ANTOINE WATTEAU
(b. 1684, Valenciennes–d. 1721)

Pilgrimage to the Island of Cythera, 1717
Oil on canvas, 50¼ × 74¾"
(128.9 × 189.9 cm)
Musée du Louvre, Paris

JEAN-ANTOINE WATTEAU (b. 1684, Valenciennes–d. 1721)

Sign-Board for the Shop of the Art Dealer Gersaint, 1720–1721
Oil on canvas, 64⅛ × 121¼″ (162.9 × 308 cm)
Staatliche Museen, Berlin

JEAN-ANTOINE WATTEAU

Pierrot (also known as *Gilles*), n.d.
Oil on canvas, 72 × 59″ (184 × 149 cm)
Musée du Louvre, Paris

59

CARLE VAN LOO (b. 1705, Nice–d. 1765)

Halt in the Hunt, 1737
Oil on canvas, 86⅝ × 98⁷⁄₁₆" (220 × 250 cm)
Musée du Louvre, Paris

FRANÇOIS BOUCHER (b. 1703, Paris–d. 1770)

Hercules and Omphale, ca. 1724 or later
Oil on canvas, 35⁷⁄₁₆ × 29⅛″ (90 × 74 cm)
Pushkin Museum of Fine Arts, Moscow

FRANÇOIS BOUCHER

The Triumph of Venus, 1740
Oil on canvas, 51 × 63½″ (129.5 × 161.3 cm)
Nationalmuseum, Stockholm

FRANÇOIS BOUCHER

The Forge of Vulcan, or *Vulcan Presenting Venus with the*
Armor for Aeneus, 1757
Oil on canvas, 126 × 129¹⁵⁄₁₆″ (320 × 330 cm)
Musée du Louvre, Paris

François Boucher

Blonde Odalisque (Louise O'Murphy), 1752
Oil on canvas, 23¼ × 28¾″ (59 × 73 cm)
Alte Pinakothek, Munich

63

VI.
Morality as a Middle-Class Value

ALTHOUGH LACKING BEAUMARCHAIS'S SENSE OF HUMOR, JEAN-BAPTISTE-SIMEON CHARDIN (1699–1779), the third painter to debut at the Salon of 1737, provided a moral counterweight to frivolous-minded rococo court art, though he was hardly excluded from court patronage. Judging from his earliest works, Chardin, who was trained at the old guild school instead of the academy, hoped to follow in the footsteps of such still-life and animal painters as Alexandre Desportes (1661–1743) and Jean-Baptiste Oudry (1686–1755), who celebrated the dogs and catches of the royal hunts. Chardin was invited to become an academician on the basis of the ambitious still lifes he displayed in an outdoor art exhibition in 1728. These paintings portrayed honest workaday trappings such as the humble battered pans and jugs in a kitchen. Hanging in the background of one of the paintings, like the stoic victim of a tyrant, a gutted skate seems to watch while the cook's cat tramples on opened oysters to stalk another fish expiring on the table. This work already indicated Chardin's ability to find epigram, fable, and drama in the humblest details of eighteenth-century life. Of course, he was accepted into the academy specifically for achievements in the lowest rank of subject matter. It may have been the challenges of membership that led Chardin to develop afterward as a figure painter, albeit one devoted to sober middle-class models that celebrated the so-called third estate, the vast middle class whose industry and taxes supported the grandeurs of the court at Versailles. By the time the Salons got under way again on a regular basis in 1737 Chardin had developed a pared-down variety of genre painting that brought him acclaim in the press and financial prosperity from the sale of engravings after his works. Several of his paintings, including *The House of Cards* and *Soap Bubbles*, were in such demand that Chardin painted five or six different versions of the same picture during the course of his career, accommodating the expanded art market with variations of a single theme that were called *répetitions*, and eventually set the precedent for the sort of painting in series for which the impressionists later became famous.

In these scenes Chardin described the sort of serious youthful curiosity that characterized the Enlightenment. For Chardin and his admirers, the sort of simple inexpensive marvels to be observed in a bubble had a pure classical beauty and symbolized fundamental laws better than did Boucher's pagan gods. Although he limited himself for the most part to a palette of browns and grays, Chardin's modest accents of bright color are especially dramatic. His decision to restrict his scenes to one or at the most two figures allowed him to achieve a powerful sense of focus absent in sprawling allegorical works. Most important, Chardin understood that academic art based on a connoisseur's knowledge of the art of the past had far more limited appeal than did art based directly on life to which a vast new audience could respond. Extending Watteau's obsession with depicting the act of looking, even as he dispensed with Watteau's love for costume and artifice, Chardin posed his models to appear to be absorbed in simple acts such as using a deck of cards not to gamble but to experiment with the elementary laws of structure. Chardin was the son of a cabinetmaker, and the sense of solid construction in his compositions results in a balanced calm that is the antithesis of the rococo mainstream of his age but points the direction for the next generation of French artists.

Out of step, Chardin was not unappreciated. The king himself purchased several paintings. But after his death Chardin's art fell into oblivion for nearly a century. Today he is perhaps most appreciated as a still-life painter. He returned with enthusiasm to that little esteemed branch of art later in his career, orchestrating vegetables and cutlery into stately geometric excercises for the painstaking study of light and form. For his great admirers Manet and Cézanne these were the enduring testament of Chardin's philosophical encounters with the visible laws of three-dimensional reality.

Chardin's important role in the development of eighteenth-century French painting also involved his encouragement of a brilliant radical thinker and writer, Denis Diderot, who, beginning in 1761, wrote extensive accounts of the annual Salons. Although newspapers already gave space to comments about academy exhibitions, Diderot's well-informed essays represent the first serious attempt in France at art criticism; when they were published later, they not only provided an important history of taste but inaugurated a new literary genre of art journalism. In Diderot's opinion, every true artist should promote virtue and denounce vice. His ideal painter was Jean-Baptiste Greuze (1725–1805), who blended the modern sensitivity of Chardin to sincere observations of modern life with the more openly virtuoso mannerisms of Boucher to perfect a sentimental, moralizing form of genre painting with the kind of attention to detail and exaggerated gestures that appear in early silent movies. Despite the support he received from Diderot and the wealth he obtained from his pictures and the engravings made after them, Greuze was embittered because the academy, of which he had become an associate in 1755, refused to recognize him as more than a genre painter. In protest, he stopped sending pictures to the Salons after 1769, initiating a strategy that many nineteenth-century painters would follow to protest the academy's restricting dogmas.

In a painting such as *The Little Girl Who Broke Her Mirror*, which appeared at the Salon of 1763, Greuze transformed Chardinesque types into antiheroines. Making a burlesque of disheveled appearance and unrestrained gestures, Greuze invented a sexist stock female character with no Enlightenment virtues: superstitious, too weak to protect herself, too self-concerned to accept her fate with dignity. Scarcely concealed or restrained, the sexual innuendo is strong and patronizing, and Greuze often catered to prevailing taste by painting would-be innocent figures in vulnerable, distressed, or regretful poses. None is more market-oriented than *The Broken Pitcher*, another titillating, albeit didactic, emblem of the loss of virginity. Where Chardin pared down details, Greuze piled them up like the best-selling novelists of the day. Indeed, at one point the artist conceived (but never carried out) a series that would tell a story with two characters carrying a complex plot through more than twenty paintings. Greuze caused a sensation at the Salon of 1761 with an elaborate novelistic genre painting treated as modern history painting. Entitled *The Village Accord*, or *A Marriage, and the Moment When the Father of the Bride Gives the Dowry to His Son-in-Law*, this painting includes a dozen figures caught up in a variety of complex emotions ranging from sibling compassion to motherly concern to fatherly fulfillment to professional objectivity. The notary seated at the table is no less an essential detail in this rural scene than are the plank floor, bare walls, and muskets. He is, of course, the alter ego of Greuze, who recorded the event with the passionate interest of a social scientist and the skill of a consummate storyteller. Restraining himself with Chardinesque colors, Greuze nevertheless indulged in a variety of pictorial conceits. For example, he had each figure touch hands with the next as if to suggest the uninterrupted passage of a shared emotional current throughout the humble room. He also showed the bride instinctively eyeing a mother hen feeding with its chicks.

Greuze's appeal to such universal virtues as family ties and motherhood epitomizes a taste for sentiment in mid-eighteenth-century French art. Even the king's aging official animal painter, Oudry, wanted to participate, and his group portrait of a bitch nursing her new puppies, exhibited at the Salon of 1753, must be understood as a prefiguration of Greuze's immensely successful campaign to appeal to the public with paintings that they could understand.

Jean-Baptiste Siméon Chardin (b. 1699, Paris–d. 1779)

The Ray, ca. 1727
Oil on canvas, 44⅞ × 57½″ (114 × 146 cm)
Musée du Louvre, Paris

Jean-Baptiste Siméon Chardin

Kitchen Table, ca. 1756
Oil on canvas, 15⅝ × 18¼″ (39.8 × 47.5 cm)
Museum of Fine Arts, Boston
Gift of Mrs. Peter Chardon Brooks

FRANÇOIS DESPORTES (b. 1661, Champigneuilles–d. 1743)

Still Life with Peaches, 1729
Oil on canvas, 35¹³⁄₁₆ × 46⁷⁄₁₆″ (91 × 118 cm)
Nationalmuseum, Stockholm

Jean-Baptiste Siméon Chardin

Soap Bubbles, ca. 1745
Oil on canvas, 36⅝ × 29⅛" (93 × 74.6 cm)
National Gallery of Art, Washington, D.C.
Gift of Mrs. John W. Simpson

Jean-Baptiste Siméon Chardin

House of Cards, 1741
Oil on canvas, 23⅝ × 28⅛" (60 × 72 cm)
Reproduced by Courtesy of the Trustees,
The National Gallery, London

69

JEAN-BAPTISTE GREUZE (b. 1725, Tournus–d. 1806)

The Broken Pitcher, 1773
Oil on canvas, 42¾ × 34″
(108.5 × 86.5 cm)
Musée du Louvre, Paris

JEAN-BAPTISTE OUDRY (b. 1686, Paris–d. 1755)

Bitch Hound Nursing Puppies, 1752
Oil on canvas, 40¾ × 52" (103.5 × 132 cm)
Musée de la Chasse et de la Nature, Paris

JEAN-BAPTISTE GREUZE

The Village Accord (A Marriage), 1761
Oil on canvas, 36¼ × 46½" (92 × 117 cm)
Musée du Louvre, Paris

VII.
Immorality, Morality, and Revolution

BESIDES GENRE PAINTING AND STILL LIFE, LANDSCAPE, WHICH ALSO WAS CONSIDERED LESS elevated than history painting, won new prominence during the mid-eighteenth century. Indeed, one of the century's most important commissions was awarded by the director of public buildings, the Marquis de Marigny (Madame de Pompadour's brother), to Joseph Vernet (1697–1792) to make "portraits" of all the great ports of France. Vernet, whose long stay in Rome had made him equally familiar with the traditions of Claude and Poussin and with the more recent triumphs in landscape realism of Canaletto, was able to complete fifteen of these paintings. In the process he inaugurated a nationalistic approach to landscape that would inspire dozens of nineteenth-century artists, beginning with Corot, to roam from village to village to find the soul and muscle of the nation away from the capital. A celebration of French commerce and the prosperity of its cities, Vernet's paintings won high praise from Diderot for truthfulness, and a work such as *The Port of Bordeaux* is a precious record of the grandiose urban renewal projects that were carried out during the reign of Louis XV. Vernet's heroic passion for landscape (he allegedly had himself tied to a ship's mast during a tempest in order to study unbridled nature as no previous artist had dared to) was enormously popular with English artists, initiating a challenge that led Turner to make landscape a popular and respected idiom for several generations to come.

The success of Vernet's "ports" may have influenced Hubert Robert (1733–1808) to submit a view of the port of Rome for his reception piece to become an academician in 1767. Supported by Marigny, Robert was admitted under a special new category as a "painter of ruins." Devoted to elevating the genre of historical landscape painting pioneered by Claude and Poussin, Robert had made a decadelong firsthand study of classical Roman ruins. Working alongside Fragonard, who came to Rome in 1759, he perfected an erudite, meditative variation of rococo landscape permeated with the reminder that worldly glories like Rome's crumble in time. This same spirit was physically embodied in fake ruins designed as decorations for gardens like those erected in the 1770s at the Park Monceau in Paris.

Following in Vernet's footsteps, Robert traveled across the French countryside to record the remains of aqueducts and temples left behind as marvels of an earlier imperial age on French soil; as first curator of the royal art collection beginning in 1784, he became obsessed with the architectural planning for the large central gallery with skylights in the Louvre. Unfortunately, Robert was imprisoned by revolutionary authorities in 1793, when the Louvre opened as the fourth public museum in the world, only to close its doors immediately for repairs to the new structure. Robert's satirical vision of the new building in ruins, exhibited at the Salon of 1796, seemed to be a fulfillment of the general warning prophesied in his earlier works, but in 1799 the great royal collection transformed into a museum for the people was reopened on a permanent basis.

Theoretical issues concerning the lessons of history and the direction painting should take were apparently of little interest to Jean Honoré Fragonard (1732–1806), a prodigy who studied briefly with Boucher and then with Chardin before winning one of the academy's coveted scholarships to study under Van Loo in Rome, where he stayed for a decade and met the brilliant

JEAN-HONORÉ FRAGONARD

The Swing, 1768–1769
Oil on canvas, 31⅞ × 25½"
(80.9 × 64.7 cm)
The Wallace Collection, London

young Robert. Enthralled with the decorative Venetian idiom perfected by Giovanni Tiepolo (1696–1770), Fragonard had a predilection for grace that often escaped the more earnest Boucher and Van Loo. As a result, while Fragonard also traded constantly in sensuality and eroticism, his less erudite works usually treat sexuality shamelessly. Never bothering to complete the requirements for becoming a full academician, Fragonard seldom sought public recognition at the Salons and showed relatively little interest in circulating engravings after his pictures. He preferred to work more whimsically. His subjects are hardly ever literary or allegorical but are better described as caprices, usually modest in scale and often rendered with a freedom that verges on sketchiness. Effortless-seeming, his pictures carry Watteau's innovations into a realm of art for art's sake that would receive full recognition only with the advent of Impressionism. In his own lifetime Fragonard chose to remain an anachronism.

A playful aquatic ballet of squirming, shifting, crouching gestures, Fragonard's *The Bathers* makes it clear that he could outdo Boucher in depicting the most arousing female poses. Yet unlike Boucher's girls posed in a fantastical setting like paid actresses, Fragonard's models seem genuinely at ease on a riverbank, as if the artist had simply portrayed teenagers unaware of being observed and thus had captured an enduring emblem of joyful feminine life returned to its natural state. Such works brought Fragonard to the attention of fun-loving patrons such as the Baron de St. Julien, who commissioned the artist to paint his mistress playing on a swing while he hid in the garden, where he could peep up her skirts voyeuristically. Fragonard turned this debased idea into a rococo frolic, with the woman defending herself by kicking her shoe at the shameless dandy reclined on his well-dressed back at the feet of a garden statue of Cupid. Fragonard animated everything from the hem of the woman's skirts to the shading branches with swinging, mock-dramatic rhythms. The silvery, slightly too green and blue tonality that he developed in this work epitomizes the cosmeticized garden-variety nature that prevailed as taste during the last decades of the monarchy.

At the Salon of 1767 Fragonard exhibited a *Head of an Old Man*, which may have been one of the first of a series of around a dozen extraordinary "fancy portraits" that have become one of Fragonard's most important legacies. The only one to be dated is the *Portrait of Monsieur de la Bretèche*, like the other individuals in this series a well-to-do patron of the arts. Dressed for the occasion in a elaborate plume-topped costume worthy of a model in Tiepolo's allegories, the sitter is presented as someone other than his real self, foremost as a model for the painter's whimsy. With dazzling speed, the strokes left as scarcely integrated ripples of paint in disregard for conventional standards of perfection, Fragonard captured his friend turning to look over his shoulder as if momentarily interrupted. Extending the brio of Rubens's renowned handling, Fragonard evidently wanted to surpass the dashing works of popular pastel portraitists such as Maurice-Quentin de la Tour (1704–1788), just as nineteenth-century masters from Daumier to Degas would make a cult of sketchlike instantaneity for oil painting, despite the medium's limitations where speed is concerned.

The idiosyncrasies of Fragonard's approach to portraiture are especially evident when his works are compared with the tasteful portraits of Tocqué, Aved, Roslin, and Duplessis, who sought to capture sitters as their real selves, posed as if for genre paintings in their homes or workplaces. Outstanding among these specialists was Louise-Elisabeth Vigée-Le Brun (1755–1842). Daughter of a mediocre painter and wife to a painter turned art dealer, Vigée-Le Brun, who became an academician in 1783, was determined to invest portraiture with the virtuosity of Rembrandt and Rubens. Loyal to her royal patrons, she left France when revolution erupted.

His extraordinary "fancy portraits" notwithstanding, Fragonard's greatest masterpiece is a panoramic record of prerevolutionary France in its final glory. This work captures the sun bursting through a clouded September sky in a crescendo to shine on the annual public festival at the park surrounding the royal palace of Saint-Cloud, not far outside Paris. Putting on their finest clothes and leaving their city cares behind, Parisians could here sample the courtly life of entertainments. Fragonard showed children urging their mothers to gape at this wonderland with a bursting fountain, a toy seller's booth, a portable stage, and a marionette theater. *The Fête at Saint-Cloud* epitomizes the pervasive "Let them eat cake" attitude that French citizens should have nothing better to do than behold the spectacles of their all-powerful kingdom.

It hardly seems possible that Louis XVI's art ministers were the primary advocates of the rigorous classical style that eclipsed Fragonard's caprices after the revolution. However, it seems no less likely that this tragic monarch, during whose reign (1774–1793) state support for the arts increased sharply and efforts were begun to turn the royal collections into a public museum, would have toppled his own government by overspending to support the American colonists in a revolt against the English king. Louis's director of arts and buildings, the Count d'Angiviller (1730–1809), sought actively to elevate the moral standards of French art and used the academy as a forum to stress decency and virtue in art through the encouragement of history painting. The year when the count took up his duties — 1774 — was marked by two singular events in art politics: Joseph-Marie Vien (1716–1809), the leading advocate of strict classical taste during the 1750s and 1760s, at best a competent artist and unpopular with most of his fellow academicians, was appointed to the influential directorship of the institution's program in Rome; and his most ambitious student, Jacques-Louis David (1748–1825), finally won the academy's scholarship prize to study in Rome after having lost the competition on three previous attempts. Grasping the principles of an international antiquarian movement centered in Rome, these two artists revolutionized painting in France, initiating a self-righteous cult dedicated to the high moral calling of artists dedicated to the noble virtues of the ancient Greeks and Romans.

As a result of David's relentless ambition and dedication, the last quarter of the eighteenth century was essentially the beginning of a new era in painting best defined by his own successes. Although David and his students are most often categorized as the impressive French contingent of the pan-European neoclassical movement in the arts, David was far more than a classicist. His remarkable works also set the tone for romantic art, usually considered as contradictory to academic principles, and for realism, often understood as contradictory to both classical and romantic values. Thus, just as the eighteenth century did not begin in earnest in the arts until 1715, it was in effect over by 1774, when David went to Rome.

David's *Oath of the Horatii*, commissioned for Louis XVI, introduced a cult of noble antiquity, portraying an imaginary scene in the spirit of the ancient historian Livy in which three young brothers swear fervent allegiance to the Roman republic before battling their cousins (who are betrothed to the Horatii's sisters, swooning at the right side of David's painting in obedience to the primacy of the state over personal loyalties). Like a Poussin inflated to a dramatic thirteen-foot-wide scale, David's composition is designed to endow human gestures with supreme powers. The three brothers act together like the arches that support the stark Doric-style room, which is darkened except where the patriotic fervor glows on the father's hands gripping the sharp swords. With unblinking self-assurance David worked every minute detail of this huge canvas to what academic teaching considered perfection. He studied each muscle of each figure like a professional anatomist; reportedly, he repainted the father's foot no fewer than twenty times!

When this sensational canvas was shown in Paris at the Salon of 1785, David was catapulted to fame, and immediately young painters aspired to follow his lead. In the hands of his most gifted pupils, such as Anne-Louis Girodet de Roucy-Trioson (1767–1824), French painting advocated an idealism based on the taut, unblemished perfection of ancient sculpture. Limited to the barest essentials required to convey its theme, Girodet's *The Sleep of Endymion*, which was exhibited at the Salon of 1793, a sort of antirococo parable of youthful chastity, exemplifies this stony, otherworldly perfection that soon became a formula.

These were hyperemotional times when every French person's political beliefs came under the sorts of tests recounted in ancient history. Louis XVI's announcement of national bankruptcy in 1788 set in motion a chain of events that would bring about his own execution at the beginning of 1793. David was a member of the Convention that voted the death of his onetime patron. Indeed, more than his rigid perfectionism in every branch of painting, it was David's uncanny political agility that permitted his preferred style to come to dominate all Europe in the next few decades.

Establishing close relations with the most dangerous revolutionaries, David immortalized the martyrs of the new republic, including Marat, the rabble-rousing pamphleteer who was assassinated while bathing in April 1793. Supernaturally illuminated (just like Girodet's Endymion visited by the incorporeal moon goddess) while life ebbs from the wound, David's propagandistic effigy of Marat in his stoic's simple surroundings appears less like a victim than like a god at peace, a secular saint whose death is represented as a noble and heroic fulfillment of life lived for the highest principles. Quickly painted as the occasion demanded, *Marat Assassinated* demonstrates how art responding to contemporary events can rival history painting and arouse the deepest passions. Nearly a half century after it was painted, David's Caravaggesque portrait, exhibited in 1846, was applauded by Baudelaire as the prototype for a realism in the spirit of Balzac that observed eternal truths in events of modern life.

Joseph Vernet (b. 1714, Avignon–d. 1789)

The Port of Bordeaux, 1759
Oil on canvas, 51¹³⁄₁₆ × 89³⁄₈″ (130 × 227 cm)
Musée de la Marine, Paris

Joseph Vernet

The Storm, 1777
Oil on canvas, 121½ × 87″ (308.6 × 220.9 cm)
Musée Calvet, Avignon

HUBERT ROBERT (b. 1733, Paris–d. 1808)

The Maison Carré at Nîmes, ca. 1787
Oil on canvas, 95¹¹⁄₁₆ × 96″
(243 × 244 cm)
Musée du Louvre, Paris

HUBERT ROBERT

*Imaginary View of the Grande Galerie
in Ruins*, ca. 1795
Oil on canvas, 128 × 157½″
(325 × 400 cm)
Musée du Louvre, Paris

JEAN-HONORÉ FRAGONARD

Portrait of M. de la Bretèche, 1769
Oil on canvas, 31½ × 25½″ (80 × 65 cm)
Musée du Louvre, Paris

Anne-Louis Girodet de Roucy-Trioson
(b. 1767, Montargis–d. 1824)

The Sleep of Endymion, 1793
Oil on canvas, 77¹⁵⁄₁₆ × 102¾″ (198 × 261 cm)
Musée du Louvre, Paris

JEAN-HONORÉ FRAGONARD

The Fête at Saint-Cloud, 1773
Oil on canvas, 85 × 131⅞″ (216 × 335 cm)
Banque de France, Paris

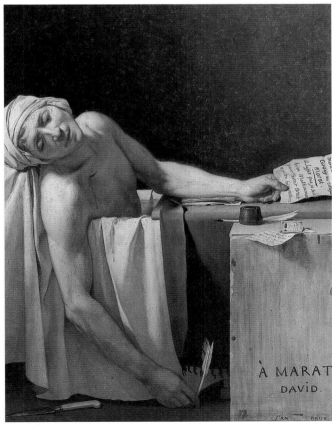

ABOVE:
Jacques-Louis David (b. 1748, Paris–d. 1825)

> *The Oath of the Horatii*, 1784
> Oil on canvas, 129¹⁵⁄₁₆ × 168⅛″ (330 × 427 cm)
> Musée du Louvre, Paris

LEFT:
Jacques-Louis David

> *Marat Assassinated*, 1793
> Oil on canvas, 65 × 50¾″ (165 × 128 cm)
> Musées Royaux des Beaux-Arts, Brussels

OPPOSITE:
Louise-Elisabeth Vigée-Le Brun (b. 1755, Paris–d. 1842)

> *Lady Folding a Letter*, 1784
> Oil on canvas, 36¼ × 29⅜″ (93 × 75 cm)
> The Toledo Museum of Art, Toledo, Ohio
> Gift of Edward Drummond Libbey

VIII.
Art Under Napoleon

JACQUES-LOUIS DAVID

Napoleon in His Study, 1812
Oil on canvas, 80¼ × 49¼"
(203.9 × 125.1 cm)
National Gallery of Art,
Washington, D.C.
Samuel H. Kress Collection

NAPOLEON'S SUCCESSFUL DEFENSE OF THE WOBBLY GOVERNMENT INSTITUTED AFTER THE REIGN of Terror launched a modern man into a Caesar-scale role. While he consolidated popular support as a conquering hero before usurping political power in 1799 (year VIII of the postrevolutionary calendar), the Corsican general demonstrated a rapacious concern for art as a symbol of authority. Treasures looted from Italian cities by his army poured into Paris in anticipation of the reopening of the Louvre as a public museum in 1799. According to one account, these treasures were paraded through the streets of Paris in "chariots bearing pictures carefully packed, but with the names of the most important inscribed in large letters on the outside, as The Transfiguration by Raphael; the Christ by Titian. The applause of an excited crowd, a heavy rumbling announced the approach of massive carts bearing statues and marble groups, the Apollo Belvedere; the Nine Muses; the Laocoön. . . . The Venus de' Medici was eventually added, decked with bouquets, crowns of flowers, flags taken from the enemy, and . . . detachments of cavalry and infantry, colors flying, drums beating, music playing, marched at intervals. . . ." No previous event in the history of French painting so intensely raised public interest in art or so elevated the ambitions of contemporary artists. As the most celebrated portraitist and art propagandist of his day, David was immediately called upon to glorify Napoleon's deeds and claims.

For his first portrait commission David presented Napoleon with the wind at this back, riding a rearing white charger and gesturing upward into the glacial Alps like a modern-day Hannibal. Not wanting this allusion to ancient history to be lost on the spectator, David inscribed the names Bonaparte, Hannibal, and Karolus Magnus into the rocks under the steed's hooves. Presented in classic silhouette, close up, the mounted general's form towers over the alpine background where the tiny figures of his troops fulfill his marching orders. In fact, Napoleon had made the crossing in March 1797 on a mule. While David was busy supervising five versions of this modern icon, his gifted students Gérard (1770–1837) and Girodet were set to work decorating the main salon of Napoleon's Malmaison Palace with equally stirring fantasies of military glory. Demonstrating the underlying romantic spirit of Davidian art, these works depict the primitive Nordic military heroes celebrated by the ancient bard Ossian, whose verses were best-sellers from their publication in the 1760s until they were later revealed as modern literary forgeries. Archetype of the artist in the service of a military state, Ossian appealed to passions and superstitions outside the rational canons of Greco-Roman art. In Gérard's hands, Ossian sings to conjure Viking legions as icy apparitions in the dark northern skies, to be interpreted as dreamland archetypes for new French superheroes.

David's favorite student despite his monarchist principles, Antoine-Jean Gros (1771–1835) was introduced to Napoleon in Italy in 1796. Awarded the rank of inspector of reviews to facilitate his firsthand research, Gros invented modern military history painting with its emphasis on intense realism and its cinematic scope. His greatest success purports to document an event that took place early in 1799 after Napoleon's victorious army was decimated by an outbreak of plague. Unafraid for himself during a visit to a makeshift field hospital, the compassionate general calmly touches the sores of one victim with the confidence of a modern-day saint capable of miraculous healing. Gros's intensely realistic rendition of the horrific pestilence with its swollen pallid bodies, the exotic setting, and the mixed emotions of hope, resignation, and repugnance observed in scores of orchestrated gestures and facial expressions catered to a growing taste for lurid suffering in art and thus heralded the advent of romanticism in French painting. Napoleon was already emperor when *The Pesthouse at Jaffa* was exhibited at the Salon of 1805 and

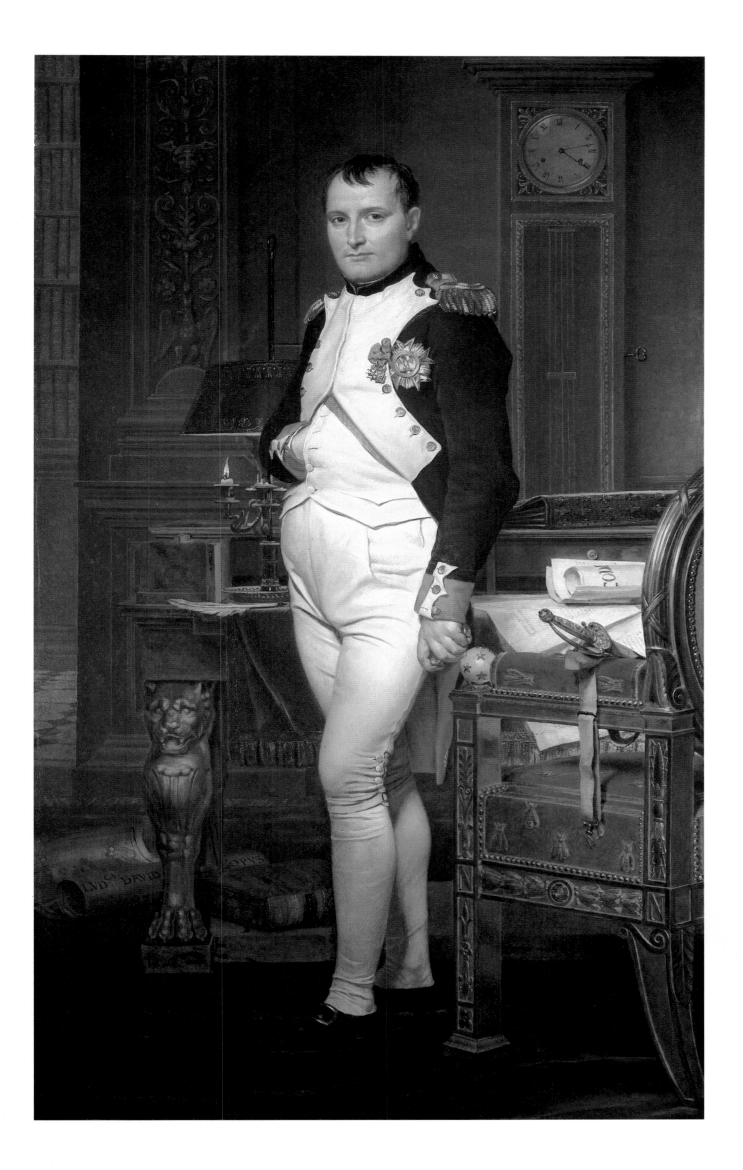

BARON FRANÇOIS GÉRARD
(b. 1700, Rome–d. 1837)

Ossian Evokes Spirits, 1809–1810
Oil on canvas, 72⁷⁄₁₆ × 76³⁄₈"
(184 × 194 cm)
Kunsthalle, Hamburg

immediately purchased for the state collection for an enormous price.

Lacking the advantage of academy schooling, Louis-Léopold Boilly (1761–1845) was not chosen to execute grandiose projects; even so, in his more modest works he exhibited the neoclassical taste that was pervasive after the revolution. His every figure drawn with elegant precision, Boilly recorded the simpler amenities of everyday life under Napoleon, anticipating the impressionists in his dedication to commonplace urban scenes. Restrained in Davidian fashion where color was concerned, *Billiards* (1807) portrays more than two dozen figures absorbed in flirtatious activities. In the spirit of the new age, the women, fashionably dressed in revealing high-waisted white shifts to appear antique and statuesque, wear virtue like a badge.

This marble-white ideal of female beauty, described by a twentieth-century scholar as the style of the "erotic frigidaire," attained perfection in *Bather of Valpinçon*, painted the following year by David's most gifted student, Jean-Auguste Dominique Ingres (1780–1867). So austere as to be exotic, as if it were a nunnery or a harem, the evenly lighted, nearly colorless setting is calculated to arouse curiosity, as is the figure's seated pose, her back turned for privacy, with no gesture whatsoever. Intensely observed and precisely painted, without any trace of brushwork to detract from the illusion, the props suggest passion in a sheerly visual way that would later challenge such abstract-minded artists as Degas and Matisse. The undulating striped pattern in the cloth wrapping the woman's hair and the crumpled sheets on which she sits agitate the superficially static mood, suggesting the restless rhythms of sexual abandon.

While the measured, understated harmonies suggest Ingres's desire to rival Renaissance masters such as Raphael, the extreme simplification is remarkably modern. Going beyond the terse concentration of David's *Marat Assassinated*, Ingres oversimplified to the point where classical clarity becomes romantically mysterious. Alone, the nude figure seems to be but a fragment of a more complex, but otherwise unrevealed, event. This picture thus introduced a new idiom of pictorial expression in which the part served to suggest a whole. Equally important, Ingres's perverse demonstration that the back of a figure can be as expressive as the face started a tradition among French painters of asserting their virtuosity by similarly restricting obviously expressive content in their subjects.

It was as a portraitist, however, that Ingres excelled, transforming details of costume and setting into symphonies of line and color. The twisting ripples and pleats of rich fabrics piled on top of one another seem to reveal an intoxicated or nervous breathing beneath the surface of the most placid sitter, whose smooth features appear to be all the more perfect in contrast to a sea of ribbons, necklaces, and rings. The interaction of areas of color and the counterpoint of linear rhythms in these masterpieces look back all the way to Fouquet and look forward to the art-for-art's-sake bias of later abstract painters — including Cézanne, whose opulent if rustic tabletop still lifes with crumpled textiles are like Ingres's portraits without the sitters.

At the beginning of the century the mute perfection of Ingres's portraits had its counterpart in the rare still-life paintings of Antoine Berjon (1754–1843). Spare, perfectly smooth neoclassical furnishings provide incongruously logical settings for cut flowers or collected seashells in Berjon's poetically charged pictures. Captive in the austere world of the well-off amateur scientist, these relics of nature seem as distressed as the chaste heroines in Ingres's exotic literary paintings.

While Napoleon remained in power, Ingres's great rival was his teacher, David, whose virtuosity as a portraitist is exemplified by his final image of Napoleon, painted in 1812, just before the disastrous Russian campaign. His sword set aside while he works into the night on papers such as his legal code, Napoleon appears like a man for all hours and seasons. Given our historical perspective, it seems that David has caught something tentative and slightly weary in the hero's face. A similar hint of the empire's downfall has been noted in the outstanding painting with which Théodore Géricault (1791–1824) made his Salon debut in 1812. Described simply as an equestrian portrait in the Salon catalog, this archly romantic work, painted with bravado as if to record every swashbuckling detail in one emotionally charged instant, amounts to a parody of David's crisply finished image in *Napoleon Crossing the Alps*, which was executed a dozen years earlier. Géricault's modern warrior strains to control a rearing animal that appears to be terrified by the roar and smoke of battle, and the soldier's backward glance to gesture his troops onward is the antithesis of the forward-facing spirit of David's earlier work. As would be all too evident the following year, when the overextended Napoleonic armies faltered, real war was full of fear and retreat.

OVERLEAF, LEFT:
THÉODORE GÉRICAULT (b. 1791, Rouen–d. 1824)

An Officer of the Imperial Horse Guards Charging, ca. 1813
Oil on canvas, 137⅛ × 104¼" (349 × 266 cm)
Musée du Louvre, Paris

OVERLEAF, RIGHT:
JACQUES-LOUIS DAVID

Napoleon Crossing the Alps, 1800
Oil on canvas, 106⅝ × 91⅛" (271 × 232 cm)
Musée du Louvre, Paris

BARON ANTOINE-JEAN GROS (b. 1771, Paris–d. 1835)

*The Pesthouse at Jaffa (General Bonaparte Visiting
the Plague-Stricken at Jaffa)*, 1804
Oil on canvas, 46½ × 65¼″ (118.5 × 164 cm)
Museum of Fine Arts, Boston
S.A. Denio Collection

Louis-Léopold Boilly (b. 1761, La Bassée–d. 1845)

Billards, 1807
Oil on canvas, 22 × 31⅞″ (56 × 81 cm)
The Hermitage Museum, Leningrad

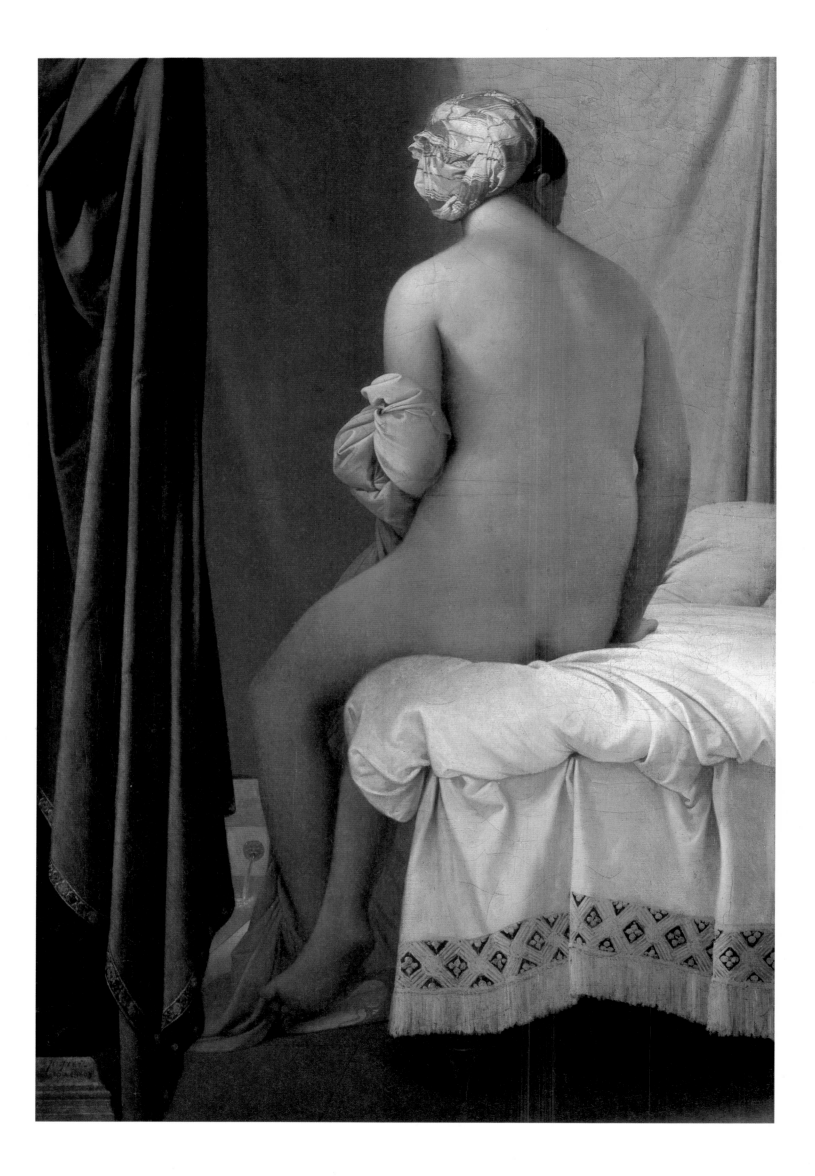

JEAN-AUGUSTE-DOMINIQUE INGRES
    (b. 1780, Montauban–d. 1867)

  Bather of Valpinçon, 1808
  Oil on canvas, 56⅝ × 38¼″ (143.8 × 97.2 cm)
  Musée du Louvre, Paris

ANTOINE BERJON (b. 1754, Lyon–d. 1843)

    Still Life of Flowers in a Basket, 1814
    Oil on canvas, 26 × 19¼″ (66 × 49 cm)
    Musée du Louvre, Paris

JEAN-AUGUSTE DOMINIQUE INGRES

    Mme. de Sononnes, ca. 1814
    Oil on canvas, 41¼ × 33⅛″ (106 × 84.2 cm)
    Musée des Beaux Arts, Nantes

IX.

Full-Blown Romanticism

With Napoleon's defeat in 1814 and the restoration of the monarchy in the person of Louis XVIII, the plundered masterpieces in the Louvre were returned to Italy. David took exile in Belgium, where he died and was buried in 1825. The empire collapsed, David apparently lost his convictions as a classicist, and his late style, first seen in a small exhibition in Paris in 1824, has never been duly acclaimed. It is best understood as a form of mock classicism, close in spirit to rococo masters such as Boucher and Fragonard, whom David had eclipsed in the 1770s and 1780s. While David never embraced their rollicking brushwork, in a large-scale painting such as *Cupid and Psyche* (1817) he demoted the gods to insincere adolescents and love to a ticklish, lighthearted sport. Caught in the bedsheets, David's Cupid wants to sneak away at dawn, leaving Psyche asleep like an antique statue with only superficial appeal. Such frank humor and irony in regard to love is surprisingly modern; not until Baudelaire and Manet would David's irreverence find its rightful heirs.

An ardent admirer who made a pilgrimage to pay his respects to David in exile in Brussels, Géricault wanted to create monumental pictures that would change art as completely as David's 1780s masterpieces had. For Géricault, however, the ultimate hero would be Everyman in his modern life struggle. Having failed to win the academy's scholarship to Rome, Géricault went there on his own in 1816 and made an intense study of the Renaissance masterpieces, such as Michelangelo's *Last Judgment*, that would form the basis of his ultraambitious works. There he decided to paint a monumental modern life scene documenting the annual pre-Lent race of the riderless horses, a pagan spectacle celebrating unrestrained bestial liberty. Like most of his projects, this was never fully realized. The remarkable drawings and painted studies for this project, works unknown to the general public until decades later, rank among the greatest pictures of the century. Observed from life, the trainers holding back the anxious steeds are contemporary versions of the relief sculptures from the Parthenon abducted with the most virtuous of neoclassical intentions from Athens to a London museum by Lord Elgin in 1803. As studies lacking inessential details, Géricault's renderings anticipate the domestic-scale modern life pictures of Manet and Degas; for example, the spectators behind the wall, indicated by mere splotches of paint in the riderless horse race studies, will reappear as blurs forty years later in their more urbane racetrack scenes.

While Géricault was in Rome, however, a shipwreck off the coast of Africa shocked the world, and the painter decided to immortalize its horrors in the form of a secular Michelangelesque requiem or a civilian *Pesthouse at Jaffa*. Completed in time for the Salon of 1819, *The Raft of the Medusa*, twenty-three feet wide, is probably the most ambitious French painting ever. Designed to shock, it amounted to an indictment of the new Bourbon regime, whose callous officers had saved themselves in boats but had abandoned one hundred fifty less fortunate passengers to a makeshift life raft that became the scene of famine and cannibalism for two weeks.

Géricault stopped at nothing to capture the ignoble suffering and insane terror. Carrying the principles of academy training to a ghoulish extreme, he visited morgues and hospitals to record the faces of death and the squalor of dismemberment in dozens of studies of amputated limbs; he even built a model of the raft for his studio and propped it at an angle to simulate the way in which ocean waves would toss it. On the raft he posed figures in the roles of the fifteen antiheroic survivors piled on top of one another to signal a distant rescue boat. Disappointed because the state did not purchase this epic from the Salon, Géricault took his controversial canvas on a commercial tour of London and then Dublin. Only five years later, at the sale of the painter's estate after his premature death, was the painting purchased for the Louvre. At this sale

the painter's extraordinary studies were briefly made public, initiating a cult among collectors and painters for this tormented genius who had staked out new realms of modern experience as the domain of painters. Missing from the sale, however, were the group of portraits Géricault had made during his last year for a doctor specializing in the treatment of the insane. Only later did these unorthodox portraits surface to be added to Géricault's heritage for posterity.

Among Géricault's most outspoken detractors was Ingres, who wanted the *Raft of the Medusa* removed from the Louvre so that it would not "corrupt the taste of the public which must only be conditioned to the Beautiful. . . . Art must be nothing but Beauty and teach us nothing but Beauty." Ingres had also exhibited a scene of horrific distress at the Salon of 1819, and the presence of beauty hardly makes it less unsettling as art.

Commissioned for Louis XVIII, Ingres's *Roger Rescuing Angelica* shares the mock-classical mood evident in David's late works. This painting, the first of many variations on the same theme that Ingres would undertake during the next forty years, illustrates an episode in Ariosto's sixteenth-century mock epic *Orlando Furioso*. In the poem, when the monster has been killed, the noble knight decides that he will rape the lady in distress as a reward for his heroism. To the reader's amusement, however, his armor has rusted tight, and he is unable to undress before Angelica is really saved. Ingres's sadistic visualization of the woman's helpless terror makes her still more arousing. Probing the darkest fantasies of the male psyche with this sharply focused image, the leading advocate of classicism invited viewers to consider the irrational interior world usually associated with his romantic contemporaries.

Of the exponents of Romanticism, the most formidable was Eugène Delacroix (1799–1863), a fellow student of Géricault at the academy's school. A lifelong archrival of Ingres,

JACQUES-LOUIS DAVID

> *Cupid and Psyche*, 1817
> Oil on canvas, 72½ × 95⅛"
> (184 × 241 cm)
> The Cleveland Museum of Art,
> Cleveland
> Leonard C. Hanna, Jr., Fund

Delacroix advocated the primacy of color where Ingres upheld the virtue of line as the ultimate foundation of painting. Of course, neither was wrong. Their opposing public positions notwithstanding, both artists held sexual fantasy to be the essence of beauty and truth. Just over sixteen feet wide, Delacroix's *The Death of Sardanapalus* was sent in January 1828, while the paint was barely dry, to join the nine other (four had been rejected by the admissions jury) archly romantic works he exhibited at the Salon of 1827, often considered a turning point away from classicism in French painting.

With the *Death of Sardanapalus* and *Liberty Leading the People* Delacroix catapulted himself to celebrity while bringing the era of grand Davidian-Napoleonic history painting to a climax. without the example of Ingres's *Roger Rescuing Angelica*. The counterpart in painting to the furious brassy scores of Berlioz, this work derived from Lord Byron's recent best-selling verse drama about a debauched Assyrian ruler who gathers all his treasures and concubines around his bed for slaughter as he sets his palace afire to thwart invaders. Nothing could be further from the moralizing stoic virtue commemorated in David's spare, stabilized compositions with their restrained use of color. In the cataclysmic, sadistic world of Sardanapalus, where insanity overrides decency, figures writhe and tumble in a sea of the brightest golds and reds. The indulgence, of course, is as much the painter's as the wicked ruler's. Delacroix must have realized that neither the state nor any private individual would have the display space, much less the tolerance for such a demented subject, to purchase this huge picture, whose relatively obscure theme obliged the painter to submit a long explanation to be printed in the supplement to the Salon catalog. Indeed, the painting went unsold for twenty years. But the artist's total independence from the conventions of taste could best be expressed in just this way; French painters ever since have sought controversy with very large (or, conversely, very small) pictures.

While *The Death of Sardanapalus* aroused a storm of controversy at the Salon, a painting by one of Gros's students, Paul Delaroche (1797–1856), was universally praised. It showed the death of Queen Elizabeth, one of the first of a series of history paintings by Delaroche designed to draw parallels between events in English history and contemporary conflicts in France between monarchists and republicans. More often than not these works show women or children in Gothic distress. None is finer than the wildly popular *Princes in the Tower*, a meticulously painted account of the terror experienced by Richard III's two nephews in the Tower of London as they sensed the executioner's approach. A master at Ingreslike suspense, Delaroche concentrated on only a fragment of the scene, revealing the remainder as a crack of light from the hallway seen under the door to the boys' tomblike cell. Given the current events of 1830, including the abdication of Bourbon King Charles X and his replacement from a different branch of the Bourbon family, Louis Philippe, Delaroche's sixteenth-century drama could not have been more topical.

It was Delacroix, however, who most blatantly capitalized on current events at the Salon of 1831, where one of the eight works he submitted was *Liberty Leading the People*. Over eleven feet wide, this modern history painting commemorates the street warfare of July 1830 that brought down the antidemocratic regime of King Charles X. Restaging the Napoleonic battle paintings of Gros in civilian dress, Delacroix sought scandal while risking severe criticism for celebrating the tricolor flag of the French Revolution in monarchist France. Clearly, his model for the painter as political activist was Géricault, and the figure of a fallen street fighter, his pants looted by someone for an unknown reason, is a clear homage to *The Raft of the Medusa*, recently acquired by the state. Incredibly, the state bought *Liberty Leading the People* from the Salon to exhibit at the museum of contemporary art, which had been inaugurated in 1818 by Louis XVIII, the ruler toppled by the events celebrated in Delacroix's picture.

Apart from the stirring command of battle painting displayed here, the work's crucial importance resides in the bare-breasted female figure leading the charge. Evidently based on accounts of a laundry girl who fought as fiercely as a new Joan of Arc for the people's cause, this figure can more easily be interpreted as a supernatural allegorical force, and the fusion in this work of realism and allegory opened up an important new realm for French painting. We shall see that many of the most controversial paintings of the later nineteenth century show naked women in the presence of dressed men, establishing a curious modern tradition.

With the *Death of Sardanapalus* and *Liberty Leading the People* Delacroix catapulted himself to celebrity while bringing the era of grand Davidian-Napoleonic history painting to a crescendo.

THÉODORE GÉRICAULT

The Race of Riderless Horses, ca. 1817
Oil on canvas, 17¼ × 23⅝" (45 × 60 cm)
Musée du Louvre, Paris

The liberalism of the contemporary art world toward Delacroix's excesses seems extraordinary in retrospect, and government support for the renegade in the form of an invitation to join a mission to north Africa in the summer of 1832 would ignite Delacroix's originality as a painter. He would spin out chromatic fantasies based on this brief trip for the next thirty years, showing future masters such as Gauguin and Matisse that the surest way to find oneself as an artist was to leave the Paris art scene for immersion into an unfamiliar world.

The Salon of 1834 contained *Women in Algiers*, an over eight-foot-wide glimpse into a shadowy stupefied harem strictly off limits to Westerners. Obsessed (in the spirit of Ingres) as much by the textile patterns as by the muffled light, Delacroix here introduced a manner of quick brushwork that had been absent from French painting since the heyday of Boucher and Fragonard. Equally important, with this picture Delacroix came to the realization, inherited by later artists, that action is not necessary to express emotion in painting. Afterward, Delacroix developed two modes, one conventionally swashbuckling and the other more modern, devoted to everyday dramas of contemplative tedium. When, over a century later, Picasso was invited to place his own paintings next to masterpieces in the Louvre when the museum was closed to the public, the Spaniard came away feeling smug, except with regard to Delacroix. "That bastard," he confessed. "He's really good." In 1955 Picasso devoted himself to a whole series of variations on *Women in Algiers*.

Delacroix's most swashbuckling works, full of tumbling and rearing horses, pouncing lions, and Arabs armed to the teeth, constitute a vast series of repetitions on a general theme, setting a precedent for careerlong specialized investigations that would extend from Degas with his dancers to Buren with his stripes. In these paintings, based on notes taken during the summer of 1832 and much more on imagination, Delacroix developed abstract ways of animating forms on a canvas with patterns of color bursting in the intense north African sunlight. The few of these works left unresolved in sketch form provide graphic demonstrations of the freewheeling harmonies that were the foundations of Delacroix's art, a reminder that he sought nothing so much as to rival in paint the abstract beauties of music. Without Delacroix's virtuoso stabs of paint to evoke glinting highlights or flickering reflections, it is doubtful whether the impressionists would have realized the potential drama in the study of light per se.

THÉODORE GÉRICAULT

The Raft of the Medusa, 1819
Oil on canvas, 193⁵⁄₁₆ × 281⅞″ (491 × 716 cm)
Musée du Louvre, Paris

EUGÈNE DELACROIX

Liberty Leading the People, 1830
Oil on canvas, 102⅛ × 128″ (260 × 325 cm)
Musée du Louvre, Paris

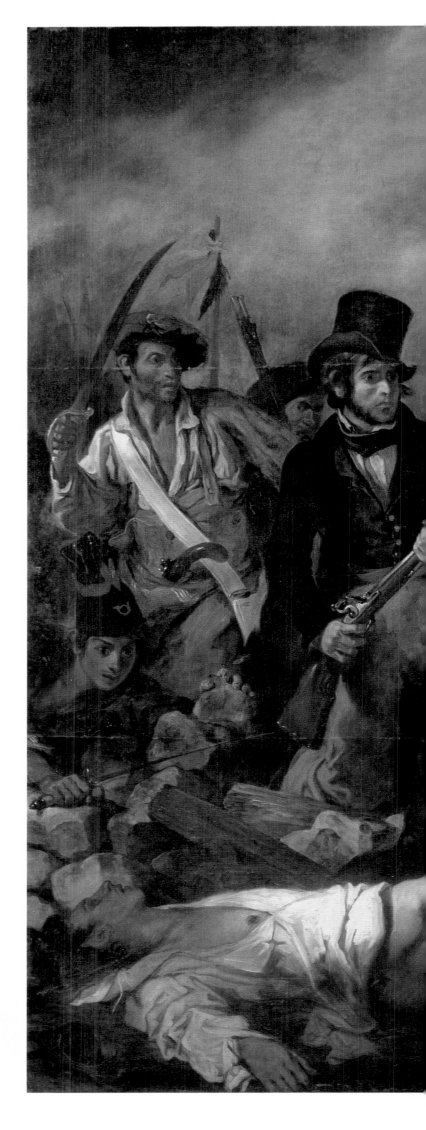

Eugène Delacroix (b. 1798, Charenton-Saint-Maurice–
    d. 1863)

> *The Death of Sardanapalus*, 1827
> Oil on canvas, 154⁵⁄₁₆ × 195¼″ (392 × 496 cm)
> Musée du Louvre, Paris

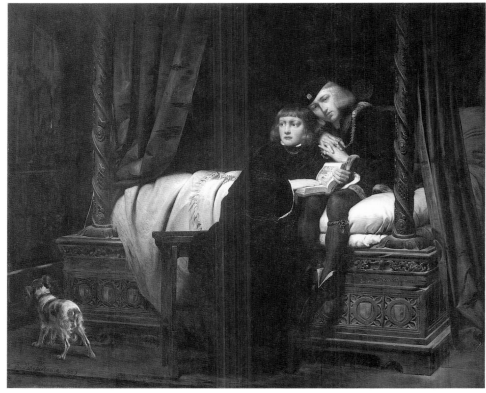

Paul Delaroche (b. 1797, Paris–d. 1856)

> *The Princes in the Tower*, 1831
> Oil on canvas, 71¼ × 84⁵⁄₈″ (181 × 215 cm)
> Musée du Louvre, Paris

EUGÈNE DELACROIX

Lion-Hunt Study, ca. 1854
Oil on canvas, 34 × 45″ (86.3 × 114.3 cm)
Musée d'Orsay, Paris

EUGÈNE DELACROIX

Women in Algiers, 1834
Oil on canvas, 70⅞ × 90⅛″ (180 × 229 cm)
Musée du Louvre, Paris

X.

Leaving Paris: From Barbizon to Ornans

THE EXTRAORDINARY POWER OF THE SKETCH ON ITS OWN TERMS, SO SELF-EVIDENT TO modern observers, was a matter of heated controversy throughout the nineteenth century. Aside from the precedent set by Géricault and Delacroix's studies, no early paintings so successfully argue in favor of spontaneity in art as those of Honoré Daumier (1808–1879), whose outstanding career as a caricaturist began in the late 1820s as Romanticism polarized taste in art. Indeed, the invention of lithography at around the time of Daumier's birth made possible the publication of satirical periodicals that fueled the political turmoil of the 1830s and 1840s. Daumier's mastery of this textured medium in which "color" was a function of black and white predisposed him to make paintings more rudimentary than any previously conceived. Around 1846, when Daumier moved into a large top-floor loft apartment on the Ile Saint-Louis, he began to paint in earnest, probably encouraged by his new neighbor, Charles Baudelaire, an ardent admirer of Delacroix who sought to find words no less passionate than his idol's colors but to devote them to descriptions of modern life. For both Delacroix and Baudelaire, Daumier, on the basis of his cartoons alone, was among the greatest artists of the age. Considered unfinished, *We Want Barrabas!*, the largest of Daumier's paintings, adapts the Middle Eastern idiom favored by Delacroix to represent the "voice of the people," no doubt in response to the abdication of King Louis Philippe in 1848 to allow popular elections. Epitomizing the theatrical looking-at-looking theme introduced into French painting by Watteau, this rudimentary sketch, in which only one face is visible in a crowd, demonstrated how painting could rival drawing in its speed and directness of expression, ushering in a new era in French figure painting.

The scope of French painting shifted dramatically to keep in step with the growing political importance of the working classes and the provinces. A new breed of painters found it intolerable that a painter would toady to such bourgeois clients as the sitters in portraits by Ingres and lead a life imprisoned in a studio to transpose history and literature onto canvas, ignoring the adventures of real life. In reaction to the cholera epidemic of 1830, country life suddenly took on the enormous appeal of good health. A genuine "portrait" of French life was the collective enterprise of a closely knit band of painters who embraced the art of landscape after they saw a celebrated example by their English contemporary John Constable at the Salon of 1824. Following this lead, artists such as Camille Corot (1796–1875), Théodore Rousseau, and Charles Daubigny (1817–1878) revived the simple genre of landscape that had been so popular in seventeenth-century Holland. The road was the ubiquitous motif in their paintings of simple villages, farms, and forests (including the Fontainebleau forest, where a colony of artists took root in the 1820s), apparently a motif that celebrated their troubadourlike existence as their work took them across the nation. Carrying the eye through space from near to far away, the road image became a major symbol in French painting throughout the century.

Before the invention of the tin tube in the 1840s, landscape painting as a genre had been limited by inherent logistical problems, including the heavy baggage of painting gear. As a result, these artists were obliged to make drawings or work on portable small canvases or panels that would not blow away in the wind. Later on painters enlarged these notes in a studio setting. This process contributed in large measure to the landscape-sketch aesthetic that developed in tandem

with the cult of Géricault for figure painters. By the 1840s Corot had become determined to exhibit his small-scale oil sketches painted out of doors with more conventionally finished works, sparking a controversy that pitted adherents of spontaneity against advocates of refinement in painting.

During the reign of Louis Philippe the rugged landscapes of artists such as Rousseau had only limited appeal, perhaps because they seemed like hymns to republicanism. In any case, these works were often denied a place at the Salons by conservative juries whose members tended nepotistically to patronize their academy-minded colleagues and their students. As a result, the so-called Barbizon (named after a village in the Fontainebleau forest) painters were obliged to exhibit refused works in protest in private studios, and they planned a private exhibition association as an alternative to the state-run Salons. Such an artists' cooperative went unrealized until 1873, when the impressionists organized themselves, but the impetus began with Rousseau and his friends. With the advent of the short-lived Second Republic in 1848, recognition finally came to these painters, and during the second half of the century their style enjoyed international popularity. The appeal can be characterized as what today is referred to as "painters' painting": Each observed shift in value in the landscape was transcribed onto canvas with a simple directness of touch that clearly remained a stroke of paint even while playing a jigsaw-puzzle-piece role in the picture's approximate representation of the real world.

Not permitted as a woman to study at the academy art school, Rosa Bonheur (1822–1899) transposed the Barbizon vision onto enormous canvases, gaining official sanction, fortune, and international fame as a specialist in animals. Indeed, *The Horse Fair*, which was exhibited in 1855, amounted to a fulfillment of Géricault's project to make a mural-scale horse painting, and it became one of the world's most expensive paintings by 1887, when a Vanderbilt bought it for the new Metropolitan Museum of Art in New York. *Plowing in the Nivernais: The Dressing of Vines* (1849), however, better represents her key position among a generation of artists determined to elevate the labors of the field to a heroic status. Daughter of a Saint-Simonian socialist family devoted to the equality of women, Bonheur supposedly chose this scene after reading *The Devil's Pool* (1846) by George Sand. It was painted on government commission for the Salon of 1849 and immediately became a highlight of the Luxembourg Palace Museum for works by living artists.

JEAN-AUGUSTE-DOMINIQUE INGRES

Portrait of M. Bertin, 1832
Oil on canvas, 45¼ × 37⅜"
(116.2 × 94.9 cm)
Musée du Louvre, Paris

HONORÉ DAUMIER
(b. 1808, Marseille–d. 1879)

We Want Barabbas! (Ecce Homo), 1849–1852
Oil on canvas, 63 × 50"
(160 × 127 cm)
Folkwang Museum, Essen

GUSTAVE COURBET (b. 1819, Ornans–d. 1877)

Burial at Ornans, 1849–1850
Oil on canvas, 122⅝ × 263″
(311.5 × 668 cm)
Musée d'Orsay, Paris

The same love of labor and the soil captivated the genius of Jean François Millet (1814–1875), whose *The Sower*, which was included in the Salon of 1850, depicts a self-assured young farmer as if his mission were as heroic as the one of Napoleon crossing the Alps that David had painted a half century before. Dominating the scene with a striding gesture to fling seeds, this image of a peasant exemplifies the symbolic nature of early realist painting in France. Tempering their shared commitment to sincerity and humility with an ambition to show working-class life as an epic worthy of Michelangelo, painters such as Millet initiated an intensely righteous version of realism that would have abiding appeal throughout the century. Indeed, van Gogh gave himself lessons in pictorial intensity by copying paintings like *The Sower*.

The self-proclaimed star of this generation was Gustave Courbet (1819–1877), whose celebrity was consolidated when he exhibited a twenty-one-foot-wide group portrait of his fellow provincial townsfolk from Ornans at the Salon of 1850. Taking advantage of a recent (and short-lived) rule that painters who had, like himself, won medals of excellence at previous Salons would be exempt from the admissions jury, Courbet threw himself into a Herculean effort to come to grips with modern French life. The subject he chose was a funeral at the brand-new cemetery just outside Ornans. The center of this anticlimactic composition is a void — the hole for the coffin — and the surviving citizens press around as witnesses. There are nearly fifty of them crammed together, none treated more importantly than any other, each portrayed with untempered realism. Their black garb had become utterly modern, standard dress throughout France in the wake of the cholera epidemics of 1830 and 1848, so commonplace had funerals become. Courbet indulged himself in the limitations of these black costumes, orchestrating nuances of black on still more black with the virtuosity of a seventeenth-century Spanish master, punctuating the general gloom only with the uncanny range of portraits, observed from every angle, without any excitement but also without any tedium. As had happened when Géricault exhibited *The Raft of the Medusa*, the cult of the ugly revived as a mainstay of French painting.

The most internationally popular of all these realist masters was Constant Troyon (1813–1865), whose mammoth *Cattle Going to Work: Impression of Morning* was a centerpiece at the World's Fair Salon of 1855 and was acquired immediately thereafter for the Luxembourg Palace Museum. Trading on the panoramic sweep of Bonheur and the confrontational antidrama of Courbet, Troyon had unprecedented success in rendering light and shadow. His achievement impressed the nineteen-year-old Claude Monet when he came to Paris to enroll in art school, but the self-taught Troyon would take on no disciples.

Years later, when Monet dedicated himself to paintings of stacked grain, he was of course fulfilling his earliest ambitions to make paintings in the quasi-religious Barbizon spirit. Paintings with haystacks enjoyed an antiestablishment glamour for beginning painters like Monet, and

Millet's *The Gleaners* was vociferously attacked by conservative newspaper critics when it was shown at the Salon of 1857. Reduced to the backbreaking labor of picking scraps left by the harvesters, these poorest of the poor were called the "three Fates of pauperdom," and for some viewers this image of social inequality aroused fears of another revolution. But given Millet's exquisitely golden rendition of the rural atmosphere, with the gleanings sparkling as highlights underfoot, the painter seems to suggest that the humblest crop provides wealth.

The moon is already risen in the gloaming sky recorded by Jules Breton (1827–1906), whose *The Recall of the Gleaners*, with its haystacks, was among the works acquired by the state from the Salon of 1859. Combining his admiration for Millet and Courbet, Breton fashioned a more generally appealing brand of realism without the pain, ugliness, and vulgarity of workers. Academic with its Italian Renaissance poses, Breton's work seems essentially at odds with the emphasis on sincerity in the best Barbizon painting, but his theatrical visions of pastoral life initiated an important form of decorative realism that would reach fulfillment in the murals of Puvis de Chavannes.

For utter sincerity, no one surpassed Daumier, whose variations on the theme of railroad passengers in *A Third-Class Carriage* bring the modern spectator face to face with the overcrowded modern world. Grasping the mechanics of the looking-at-looking theme with his masterful sense of drama, Daumier arranged these compositions so that viewers would imagine themselves seated in the position of a fellow passenger directly across from a nursing woman, whose mother returns the viewers' glance as if to protect the scant peace and privacy they have made for themselves under less than ideal modern circumstances.

HONORÉ DAUMIER

A Third-Class Carriage, 1863–1865
Oil on canvas, 25¼ × 35½" (65.4 × 90.2 cm)
The Metropolitan Museum of Art, New York
Bequest of Mrs. H.O. Havemeyer, 1929
The H.O. Havemeyer Collection

JEAN-BAPTISTE-CAMILLE COROT
(b. 1796, Paris–d. 1875)

Saint-André-en-Morvan, 1862
Oil on canvas, 12³⁄₁₆ × 23¼″
(31 × 59 cm)
Musée du Louvre, Paris

THÉODORE ROUSSEAU (b. 1812, Paris–d. 1867)

Village of Becquiny, ca. 1857
Oil on panel, 25 × 39⅜″ (63 × 100 cm)
The Frick Collection, New York

CONSTANT TROYON (b. 1810, Sèvres–d. 1865)

Cattle Going to Work: Impression of Morning, 1855
Oil on canvas, 102¼ × 157½″ (260 × 400 cm)
Musée d'Orsay, Paris

ROSA BONHEUR (b. 1822, Bordeaux—d. 1899)

Plowing in the Nivernais, 1849
Oil on canvas, 52¼ × 102¼" (134 × 260 cm)
Musée d'Orsay, Paris

JEAN-FRANÇOIS MILLET (b. 1814, Gruchy–d. 1875)

The Sower, 1850
Oil on canvas, 40 × 32½″ (101.6 × 82.6 cm)
Museum of Fine Arts, Boston
Gift of Quincy Adams Shaw through Quincy A. Shaw,
Jr. and Mrs. Marian Shaw Haughton

JULES BRETON (b. 1827, Courrières–d. 1906)

Recall of the Gleaners, 1859
Oil on canvas, 35½ × 69¼″ (90.2 × 175.9 cm)
Musée d'Orsay, Paris

JEAN-FRANÇOIS MILLET

The Gleaners, 1857
Oil on canvas, 32¼ × 43¼″ (83 × 111 cm)
Musée d'Orsay, Paris

XI.
Real Allegories

ON DAYS WHEN THE WEATHER WAS BAD, COROT, THE BARBIZON ARTIST COMMITTED TO sincerity and truth, was of course obliged to work in a studio like an old-fashioned landscape painter. Most often he would civilize these Claudelike landscapes with dancing figures in antique costumes, evidently based on the ballet dancers he liked to sketch at the Paris Opéra. Works like these link a poetic Renaissance vision of nature to the brash fantasies of Matisse at the outset of the twentieth century. These artificial works suggest how realist painters were sometimes obliged to put aside their aesthetic principles because of practical concerns such as bad weather and the complications of staging models.

Since reality does not stand still, realism is at odds with the time-consuming act of painting, obliging its adherents to accept hypocrisies, forcing them, for example, to require models in everyday costumes to hold long "realistic" poses, similar to the way in which history painters worked. Baudelaire, the most vigorous advocate among critics of painting from modern life, urged artists to immerse themselves in the crowd to familiarize themselves with the details of nineteenth-century life, but such advice was next to impossible to follow for painters who needed space, privacy, and time. Not surprisingly, the artists Baudelaire singled out for special praise, including Daumier and Constantin Guys (1802–1892), were draftsmen who could work with portable pen and paper. When Baudelaire endorsed Eugène Boudin (1825–1898), it was for his pastels rather than his oil paintings.

One of the oddest aspects of realism is the large percentage of pictures with reclining or sleeping figures, since the unusual popularity of such poses reflects the demands of models unwilling or unable to hold more strenuous poses as long as a painter might like. Courbet's life-scale depiction of two young women collapsed on a shady riverbank is a case in point. In 1857, when the picture was first shown at the Salon, viewers were shocked by what they took as Courbet's frank portrayal of two prostitutes, one of whom has removed her dress to use as a sheet for her nap on the grass (hardly realistic behavior even for a whore). Whereas nineteenth-century observers might tolerate statuesque nudes in the name of classicism, chubbier, more matter-of-fact models only slightly undressed like Courbet's were evidently too familiar to these viewers and thus were liable to condemnation as slothful sluts. Obsessed with the discrepancy between art and daily life, Courbet had in 1855 exhibited a nearly twenty-foot-wide portrait of himself at work in his studio, surrounded by his supporters and the ordinary working people who came to pose for his pictures. Although the Salon jury accepted eleven of the fourteen paintings Courbet submitted, they refused this and two other very large works, probably in order to divide the available wall space more equitably: More than seven thousand paintings had been submitted that year, and in the end there was room for only 1,867. More than nine hundred thousand visitors came to see the Salon of 1855, which was a centerpiece to the World's Fair held in Paris. Furious at the rejection, Courbet decided to have a temporary building constructed for his own one-artist exhibition, confident that the entrance fees would cover the costs. They did not come close, but Courbet's grand unprecedented gesture of independence from the official taste of the Salon jury made him a hero for young artists everywhere, and by the end of the century such independent exhibitions had become an essential feature of contemporary art.

In his privately printed catalog Courbet entitled the rejected self-portrait *The Painter's Studio: A Real Allegory*. Judging from the elaborate scene, "real" and "allegory" are inseparable terms: Although a real model is standing behind Courbet, her clothes on the floor in a pile, he ignores her to work on a landscape painted not directly from nature in realist fashion but from memory and imagination. Apparently he will soon need her to pose like the women on the

riverbank so that he can add her to the landscape. With her dimpled figure, she will surely not be mistaken for a classical nymph, and as a modern woman, her nudity will seem immodest. As for Baudelaire, Courbet included his friend at the far right, ignoring reality with his nose in a book!

Modern life often imitates art and thus makes a mockery of realism. Such ironic situations had special appeal for painters in the middle of the nineteenth century, including the conservative academician Jean-Léon Gérôme (1824–1904). His *Duel After the Ball*, painted in his studio no doubt, shows the sort of blurry predawn landscape outside Paris that would so appeal to the impressionists in the following decades. Well-to-do revelers from a costume party have assembled to settle a nineteenth-century account of honor in ancient fashion with swords. Their ill-sorted costumes notwithstanding, the figures portray a very real, if anachronistic and horrible, fact of contemporary life.

With his unerring sensitivity to sham, Daumier would devote his paintings to putting tear-jerking realist efforts like Gérôme's into perspective. Imagining himself a spectator at the theater, Daumier rendered the silhouetted reactions of fellow spectators in the mute darkness to the melodramatic realist play both he and they observe on the artificially lighted stage in the background of the painting. Only by including both real and artificial terms in the same frame (thus constructing what Courbet called "real allegory") could he document paradoxes of modern life in painting. Daumier (and Baudelaire, who published an essay stressing how no living creatures except human beings are blessed with an understanding of humor) set a precedent for artists to address absurdity and foolish inconsistency as essential elements of real life. Daumier's very greatest painting is among those he based upon *Don Quixote*, by Miguel Cervantes, about a seventeenth-century nobleman who sees not reality but what he wants to see and, hence, charges windmills as if they were giant-sized foes.

JEAN-BAPTISTE-CAMILLE COROT
Morning — Dance of the Nymphs, 1850
Oil on canvas, 38½ × 51½ (98 × 131 cm)
Musée du Louvre, Paris

No antiacademic artist under Courbet's spell better understood this new freedom than Edouard Manet (1832–1883), who enjoyed breaking rules in order to shock viewers into looking afresh at the wonderful mechanisms of illusion that guide all perceptions. Utterly misunderstanding Manet, his earnest classical-minded colleagues laughed not with him but at him, refusing his pictures admission to the Salon of 1863. That year so many painters were refused that the Emperor Napoleon III (elected in 1852) decided for once to provide state support for a alternative Salon des Refusés to display works unacceptable to the official jurors. Here the public encountered Manet's strange masterpieces alongside works by other young mavericks such as Camille Pissarro and James Whistler. In one of Manet's works his favorite model, Victorine Meurent, is posed in comic semi-transvestiture as a male bullfighter with a lavender bandanna. She has no idea how to hold the red toreador's cloth, which serves Manet as an art-for-art's-sake accent of color. The only authentically realistic detail in this spoof is the horseman jabbing a bull in the background, and this Manet took from art, not life, plagiarizing a famous etching by the Spanish realist artist Goya.

No less shocking, *Luncheon on the Grass*, first shown in the same Salon des Refusés and since become the most famous modern French painting, is a "real allegory" with a naked woman amid dressed men, in the tradition established by Delacroix and Courbet. A parody of a detail in a

work by the Renaissance master Raphael, Manet's weird would-be realist scene again features Victorine Meurent, this time in her studio model's role, staring back out of the picture at the painter-spectator rather than participating in a conversation with her comodels. So brightly lighted as to appear more two-dimensional than real, her flesh (obviously painted under studio conditions rather than out of doors) seems out of place in the shady bower. Needless to say, critics considered this departure from the rules of consistent illusion a sign of ineptness.

No work by Manet was more offensive in terms of both its subject and how it was painted than *Olympia*, which actually was accepted for the Salon of 1865. A spoof of Titian's celebrated *Venus of Urbino*, *Olympia* portrays Victorine Meurent in the role of a whorish goddess, as scrawny and unlucky as the hissing black cat at her feet. Playing the idiot artist's role to the hilt, Manet painted the cat (and a black woman servant) silhouetted against black curtains to appear hardly visible while showing his favorite model silhouetted against white bed linens, thus minimizing her bodily appeal. Again she stares out of the picture, suggesting an awareness of the spectator's presence and indicating that the painting shows only one part of a larger encounter, a fragment of some mysterious whole. Just how awkward Manet's works seemed to contemporaries can be sensed by comparing them with Ingres's *Turkish Bath*, which was presented at the Salon of 1863. Voyeuristic rather than confrontational, this hothouse of perfect female bodies collapsed in limp abandon was anathema to many members of the realist generation. For them, such imaginary fantasies had nothing to do with real experience and such precise rendition of form had little more personality than the mechanically engendered images of photography that appealed to a public uninterested in the subtleties of brushwork.

GUSTAVE COURBET

The Painter's Studio: A Real Allegory..., 1855
Oil on canvas, 142⅛ × 235⁷⁄₁₆"
(361 × 598 cm)
Musée d'Orsay, Paris

Jean-Léon Gérôme (b. 1824, Vesoul–d. 1904)

Duel After the Ball, 1857–1859
Oil on canvas, 14¹⁵⁄₁₆ × 21¾″ (37.9 × 55.2 cm)
Walters Art Gallery, Baltimore

HONORÉ DAUMIER

Don Quixote and Sancho Panza, 1864–1866
Oil on canvas, 56 × 84″ (142.2 × 213.3 cm)
From the Collection of Joan Whitney Payson,
New York

HONORÉ DAUMIER

The Drama, ca. 1860
Oil on canvas, 38½ × 35⅞″ (98 × 90 cm)
Neue Pinakothek, Munich

EDOUARD MANET

    Luncheon on the Grass (Déjeuner sur l'Herbe), 1863
    Oil on canvas, 82 × 104″ (208 × 264 cm)
    Musée d'Orsay, Paris

EDOUARD MANET (b. 1832, Paris–d. 1883)

    Mademoiselle Victorine in the Costume of an Espada, 1862
    Oil on canvas, 65 × 50¼″ (165.1 × 127.6 cm)
    The Metropolitan Museum of Art, New York
    Bequest of Mrs. H.O. Havemeyer, 1929
    The H.O. Havemeyer Collection

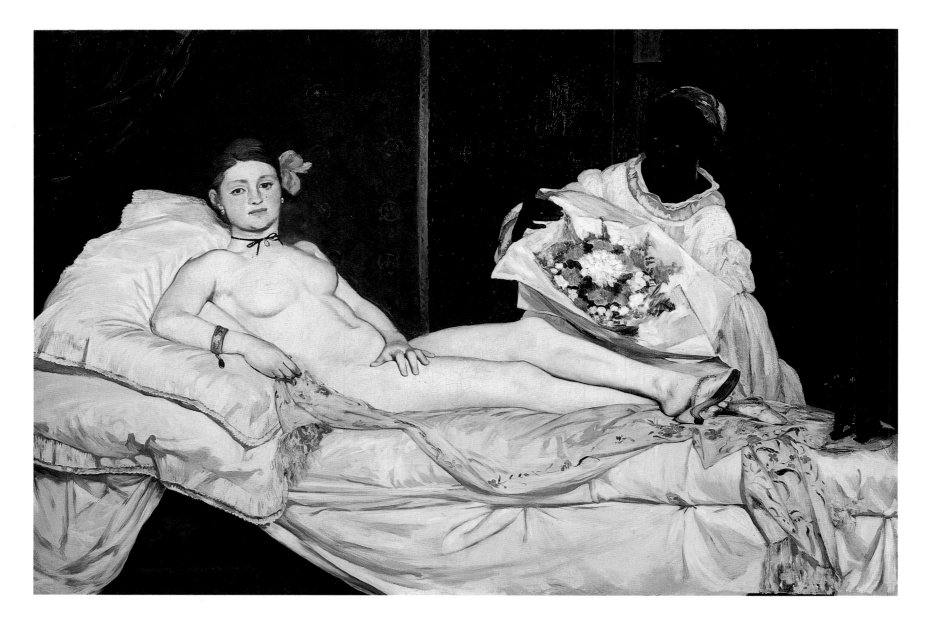

EDOUARD MANET

Olympia, 1803
Oil on canvas, 51⅜ × 74¼″ (130.5 × 190 cm)
Musée d'Orsay, Paris

JEAN-AUGUSTE-DOMINIQUE INGRES

Turkish Bath, 1863
Oil on canvas, 43⁵⁄₁₆ × 43⁵⁄₁₆″ (110 × 110 cm)
Musée du Louvre, Paris

XII.
Brushwork in the 1860s

BRUSHWORK IN ALL ITS GLORIOUS VARIETY, WHICH MIGHT BE UNDERSTOOD AS DRAWING WITH color — feathered, twisted, speckled — was seldom more spectacularly demonstrated than in a chapel of the Church of Saint-Sulpice in Paris for which murals were commissioned from Delacroix. When they were unveiled in July 1861, the cult of Delacroix reached its height, and the vigorous energy of light and color with which he evoked an imaginary biblical landscape would inspire painters from Degas to van Gogh to intensify their on-the-spot perceptions of French locales closer at hand. Delacroix's death in 1863 was marked by a Rembrandtesque group portrait of the modern school by Henri Fantin-Latour (1836–1904). Exhibited at the Salon of 1864, this group included Baudelaire, Manet with his red hair, and Whistler holding a bouquet and cultivating a resemblance to Delacroix, whose portrait on the wall seemingly magnetizes the mavericks of the next generation.

Missing was Courbet, whose magnificent hunting scenes are hardly less obvious gestures to Delacroix's genius than is Fantin-Latour's group portrait. Substituting hounds and stags in the snow for Delacroix's tigers jumping at horses in torrid Araby, Courbet sought to beat the great romantic at his own game. Moreover, the chief realist indulged no less in brush virtuosity, rendering a white-on-white world with every conceivable texture, including passages scraped across the canvas from the blade of a palette knife to reveal flickers of underlayers, suggesting the richness of light in an unprecedented way.

Even artists opposed to romantic brushwork, such as Gérôme, might be caught under the Delacroix tradition. No less concerned about realism than was Courbet, Gérôme was obsessed by the need to impress viewers with his meticulously fine craftsmanship, so smoothly finished as to rival the perfect illusion created by photographs. If Courbet loved to boast how he could paint wild, inaccessible scenes way off in the French provinces, Gérôme for his part would climb to the rooftops in Cairo for a good painting and secretively observe the faithful turned to some invisible Eastern spirit manifest to their foreign eyes. While Gérôme would live out the century to become the personification of archconservative taste, his rival in dramatic exactitude, the precocious Henri Regnault (1843–1871), would become a victim of the war with Prussia that brought down the Second Empire. More explicitly lurid than anything Delacroix ever painted, Regnault's sensationalistic *Execution Without Trial under the Moorish Kings of Granada* is both too horrible to look at and too beautiful not to. Had Regnault lived, Delacroix's heritage would have been that much richer.

For realists, however, such charged historical dramas lacked sincerity and smacked of commercialism. Ernest Meissonier (1815–1891) was a paragon of virtuosity for virtuosity's sake. Lampooning Meissonier's magnificent, proto-cinematic history painting *The Campaign of 1814*, showing Napoleon leading his remaining troops in retreat through a frozen landscape, the novelist Edmond Duranty suggested that the painter was rich enough to rent a herd of horses and enough riders and costumes to stage the vast event at his country estate in realist fashion and that in order to keep up with the movement of the column, he had had a little railroad built that carried his easel in tandem with his models.

Although Duranty was exaggerating for literary effect, Salon artists such as Gérôme, Regnault, and Meissonier would go to almost any length to be sensational in the increasingly competitive Parisian art world of the 1860s. Duranty's friends Degas and Manet sought to simplify the business of being a painter, to concentrate on the fundamentals of art rather than on showmanship. Whereas Meissonier would pretend to take up his painter's position in front of the

slow march of history, Manet would pretend, with humor, to risk his realist painter's life for something as trifling as a race, awaiting the victor at the finish line fearlessly while a pack of horses hurtled down on him. A spoof on the theatrics of Salon artists, Manet's painting is an extraordinary rendition of the appearance of movement, so seldom attempted in art. Concentrating on the instantaneous event, he recorded a blur of shapes, scumbling imprecise details with his brush and only occasionally recognizing a specific detail such as a parasol or a spectator with field glasses in the stands. His bold departure from convention, however, initiated a crucial enterprise for French painters: the need to record the simple glance, the basic unit of everyday sight, unpremeditated, unfocused, but hardly unimportant when recognized as the atom unit of all perception.

No less willing to leave fallen historical heroes to the Salon darlings, Manet's young colleague Edgar Degas (1834–1917) accompanied him to the local racetracks. For Degas the greatest dramas were the play of light and the rotation of forms as the parading horses and silk-suited jockeys cast wild shadows in front of the crowd of spectators before the race. Such civilized settings were as far afield as Degas would go to paint out of doors. Indeed, he even suggested in anti-impressionist jest that the police be empowered to make arrests to control the explosion of landscape painters littering the French countryside.

Like Daumier, Degas loved to meditate on the mechanics of spectatordom, and he put the looking-at-looking theme at the service of portraiture, transforming its conventions into a glancing form of modern realism. *The Orchestra of the Opéra*, which seems at first to record a random close-up glimpse through opera glasses into the orchestra pit during a ballet performance, is actually a "portrait" of the painter's musician friends observed as themselves rather than formally posed the way Fantin-Latour might have presented them. The fact that a spectator of Degas's picture is obliged to imagine himself or herself in a particular seat at the theater extends Manet's discovery that a realist painting can include only half a scene: The act of looking obliges the spectator to stand apart from what is seen; to record the act of looking, painters must evoke the continuation between the space observed (and therefore in the picture) and the observer's

HENRI FANTIN-LATOUR
(b. 1836, Grenoble–d. 1904)

Homage to Delacroix, 1864
Oil on canvas, 63 × 98⅞"
(160 × 250 cm)
Musée d'Orsay, Paris

space (implied by details in the picture but outside it by definition). To suggest real experience, the painter must take both parts of the visual act into account.

Degas's profound study of how space extends beyond a painting's limited visual field began with a group portrait of his uncle's family on which he worked for nearly a decade. Partly a formal portrait, partly an informal genre scene, this painting portrays the awkwardness of modern domestic life as much as it portrays a particular family. Each of the four figures looks away from the others, scattering the spectator's focus across and beyond the room as surely as the mirror with its image of the space outside the picture, the doorway to another room at the left, and the little dog partly visible at the right. Disregarding Degas, this headless dog is a sort of symbol for the continuation of space outside the confines of a painting as well as for the instantaneous unrehearsed moment this painter sought to capture with the strict objectivity of a social scientist. Despite the vast differences in subject, Degas's accomplishment in works such as *The Bellelli Family* parallels what Courbet accomplished in his light-dappled landscape paintings with sheltered groups of deer. No less a family scene, Courbet's *Thicket of Deer*, which was exhibited at the Salon of 1866, likewise captures an utterly candid instant, with the skittish animals unaware of the painter's presence. While neither painter would have been able to stalk his subject firsthand as these pictures suggest, both subscribed to the decade's obsession with instantaneity as the fundamental condition of experience and thus the touchstone for truth.

JEAN-LÉON GÉRÔME (b. 1824, Vesoul–d. 1904)

Prayer on the Rooftops, 1865
Oil on panel, 19⅝ × 32″ (50 × 81 cm)
Kunsthalle, Hamburg

HENRI REGNAULT (b. 1843, Paris–d. 1871)

Execution Without Trial Under the Moorish Kings at Grenada, 1870
Oil on canvas, 57½ × 19⅝″ (146 × 49.8 cm)
Musée d'Orsay, Paris

EUGÈNE DELACROIX

Jacob Wrestling with the Angel, 1853
Oil and wax, 110⅝ × 75³/₁₆″ (281 × 191 cm)
The Church of Saint-Sulpice, Paris

GUSTAVE COURBET

L'Hallali of the Stag, 1867
Oil on canvas, 139¼ × 198¹³/₁₆″ (366 × 505 cm)
Musée des Beaux-Arts, Besançon

EDGAR DEGAS

The Orchestra of the Opera, ca. 1870
Oil on canvas, 22¼ × 18¼″ (56.5 × 46.2 cm)
Musée d'Orsay, Paris

EDOUARD MANET

Racetrack Near Paris, ca. 1865
Oil on canvas, 17¼ × 33¼″ (43.9 × 84.5 cm)
The Art Institute of Chicago, Chicago
Potter Palmer Collection, 1922

EDGAR DEGAS (b. 1834, Paris–d. 1917)

Racehorses Before the Stands, 1866–1868
Essence on paper mounted on canvas, 18⅛ × 24″
(46 × 61 cm)
Musée d'Orsay, Paris

ERNEST MEISSONIER (b. 1815, Lyon–d. 1891)

The Campaign in France, 1864
Oil on canvas, 20¼ × 30″ (51.4 × 76.2 cm)
Musée d'Orsay, Paris

XIII.
Landscape Becomes Modern

FRÉDÉRIC BAZILLE (b. 1841,
Montpellier–d. 1870)

The Village View, 1868
Oil on canvas, 51³/₁₆ × 35″
(130 × 89 cm)
Musée Fabre, Montpellier

THE CHALLENGE OF FINDING WAYS TO COMMUNICATE THE INSTANTANEOUS AND PANORAMIC dimensions of experience dominated more modest landscape painting as much as it did the elaborate "machines" devised by academic and realist-minded figure painters alike. Wanting literally to get inside his paintings, Daubigny outfitted a studio boat, setting a precedent for later landscape masters, including Monet. In Daubigny's paintings made in this way, the foregrounds are always expanses of water. They can be understood as "floating worlds" in the spirit of the popular Japanese landscape prints that were imported in quantity during these decades. His vantage point provided Daubigny with a double image of virtually every scene: the physical reality stretching along the banks and its two-dimensional reflection in the water's mirror surface, a sort of natural optical "painting" within the painting. As a result, his unpretentious landscapes became meditations about the translation from three to two dimensions as a painter copies reality onto a canvas. The motif of a distant image transposed toward the spectator in space by reflection and thus bridging the distance between the spectator and the image perceived became a mannerism of midcentury French landscape painting. Even without a boat studio, painters such as Corot could set their easels on one bank of the Seine and look across the water's mirror surface to villages nestled among trees, escaping from the "progress" of modern life with its bustling cities.

To fully appreciate the appeal of tranquil landscapes such as Corot's and Daubigny's, one should recall that during the 1850s and 1860s Paris was a topsy-turvy world, with old buildings destroyed to make way for broad new boulevards, sewers, and parks in one of the most extensive urban renewal projects in history. The lure of the countryside with its simple, healthy way of life was a ubiquitous theme beginning in the 1850s. Verdi's opera *La Traviata* (1853), based on an 1848 novel by the younger Dumas, was perhaps the most popular manifestation, its unforgettable songs telling the story of a man who would save his beloved's health by abducting her to the countryside. Meanwhile, the hero's father plots to save him from Paris by forcing his return alone to rural Provence. Paul-Camille Guigou's (1834–1871) dazzling landscapes of that region in the south of France (where Cézanne was born) appeal eloquently to what became a quasi-religious cult of clarity, simplicity, and freedom, all threatened by the onslaught of industrialization and urbanization.

Looking over the shoulder of Camille Pissarro (1830–1903) as he stands along the side of the road outside the village where he lived when he painted *The Hillsides of L'Hermitage, Pontoise*, we are witness to the little encounters of modern life outside the modernistic capital. From this vantage the road curls into space, across, around, down, up, and over it, like a constantly changing preposition, threading one bit of the landscape to the next. This nonsymmetrical, irregular antiurban liberty of space is the ultimate drama for Pissarro, whose paintings depicting clusters of simple little buildings would inspire Cézanne to paint nearly identical motifs that would in turn ultimately provoke a complex study of the irregularity of space in art called cubism at the beginning of the next century.

Boudin supported himself as an art supply dealer in Le Havre, catering to landscape painters attracted to the rugged Normandy coast, but his real passion was painting out of doors

CAMILLE PISSARRO
(b. 1830, St. Thomas–d. 1903)

The Hillsides of L'Hermitage, Pontoise,
ca. 1867–1868
Oil on canvas, 59⅝ × 79″
(151.4 × 200.6 cm)
Solomon R. Guggenheim Museum,
New York
Justin K. Thannhauser Collection,
1978

directly from nature, and he introduced the young Monet to this challenging enterprise. Working at breakneck speed to record shifting colors and shapes such as the passing clouds, Boudin was among the most influential impressionist pioneers. By the mid-1860s he had developed a single motif that he painted over and over, documenting the groups of fashionably dressed tourists who came to the Normandy beaches with their children and pets, sitting on their chairs and shading themselves with parasols while observing the boats and the spectacle of surf and sky. Quickly and simply painted, with each brushstroke corresponding to a specific element, from a rippling flag to a straw hat, these beach scenes introduce the crowd-as-spectator theme that would lead Manet and Degas to develop Impressionism at the racetracks.

Extending Boudin's motif of figures on the beach, usually executed with a predominently gray palette of closely related tones, Monet in 1867 painted a highly colorful group portrait of his family in their garden watching the ships on the Channel. The portrait is unconventional in that his father and aunt, the ostensible protagonists, who hardly approved of Monet's impovishering career, are seated in the foreground with their backs to the painter. Asserting his independence from both family and mentor in this work, Monet fused Boudin's lessons with the stylistic liberties that Manet had developed for his controversial seascapes and racetrack subjects. Hostile to this new way of painting, Monet's family could hardly guess that twenty years later their "black sheep" would have a world-famous garden of his own or that this very painting would sell a century later for a record-setting, million-dollar-plus price to New York's Metropolitan Museum of Art.

Among Monet's more immediate ambitions was to develop the manual dexterity and hand-to-eye coordination necessary to work directly out of doors in order to capture the most difficult and elusive landscape subjects. Moreover, like his colleagues, he was determined to finally

132

paint figures out of doors in the landscape rather than in the studio. According to the young art critic and novelist Emile Zola (1840–1902), this was the dream of every painter of his generation. Finally, Monet and his friends wanted to combine Western pictorial conventions and those characteristic of Eastern art in order to find a universal visual language. The simplifying design principles common to Japanese art, such as the woodblock prints of Ando Hiroshige (1797–1858), became as popular during the Second Empire as Japanese electronic goods have become in our time. Monet's *The Magpie*, depicting a visual world of glaring light and flat shadows, exemplifies so-called Japonisme with its emphasis on broad areas of a single color. Without extraordinary athletic stamina, however, Monet could hardly have recorded these delicate nuances of white; painting out of doors in the snow was a challenge few previous landscape artists had ever faced.

Keeping precedents by Courbet and Daubigny in mind, Monet sought to record the rapid experience of the glance in full-size paintings, aware that his abbreviated notations of form and color with dots and strokes of every size and shape would challenge the public. Indeed, outrage at his work stimulated him to be still more daring. Comparing paintings with nearly identical premises, one by Monet and the other by his roommate, Frédéric Bazille (1841–1870), illustrates the extent of Monet's unconventionality. Working separately, both decided to pose a woman in a striped dress seated under a shady tree beyond which a village along a river sparkles in the sunshine. Unlike Bazille, Monet worked too fast to worry about details like the textures of bark and silk. Instead, Monet's picture appears hardly less rough and fluid than the pictorial reflection mirrored on the rippled surface of the river. It is that upside-down reflection of a building on the river's far bank that seems to absorb the attention of Monet's mistress and model, Camille Doncieux, whose face in this picture is recorded merely as a single slash of reddish paint. Monet's extreme simplification of forms can be understood as an attempt to convey in a painting the raw retinal sensations of his own quick glance, with all the surprise and uncertainty inherent in the visual act before the mind begins to select, arrange, and focus.

A pair of closely related city views by Monet and his other roommate, Auguste Renoir (1841–1919), both painted in 1867, the year of another World's Fair in Paris, indicate how all the hallmarks of their style were already developed nearly a decade before the famous group exhibition at which the term "Impressionism" was coined. Literally turning his back on the masterpieces nearby, Monet arranged for permission to paint his view from the balcony of the Louvre, preferring to observe the movements of pedestrians below on the quay, visible only as little dots and dashes of blue or black. Renoir protected himself from the sun's heat by setting up his easel under one of the bridges across the Seine to observe tourists lining up to board a sight-seeing boat. Itself a rough "image" made by daylight, the shadow in the foreground of this extraordinary work, *The Pont des Arts*, indicates the pedestrians and street lamps overhead, capturing a dimension outside Renoir's primary field of vision to suggest the fullness of space so much at issue with Manet and Degas.

Observed from afar, the way Boudin observed tourists on the Normandy beaches, the figures in Monet's and Renoir's paintings lose any narrative interest as human beings and melt into a rich visual fabric as accents no different from chimneys or tree trunks. Atomized this way into a perfectly egalitarian world of raw sensations, without concern for what the sensations convey other than abstract form and color, the world of French painting had become impressionist. The full impact of the change was delayed by the outbreak of war in the summer of 1870. Bazille was among the casualties in the quick, humiliating defeat of France by Prussia.

JEAN-BAPTISTE-CAMILLE COROT

Ville d'Avray, ca. 1867–1870
Oil on canvas, 19⅜ × 25⅝″ (49.2 × 65.3 cm)
National Gallery of Art, Washington, D.C.
Gift of Count Cecil Pecci-Blunt

PAUL-CAMILLE GUIGOU (b. 1834, Villars–d. 1871)

Scene on the Durance River, 1866
Oil on canvas, 26 × 46⅛″ (66 × 117.8 cm)
Kimball Art Museum, Fort Worth, Texas

CLAUDE MONET

Garden at Sainte-Adresse, 1867
Oil on canvas, 38⅝ × 51⅛″ (98.1 × 129.9 cm)
The Metropolitan Museum of Art, New York
Purchased with Special Contributions and Purchase
Funds Given or Bequeathed by Friends of the
Museum, 1967

EUGÈNE BOUDIN (b. 1824, Honfleur–d. 1898)

Beach Scene at Trouville, 1863
Oil on canvas, 13¼ × 22¼"
(34.9 × 57.8 cm)
National Gallery of Art,
Washington, D.C.
Collection of Mr. and Mrs.
Paul Mellon, 1983

PIERRE-AUGUSTE RENOIR (b. 1841, Limoges–d. 1919)

The Pont des Arts, Paris, ca. 1867–1868
Oil on canvas, 24½ × 40¼″ (62.2 × 102.2 cm)
The Norton Simon Museum, Pasadena
The Norton Simon Foundation

CLAUDE MONET

On the Seine at Bennecourt, 1868
Oil on canvas, 31⅞ × 39½″ (81.5 × 100.7 cm)
The Art Institute of Chicago, Chicago
Potter Palmer Collection, 1922

CLAUDE MONET (b. 1840, Paris–d. 1926)

The Magpie, 1867–1868
Oil on canvas, 35 × 51³⁄₁₆″ (89 × 130 cm)
Musée d'Orsay, Paris

XIV.
Time and Series in the 1870s

MANY OF THE UNFORGETTABLE FRENCH PAINTINGS OF THE MID-NINETEENTH CENTURY measure invisible time with visual details. This awareness of time as a precondition of visual experience was revolutionary. Courbet, exiled from France for his role in the civil war that followed the peace treaty with Prussia, apparently identified with the agonies of imprisonment when he painted a picture of a hooked trout. Rendered with flickered, feathered brushwork, the shadowy riverbeds and the fish's spotted scales symbolize an instantaneous life-and-death encounter.

Indebted to Courbet's example, Cézanne at the outset of his career liked to endow ordinary things with high drama. Around 1870, when he painted *The Black Clock*, Cézanne was hiding in the south of France from military police tracking recruits. This odd still life asserts an art-for-art's-sake philosophy by presenting objects in nonsensical relationships: In real life no one would arrange a tablecloth on a mantelpiece or place a vase on top of a clock. The clock in question is as charged with symbolism as is the hooked trout in Courbet's variations. Juxtaposed here with a large seashell as a metaphor of time and tide, this clock without hands seems to imply death. The absence of the hands, however, may simply be Cézanne's way of stressing that the hands moved while he was painting the picture and therefore he could not include them without violating the principles of strict realism.

Cézanne's subsequent career has been understood as a painter's stubbornly honest attempt to account for time as a factor in his observations and his transcriptions of them with paint. The clock without hands amounts to a sort of fantasy tailored to impressionist painters, and *The*

GUSTAVE COURBET

The Trout, 1872
Oil on canvas, 20¹¹⁄₁₆ × 34¼″
(52.5 × 87 cm)
Kunsthaus, Zurich

Hanged Man's House, which was exhibited at the first impressionist group show in 1874, exemplifies their unorthodox efforts to get time into their pictures. Its grim title aside, this painting extends the rustic idiom developed by Corot and Pissarro to the breaking point. Observed from the elbow of a sharply turning road, the scene is full of spatial suspense. Using a variety of techniques to apply paint with both brush and knife, scraping, dragging, feathering, and smudging, Cézanne managed to indicate, besides the instantaneous play of light, a sense of his surprise upon encountering the scene suddenly before him, blurring the forms in the foreground into patches of green and pale orange that make sense only as things observed but not yet recognized for what they are. The same historic exhibition contained what may be Pissarro's greatest masterpiece, *Hoarfrost*, also a meditation on time and visual experience. Pissarro chose to represent the fragile, semitransparent presence of a frost layer as the rising sun melts it away, transforming one brief visual sensation into another by means of light.

Clouds scudding across the sky and boats drifting downriver are perhaps the specific details used most frequently in these pictures to imply the ticks of the impressionist clock, but more abstract devices, such as the fragment, are just as prevalent. In a landscape like Sisley's (1839–1899) *Bridge at Villeneuve-La-Garenne*, the bridge extending in or out of the field of vision at the left needs to be completed in imagination by a viewer the way an ambulatory spectator in real life might anticipate or remember what was about to come into view or had just passed from sight. Imprecise forms — such as dashes of dark paint on a lighter field that suggest the shadow sides of a river's ripples or scumbled white curlicues along a form's edge that suggest distortions from glaring sunlight — seemed absurd to many of the earliest viewers of impressionist works. They were unprepared to accept what they regarded as childish scrawls for accurate transcriptions of intense and instantaneous visual stimuli. Sheltering herself from the sunlight with a parasol,

PAUL CÉZANNE
(b. 1834, Aix-en-Provence–d. 1906)

The Black Clock, ca. 1870
Oil on canvas, 21¼ × 28¼″
(54 × 73 cm)
Private Collection, London

*Woman with a Parasol — Madame Monet
and Her Son*, 1875
Oil on canvas, 39⅛ × 31⅞"
(100 × 81 cm)
National Gallery of Art,
Washington, D.C.
Collection of Mr. and Mrs.
Paul Mellon

Monet's wife seems to dissolve before the painter's unsheltered eyes while he races the clock to paint a brief pause in her stroll with a welter of strokes. Like an unraveling tapestry in appearance, the resulting medley of sensory atoms records what Monet and his colleagues called the "envelope" of palpable space as a matrix experienced on a par with any objects or figures within its expanse.

Louis Leroy, the humorist critic who coined the term "Impressionism," which refers to raw sense data registered on the retina, described the little figures in Monet's *Boulevard des Capucines* as "black tongue lickings." Observed in motion from the upper-floor studio of the famous photographer Nadar (1820–1910), where the first impressionist exhibition was held, these urban pedestrians are seen out of the corner of Monet's eye, glimpsed rather than studiously observed in the photographic spirit of conventional realist painting. Today, seen from the distance from which a viewer would look at a picture by Ingres or David, Monet's painting still looks like flat little spots of paint carelessly arranged in a vaguely recognizable order; observed from farther back, the strokes magically coalesce to produce an illusion of striking, nearly stereoscopic, reality. It is worth noting that Monet painted two versions of this same scene, although only one of them was included in the famous group exhibition held outside the Salon by artists whose unorthodox techniques seemed threatening to the jurors. Presumably the variations are demonstrations of the shifting appearances of a single scene confronting any painter of modern life on the fly.

Degas, whose participation in the exhibition seems uncalled for and thus perverse given the enormous popular appeal of his predilection for photographic realism, also began around this time to produce nearly identical variations on a single scene. Since he never showed them together, it seems reasonable to suppose that he made them to satisfy market demand, just as Ingres, Delacroix, and Courbet had done. (Incidentally, when the Academy began in the 1860s to organize the first retrospective memorial exhibitions of great French painters, sometimes several variations were hung near to one another, and this may have given license to the impressionists' variations on single themes.) Unlike Monet, who was determined to show the quick process of painting in his pictures, Degas sought to fool viewers with virtuoso precision, suggesting that he had captured to perfection a random instant no longer than that needed to yawn or scratch the back. Yet with his love for perversity and paradox, the anti-impressionist Degas advocated the beauty of what was unfinished; his favorite subjects were dimly lighted ballet rehearsals, which can be understood to be analogous to the undeveloped sketches in paintings by his impressionist colleagues.

Slapdash Impressionism was carried to its most extreme form by the only woman painter in the group, Berthe Morisot (1841–1895), who showed five variations of the same harbor scene at the second impressionist exhibition in 1876. Each painting was hurried in order to represent her own act of seeing as accurately as it represented the strollers who crossed her field of vision while boats and flags shifted and fluttered in the distance. Committed to not stopping whatever happened, Morisot scratched over and wiped out areas that changed too quickly to record any other way. This group of sequential views initiated what would be the most important trend in painting from then on: the concept of working in series. Monet, who presented a group of related paintings of the Saint-Lazare train station in Paris at the third impressionist exhibition in 1877, usually receives credit for this innovation.

As if the challenge of capturing complex changes in form were not enough for him, Monet opted to portray a bustling urban center where billowing smoke scatters like rolling mercury to blot and distort recognizable objects into abstract patches of color. With one train arriving and another leaving in the best of these variations, Monet recorded two superimposed times at once: modern urban timetable existence, with its logic and predictability, and the shifting sensations of light and shadow oblivious to this new man-made order. Here at last was the fulfillment of Baudelaire's appeal for kaleidoscopic paintings of city life.

PAUL CÉZANNE

The Hanged Man's House, Auvers-sur-l'Oise, ca. 1873
Oil on canvas, 21⅝ × 26" (55 × 66 cm)
Musée d'Orsay, Paris

CAMILLE PISSARRO

Hoarfrost, 1873
Oil on canvas, 25⅝ × 36⅝" (65 × 93 cm)
Musée d'Orsay, Paris

ALFRED SISLEY (b. 1839, Paris–d. 1899)

Bridge at Villeneuve-La-Garenne, 1872
Oil on canvas, 19¼ × 25⅝" (49.5 × 65.4 cm)
The Metropolitan Museum of Art, New York
Gift of Mr. and Mrs. Henry Ittleson, Jr., 1964

EDGAR DEGAS

The Rehearsal on the Stage, ca. 1874
Pastel over brush and ink drawing on paper,
21 × 28½″ (53.3 × 72.3 cm)
The Metropolitan Museum of Art, New York
Bequest of Mrs. H.O. Havemeyer, 1929
The H.O. Havemeyer Collection

CLAUDE MONET

Boulevard des Capucines, Paris, 1873
Oil on canvas, 31¼ × 23¹³⁄₁₆″ (79.4 × 60.6 cm)
The Nelson-Atkins Museum of Art, Kansas City
Acquired through the generosity of the Kenneth A.
and Helen F. Spencer Foundation Acquisition Fund

RIGHT:
BERTHE MORISOT (b. 1841, Bourges–d. 1895)

Harbor Scene, Isle of Wight, 1875
Oil on canvas, 17¼ × 25½″
(43.8 × 64.7 cm)
Newark Museum, Newark, New Jersey
Gift of Mrs. Esther U. Johnson, 1979

BELOW:
CLAUDE MONET

The St. Lazare Railroad Station, 1877
Oil on canvas, 29¼ × 41″
(75.5 × 104 cm)
Musée d'Orsay, Paris

XV.
Impressionist Figure Painting

GUSTAVE CAILLEBOTTE

The Man at the Window, 1876
Oil on canvas, 46¼ × 32⅝"
(117.5 × 82.8 cm)
Private Collection

AT THE SAME 1877 GROUP SHOW WHERE MONET PRESENTED HIS RAILROAD STATION variations, Degas's disciple Gustave Caillebotte (1848–1894) presented large works that could never have been painted directly from nature in impressionist fashion. Indeed, the largest of these, *Paris Street: A Rainy Day*, was probably intended as a clever rejoinder to the sunshine mood of classic Impressionism. Based on dozens of highly specialized studies of details, some undertaken to observe the play of filtered light on a few drenched paving stones, this picture raised the stakes for would-be modern life painters, challenging them to work on a monumental scale as Salon artists did. Caillebotte was well enough off to afford big canvases and ample paints even if his ambitious works attracted no buyers. Notwithstanding the remarkable command of perspective in this picture, it is in the figures in the foreground that the most curious details are found. The feet of these three all fall outside the frame, suggesting the continuation of the space inside the picture into the adjacent spectator's space. Looking at something outside the picture to the left, the couple sharing an umbrella are oblivious to the man sharing the sidewalk with them and force him out of their way (and out of Caillebotte's painting to the right). The Daumieresque humor is impossible to overlook, as are premeditated compositional devices used by Caillebotte to heighten the illusion of realism by suggesting the extension of space beyond the frame.

In his own anti-impressionist way, Degas around 1877 began to paint nocturnal scenes, with ultramodern artificial gas lighting to guide ladies' men and ladies of the night on their rounds through dance halls and cafés. Degas calculated these pictures carefully, limiting himself to fragmentary images of urban night crawlers as if he had infiltrated their world in the role of a disinterested ambulant spectator who paid them no more attention than a glance. Columns and lampposts divide Degas's novel compositions into geometrical zones, stripes, and squares that anticipate the rigorously abstract beauties of Mondrian fifty years later.

The number of French paintings of whores during the 1870s and 1880s defies explanation despite the fact that prostitution had become a rampant symptom of urban decay. Even one of the bourgeois little girls painted as a specialty by Mary Cassatt (1843–1926), Degas's American disciple, posed wantonly, as if playing a grown-up model in the role of a courtesan for a modern life painter. Surely humor is present in this sort of picture, which addresses the crux of realism: the analysis of real-life behavior designed to attract attention or, put another way, the extensive presence of pose, costume, and mask in everyday life. Scarcely an issue for landscape painters, allure and desire are powerful and fundamental aspects of the visual act that concerned figure painters dedicated to analyzing how looking works.

Caillebotte's *The Man at the Window* is a remarkable attempt to describe these complex issues. More than just a virtuoso demonstration of his ability to capture firsthand observations of both indoor and outdoor light effects, it is an emblem of modern loneliness. The male protagonist, accompanied only by his reflection in a pane of an open window, has nothing better to do than pull his expensive chair to where he can play the voyeur from his balcony. Although Caillebotte used only the figure's back to tell this story, its slight tilt leftward is enough to show that his sights are turned to contemplate a female prey crossing the shadow-covered street below.

Once a spectator sees what the man in the painting is looking at, the mathematical logic of the space is distorted by the implication of an emotional telescope.

For several of the impressionists the looking-at-looking theme served as both a narrative device and a compressive spatial device, bringing something far away to close attention. Renoir's *The Theater Box* is an especially impressive example. The vaguely sad woman appears close at hand in this painting, like the sitter for a conventional portrait, but the setting, costume, and props indicate a modern life genre scene. In reality, however, this woman would be far removed from a spectator across the theater unless the spectator were observing her through opera glasses like those she holds. Her escort, seated behind her and looking out across the house through his own opera glasses, in effect mirrors the role of the spectator of the painting. Together, the two figures crammed into the shallow space of their box imply an extension of space outside the painting, addressing the spectator's consciousness of the surrounding nature of space in reality. On a less abstract level, Renoir's portrait of spectators becoming the spectacle stressed the somewhat trite "all the world's a stage" theme that obsessed this generation of realist artists.

Renoir was at his best when he painted real-life situations involving large groups, and his nearly six-foot-wide *Dancing at the Moulin de la Galette, Montmartre*, which was exhibited at the same impressionist group exhibition with Caillebotte's *Rainy Day*, successfully demonstrated how quick virtuoso brushwork could record the movement and sparkle of modern life at Salon scale. Of course, Renoir could not have set up a large canvas to work at the side of this outdoor dance hall but had to stage the scene bit by bit. Even so, his feathery strokes, themselves "dancing" across the canvas like dappled sunlight, symbolize the instantaneity of a glance. Glancing is Renoir's ultimate subject in this extraordinary work, and the scattered glances of the dozens of figures animate the scene in every direction, suggesting, besides the true-to-life appearance of the scene, the intoxicated, distracted feeling that is a fundamental dimension of perceptual experience in a crowd.

The virtuoso rendition of light and commentaries on its role in guiding and even heightening perception were not the exclusive domain of the impressionists during the 1870s. The best Salon artists addressed the same issue in their own fashion. For example, at the Salon of 1876 the decadent classical artist Gustave Moreau (1826–1898), who would much later become Matisse's teacher, showed a fantastical watercolor representing the apparition of John the Baptist's head to the murderous Salome. A large oil study for this theatrical picture set in a dim vaulted Eastern palace has much in common with Degas's ballet variations and even with his nocturnal scenes. Haunted by guilt, the seminaked young woman amounts to a prototype for the actresses and whores in fantasy costumes that appear in modern life art. At the Salon of 1879, Jules Bastien-Lepage (1848–1884) presented something like an out-of-doors impressionist history painting. Too earnest to limit himself to the portrayal of an anonymous modern-day woman with a parasol, he conjured up a Joan of Arc dressed just as peasant farmers still dressed in contemporary France. The intense expression on Joan's face, however, as she searches for a hovering supernatural apparition makes high drama of the looking-at-looking theme.

Unaware that they are being observed as part of the human comedy, the figures in Manet's café paintings are looking outside the frame of vision. These figures either disregard their surroundings by turning inward in thought or turn to watch something, presumably the performer, whose image reflected in the mirror in the background helps explain the whole from which Manet's fragment of modern life has been extracted as a specimen of real-life perception. Manet's ultimate masterpiece, *The Bar at the Folies-Bergère*, which was exhibited at the Salon of 1882, invites the spectator to confront a young barmaid on the job at a chic night spot. Her distant expression suggests a prisoner's lack of interest in what she does and where she is, yet Manet devotes considerable skill to describing the space surrounding this woman, behind whom is a vast, sparkling mirror reflecting what is in front of her and thus outside the picture. Her role is little different from that of the merchandise on display on her countertop. We know this because in the mirror Manet has painted the reflection of a gentleman customer who must be imagined to stand just across from her, where the artist himself or the painting's eventual spectator would have to be to take part in this encounter. Disregarding the laws of optics, Manet incorrectly situated this reflection off to the right, stressing the discrepancy between truth in art and truth in life that can make the best paintings more enjoyable and meaningful than what they purport to represent. One of the most fascinating offshoots of Manet's picture is James Tissot's

(1836–1902) *The Young Lady of the Shop*. The working girl in this picture confronts spectators with her eyes while holding open a door as if to allow them in imagination to walk into, through, and out of the painting. A gentleman in the background who looks through the shop window from the sidewalk outside adds to the complex situational illusion addressed to the painter-spectator.

While such gimmicks could enhance the sense of realism, the underlying significance of what we take for reality in relationship to illusion required a different approach. After all, modern life in public places amounts to a form of theater at odds with true reality, which is something private that each individual keeps hidden. Understanding the more profound dimension of behind-the-scenes reality, Degas was most fascinated by rehearsal or dressing room situations. In the 1880s he honed such episodes to pictures of single nude female figures bathing themselves in the crammed privacy of their own homes. Realizing that nudity had always been a symbol for truth in art, Degas conceived these works to suggest a voyeur's intrusion through a keyhole to see modern woman as she really is before dressing with wigs and corsets to appear in the outside world in whatever role she accepts. Degas observed his models from odd angles to make many of these realist masterpieces, claiming that novel viewpoints prevented him from falling victim to blinding habits of perception. To reinvent the nude in this manner as a subject for modern painting, Degas took his inspiration from his idol, Ingres, using his abstract understanding of the figure as a touchstone to create a classical mode of Impressionism.

GUSTAVE CAILLEBOTTE
(b. 1848, Paris–d. 1894)

Paris Street: A Rainy Day, 1876–1877
Oil on canvas, 84¼ × 118½″
(212.2 × 276.2 cm)
The Art Institute of Chicago, Chicago
Charles H. and Mary F.S. Worcester Collection, 1964

EDGAR DEGAS

Women on the Terrace of a Café —
Evening, 1877
Pastel on monotype,
21½ × 28⅛″ (54.5 × 71.5 cm)
Musée d'Orsay, Paris

EDGAR DEGAS

The Bath, ca. 1890–1895
Oil on canvas, 32 × 45¼″
(81.2 × 116.2 cm)
The Carnegie Museum of Art,
Pittsburgh
Acquired through the generosity
of Mrs. Alan M. Scaife

JAMES TISSOT (b. 1836, Nantes–d. 1902)

The Young Lady of the Shop (The Milliner's Shop), 1883–1885
Oil on canvas, 57½ × 40″ (146 × 101.6 cm)
Art Gallery of Ontario, Toronto
Gift from Corporations' Subscription Fund, 1968

MARY CASSATT (b. 1845, Pittsburgh–d. 1926)

Little Girl in a Blue Armchair, 1878
Oil on canvas, 35¼ × 51⅛″ (89.5 × 129.8 cm)
National Gallery of Art, Washington, D.C.
Collection of Mr. and Mrs. Paul Mellon

PIERRE-AUGUSTE RENOIR

The Theater Box, 1874
Oil on canvas, 31½ × 24¹³⁄₁₆″ (80 × 63 cm)
The Courtauld Institute of Art, London
The Courtauld Collection

JULES BASTIEN-LEPAGE (b. 1848, Damvillers–d. 1884)

Joan of Arc, 1879
Oil on canvas, 100 × 110″ (254 × 279 cm)
The Metropolitan Museum of Art, New York
Gift of Erwin Davis, 1889

GUSTAVE MOREAU (b. 1826, Paris–d. 1898)

The Vision (Dance of Salome), 1874–1876
Oil on canvas, 55⅞ × 40½″ (142 × 103 cm)
Musée Gustave Moreau, Paris

PIERRE-AUGUSTE RENOIR

Dancing at the Moulin de la Galette, Montmartre, 1876
Oil on canvas, 51⁹⁄₁₆ × 68⅞″ (131 × 175 cm)
Musée D'Orsay, Paris

EDOUARD MANET

The Bar at the Folies-Bergère, 1881–1882
Oil on canvas, 37¾ × 51¼" (95.9 × 130.2 cm)
The Courtauld Institute Galleries, London
The Courtauld Collection

XVI.
Beyond Instantaneity

RENOIR'S *LUNCHEON OF THE BOATING PARTY*, WHICH WAS EXHIBITED AT THE IMPRESSIONIST group show of 1882, is the last great painting of modern life observed in a glance. Perhaps it is only a coincidence, but experiments to record motion with split-second photography by Eadweard Muybridge (1830–1904), for example, captured attention in the 1880s, in a sense making what Renoir was attempting seem obsolete. Like a randomly frozen frame from a film set on the terrace of a rustic restaurant outside Paris on the Seine, this magnificent work glorifies the charms of such trivial activities as blowing kisses at a lapdog and covering the ears to avoid hearing a too-bold jest. All the figures are ruddy with the afternoon wine and fruit, and in the distance sailboats are skimming. Oblivious to the glistening still life of dessert, the satiated youths watch one another watching one another, as if modern life were a visual feast.

Whereas during the 1870s Monet had favored ordinary motifs, now he preferred the most dramatic, often remote, locales. It is worth pointing out that Monet, along with Cézanne and Degas, was an avid reader of *The Thousand and One Nights* for its fairy-tale qualities; like his colleagues, he began to prize perceptions when reality appeared too fantastic to believe. The term *féerique* ("fairytalelike") was widely used by critics and theorists to describe the painting of reality at its most dreamlike. The extraordinary rock formations at the Normandy beach of Etretat, a Mecca for painters since before the time of Courbet, had such qualities for Monet, who hiked and scaled to reach vantage points unknown to his predecessors. From these sites Monet observed the play of light in flickers from slapping waters and white cliffs that had been sculpted into shapes resembling Gothic cathedrals. Sparkling like jewels, these impressionist landscapes are records of a brief moment of perception; however, they are also commentaries on centuries of geological time as it slowly weathers and changes the world's most solid physical facts.

No less concerned with the interacting verities of instantaneity and permanence, Cézanne in the 1880s both developed his unique use of a patch of thin color to mark the subtlest shift of light from one plane to an adjacent one and invented structured compositional motifs to anchor those observations. His favorite view was across the Provence plains to Mont Sainte-Victoire, and in the best of these pictures the mountain's distant silhouette is repeated by the intertwining branches of trees in the immediate foreground. Cézanne compared his compositions in which near and far were interwoven to hands joined with the fingers inserted into one another. "There must not be a single link too loose, a hole through which the emotion, the light or the truth may escape," he explained.

While these impressionist pioneers sought in their 1880s landscapes to express overtones of eternity evident in the simple and awesome patterns of nature, other painters transposed the same elegiac mood into scenes of modern life. Determined to go beyond mere description, these artists often drew upon the elementary conventions of art from the past that had emphasized spiritual values above all else. The relative rigidity of Gothic or even Egyptian art appealed to artists as expressions of the universal moral values that were missing in contemporary life and recent art based directly on it. Pierre Puvis de Chavannes (1824–1898), who started around 1860 to combine the allegorical emphasis of academic painting with the simplicity and clarity valued by his impressionist friends, became the most successful muralist of his generation. By the 1880s he had become a model for painters who wanted to go beyond instantaneity to represent more general truths. Puvis's *The Poor Fisherman*, which was shown at the Salon of 1881, stresses piety, family ties, and labor as virtues. Sustained by their immediate contact with nature, the baby sleeps, the wife gathers wildflowers, and the husband on his boat bends his head for the morning prayer. A stillness foreign to Impressionism pervades the riverside scene, without a ripple on the water's surface and with serene, colorless light revealing simple forms as symbols of honesty and universality.

An ardent admirer of Puvis's works, Georges Seurat (1859–1891) presented a nearly ten-foot wide impressionist mural to the Salon of 1884, only to have it refused by the jury. The unworthy picture, which Seurat showed that same spring in an exhibition of the newly organized jury-free Society of Independent Artists, represents a slice of modern urban life set just outside Paris on the Seine. The establishment of this alternative Salon open to all artists, encouraging more and more unorthodox experiments without concern for censorship, was an event of inestimable importance. The ultranaive paintings of Henri Rousseau (1844–1910) are a case in point: Slashed when they were exhibited at the official Salon in 1885, his unique fantasy paintings were welcomed for their odd originality at the Independents' Salons in subsequent years.

Seurat's refused *Bathers, Asnières* must have seemed far less controversial but far more ambitious and therefore potentially dangerous to standards of serious taste. Ignoring the row of smokestacks impinging on their little oasis of nature in the metropolis, the figures pause, and some even strip away their modern clothes to rest and refresh themselves by the water. The setting, rendered in orthodox impressionist fashion with feathery brushstrokes to evoke the vibrating play of daylight, is at odds with the motionless figures, whose simple contours in the spirit of Puvis are closer to the timeless monumentality of Italian Renaissance mural painting than to the instantaneity of recent French art. The total absence of drama or focus is what makes Seurat's huge image unconventional. The most striking details are the silhouetted shapes of the figures' backs or their hats, causing the decorative interrelationships of form and color to take on an unprecedented importance.

Encouraged by a fellow exhibitor at the Society of Independent Artists, Paul Signac (1863–1935), to paint with brighter colors, Seurat immediately set to work on *Sunday Afternoon on the Island of La Grande-Jatte*, the same unsalable size as *Bathers* and representing another ensemble of ordinary Parisians, this time observed on an island in the Seine that is barely visible at the far right of the earlier picture. Working from scores of drawings and portable studies for individual details, Seurat developed a scene with over forty fashionably dressed figures frozen in relaxed attitudes. They appear to have nothing more important to do than stroll with their children and pets. Despite the absence of significant action, the painting was immediately compared to Egyptian murals and the sculptural reliefs of the Parthenon frieze because Seurat had so studiously simplified every shape along its silhouette.

Most astonishing when this painting was exhibited at the final impressionist group exhibition in 1886, however, was the surface of uniform little dots that replaced the variety of short strokes characteristic of works by Monet, Morisot, and Renoir. These points (hence the term "pointillisme" to describe this style) of contrasting colors in the works exhibited by Seurat and Signac seemed impersonal, insincere, and even mechanical at first. However, their fastidious, time-consuming system, devised in the name of scientific accuracy, followed laws governing the mixing and interacting of the basic primary and secondary colors to achieve a new degree of accuracy and intensity in the transcription of observations. The fast-drying dots were a way for these so-called neo-impressionists to measure the components of any color with precision.

Seurat added a curious framing border of dots painted in complementary colors around his big painting. Framing had become an issue around 1880, and Seurat kept pace with Renoir, Gauguin, van Gogh, and others by opting for a white rather than a conventional gold frame. Moreover, rather than varnish (and eventually yellow) his huge picture, he covered it with an expensive protective sheet of glass. Presented this way, the painting must have appeared aggressively modern on the standard red fabric walls used throughout the nineteenth century. Whistler and Gauguin around this time even tried decorative yellow walls as another strategy to shock viewers out of old habits.

Ironically, the systematic pursuit of truth in representation led Seurat and Signac to a fantastical new kind of decorative abstraction, and their greatest works seem tapestrylike or "fairytalelike." For example, Signac's *Gas Tanks at Clichy*, which heralds a cynical new genre of industrial landscape, seems otherworldly in its brightness, a result of the juxtaposition of complementary red and green tones to transcribe daylight more intense than even the most powerful gas lighting could ever hope to rival. The same painter's *Parisian Sunday*, exhibited at the Independents' Salon of 1890, applies the new system to the rendition of interior lighting. Here

Henri de Toulouse-Lautrec (b. 1864, Albi–d. 1901)

In the Circus Fernando: The Ringmaster, 1888
Oil on canvas, 39½ × 63½″ (100.3 × 161.3 cm)
The Art Institute of Chicago
The Joseph Winterbotham Collection, 1925

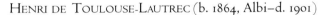

the blue shadows create a cool mood in perfect harmony with the self-centered figures turned away from one another — she to peer out the window for more brightness, he to muse at the fireplace. (Even the cats are absorbed by the play of lights, in the mirror and on the floor.) Signac's abstract use of line is equally sophisticated. While, according to modern theories, upward-turned lines suggest joy and horizontals indicate calm, downward-turned lines like those everywhere in Signac's painting denote sadness. Their perfectly decorated townhouse notwithstanding, happiness eludes the couple in this masterpiece of modern-life painting.

Henri de Toulouse-Lautrec (1864–1901) was among several of Seurat and Signac's

extraordinary contemporaries fascinated by their systematic investigation of the emotional forces inherent in individual colors, lines, and shapes that in themselves expressed a spectrum of distinct moods. Highlighting his *In the Circus Fernando* with hot oranges and reds and exaggerating the rhythms of rising curved shapes, Lautrec sought to express the essential excitement of experience in modern life, even if that meant departing from a strictly accurate transcription of appearances. A work Lautrec hoped to expand to mural scale, this stylized image captures movement with more drama than any previous painting had. Extending devices introduced by Degas a decade before, Lautrec cropped figures at every side of his composition, from the footless ringmaster, to the armless clown, to the headless spectators in the grandstands, implying the extension of space in every direction at once. Observed from above, silhouetted against the floor, the ringmaster seems to float like a figure in a Japanese print, and the curving snap of his whip appears to initiate a rippling of ever wider curves continuing along the arena's perimeter at an abstract gallop.

Even to his admirers, Lautrec's graphic style seemed more suitable to advertising posters than to painting, with the result that in 1891 he quickly emerged as one of the world's greatest lithographers with a huge poster to promote a new dance hall called the Moulin Rouge. So popular have his works on paper remained ever since that Lautrec's greatness as a painter is sometimes overlooked; that is all the more extraordinary since his posters at first were developed from paintings such as *At the Moulin Rouge: The Dance*. Aware that contrasts of all sorts (not just contrasts of complementary colors) intensify visual design, Lautrec placed a woman wearing a shocking pink coat in a dim, smoke-filled gaslit interior otherwise crowded with dark-suited drinkers. It is as if he had superimposed Seurat's *Sunday Afternoon on the Island of La Grand-Jatte* with Courbet's *Burial at Ornans*, capturing the mixed but fundamentally decadent mood of the end of the century.

The tragicomic mood was perhaps best caught in Seurat's *Invitation to the Sideshow*. This gaslit scene outside a circus seems far removed from Paris. The dark trombonist transports the crowd of mundane spectators to a dim fantasy world. Both the leafless tree at the left and the stylized flames of the gas lamps overhead seem to dance a dirge to his music. Hardly a fitting prologue for a circus, the lugubrious scene can be understood as a departure from realism in order to make a doleful commentary about modern life.

PIERRE-AUGUSTE RENOIR

The Luncheon of the Boating Party
(La Grenouille), 1881
Oil on canvas, 51 × 68" (130 × 173 cm)
The Phillips Collection, Washington, D.C.

GEORGES SEURAT (b. 1859, Paris–d. 1891)

Bathers, Asnières, 1883–1884
Oil on canvas, 79⅛ × 118½″ (201.2 × 301 cm)
Reproduced by courtesy of the Trustees,
The National Gallery, London

172

PAUL SIGNAC (b. 1863, Paris–d. 1935)

Gas Tanks at Clichy, 1886
Oil on canvas, 25½ × 31⅞″ (65 × 81 cm)
National Gallery of Victoria, Melbourne
Felton Bequest, 1948

PAUL SIGNAC

Parisian Sunday, 1889–1890
Oil on canvas, 59 × 59″
(150 × 150 cm)
Private Collection, Paris

GEORGES SEURAT

Sunday Afternoon on the Island of
La Grande Jatte, 1884–1886
Oil on canvas, 81 × 120⅜″
(207.6 × 308 cm)
The Art Institute of Chicago,
Chicago
Helen Birch Bartlett Memorial
Collection, 1926

HENRI DE TOULOUSE-LAUTREC

At the Moulin Rouge: The Dance, 1890
Oil on canvas, 45½ × 59″ (115.5 × 149.8 cm)
The Philadelphia Museum of Art, Philadelphia
The Henry P. McIlhenny Collection
in memory of Frances P. McIlhenny

XVII.
Martyrs for Modern Art

SEURAT'S EXAMPLE IMMEDIATELY EXCITED A YOUNG DUTCH PAINTER NAMED VINCENT VAN Gogh (1853–1890), who came to the international art world of Paris in early 1886, while *Sunday Afternoon on the Island of La Grand Jatte* was on exhibit. Moved in with his brother, Théo, a contemporary art dealer, van Gogh painted dots of yellow paint on his blue workingman's shirt as a sign of support for the theoretical use of color, including the juxtaposition of complementaries (such as yellow and blue) to achieve intensity. In one of his many telling self-portraits he identified still more explicitly with such color theory, showing himself as an out-of-doors painter, with a broad-brimmed yellow hat painted in regimented strokes to render the woven straw. Set against a sky symbolized by a pattern of long blue strokes, van Gogh's face seems to radiate brightness as if it were surrounded by the halo of a medieval saint. Having absorbed Seurat's ideas, van Gogh instinctively pushed them into a hyperintense realm usually referred to as Expressionism.

Paul Gauguin (1848–1903), a sailor turned stockbroker turned contemporary art collector turned impressionist artist, was among the participants at the final impressionist exhibition of 1886. He reacted to Seurat's works as a challenge to go even further beyond classical Impressionism and transform the fundamentals of painting to establish a new visual order for the future. Distrustful of art world intrigues and contemptuous of modern urban values, Gauguin left his job and abandoned his large family to move to the picturesque village of Pont Aven in Brittany, where he established himself as the daring, charismatic leader of an art colony. Holding a viper in his self-portrait as a fallen angel meditating on the green apples of knowledge and sin, he opted for a style diametrically opposed to Seurat's fastidious dots. Gauguin sought still more dramatic intensity through stylization and the use of large areas of unmodulated color like those found in Japanese prints and Gothic stained-glass windows. Such references to different cultures contributed to Gauguin's goal of synthesis, incorporating even the most primitive and exotic forms to express the ancient, sacred invisible truths evident to all people in every age. Disregarding the commonsense logic of representational art, Gauguin fashioned mysterious dreamlike images as crudely rendered as a child's drawings. His *Still Life with Three Puppies* not only revolutionized still-life painting, it introduced a cult of outline and pattern as the touchstones for abstract art in our own century.

The precocious teenager Emile Bernard (1868–1941), a fellow student of van Gogh, introduced him to Gauguin, and soon the three artists were corresponding with one another, dreaming together of founding a medieval artists' brotherhood, if possible in a remote, utterly noncivilized tropical setting. Working in tandem in Brittany, Bernard and Gauguin spurred each other to ever more shocking departures from convention. Bernard's *Buckwheat Harvesters*, with its coarsely outlined figures of farmers in their local costumes (no different in 1888 from what they had been in earlier centuries), is painted with such broad flat areas that it has no more illusionistic depth than a stained-glass window, and the intense red used throughout conjures up an exaggerated, miraculously transubstantiated daylight. Gauguin used the same models to paint an altarpiece so unorthodox that local church officials refused to accept it as a gift. It shows women coming out of church in their strange bonnets, emblems of their pious minds that can summon up an Old Testament vision of Jacob wrestling with the angel of the Lord. As earnest as Manet had been full of humor in painting *Mademoiselle Victorine in the Costume of an Espada* twenty-five years before, Gauguin contrasted these real-life women with red grass and illogically small background figures, initiating an anything-goes freedom addressed to the supernatural, to miracles, faith, and superstition. Urging young disciples such as Paul Sérusier (1864–1927) to transform nature as they transcribed it, using intense colors, Gauguin initiated a radical new conception of landscape as an internalized fantasy space.

Since early 1888 van Gogh had been installed in the southern town of Arles, not far from where Cézanne was at work in similar isolation from the Paris art world. There the Dutch artist invented an intense form of symbolism all his own, epitomized by his still lifes with crockery vases full of withering sunflowers, intensely drawn and colored so as to writhe and shine from within like vegetable stars. He inscribed his paintings with his first name, "Vincent," as a sign of brotherhood. (French collectors probably could not pronounce his last name.) For some of the sunflower pictures he signed the vase, suggesting that he identified with the dark container of these light-worshiping wildflowers. Almost all his works are self-portrtaits by proxy. For example, his blue and yellow bedroom, composed as an image to rest the mind of a viewer, as Matisse would later try to make paintings like armchairs to refresh nerves tired by modern life, is another form of self-image, stressing his preference for old-fashioned comforts over modern luxuries. As for modern life removed from nature, even in Arles van Gogh found vestiges of its psychic depravities, and color plays a crucial role in his tormented rendition of the local pool hall. "I have tried to express the terrible passions of humanity by means of the red and green," he explained in one of his letters.

Just days after van Gogh finished his first bedroom painting, Gauguin arrived as a guest, thanks to financial support from Théo van Gogh. The month these two hyperemotional painters spent together in Arles was probably the most intense and influential month in the history of French painting, and the story of how van Gogh, too eager to impress Gauguin for friendship's sake, went mad and mutilated himself does not need repeating. Committing himself to an asylum in April 1889, van Gogh sought health by painting landscapes that often reach a fever pitch, as in *The Starry Night*, an apocalyptic vision more commanding than any imagined by Gauguin's peasant women. Hurtling on wind currents, light pulses like cells in a life stream through the heavens above and animates the darkened earth below with profound rhythms. Laying down his paint in thick strokes with the opulent abandon of a pastry chef, van Gogh initiated a whole new way of painting with palpable pure colors that take on lives all their own. As if he had completely emptied himself in his rush to bring painting into uncharted areas of technique and meaning, van Gogh took his life in the summer of 1890. Understood by many as a sacrifice for art, his death inspired subsequent generations of artists to emulate his independence and reckless commitment to self-expression as the highest form of universal truth.

VINCENT VAN GOGH (b. 1853, Groot-Zundert–d. 1890)

Self-Portrait with Straw Hat, 1887
Oil on canvas, 16 × 12¾″ (40.5 × 32.5 cm)
Vincent van Gogh Foundation
Rijksmuseum Vincent van Gogh, Amsterdam

PAUL GAUGUIN (b. 1848, Paris–d. 1903)

Self-Portrait, 1889
Oil on wood, 31¼ × 20¼″ (79.2 × 51.3 cm)
National Gallery of Art, Washington, D.C.
Chester Dale Collection

Paul Gauguin

Still Life with Three Puppies, 1888
Oil on wood, 36⅛ × 24⅝" (91.8 × 62.6 cm)
The Museum of Modern Art, New York
Mrs. Simon Guggenheim Fund

EMILE BERNARD (b. 1868, Lille–d. 1941)

The Buckwheat Harvesters, 1888
Oil on canvas, 28¼ × 35½″ (73 × 90 cm)
Josefowitz Collection

PAUL GAUGUIN

    The Vision After the Sermon, 1888
    Oil on panel, 28¾ × 36¼″ (73 × 92 cm)
    National Galleries of Scotland, Edinburgh

PAUL SÉRUSIER (b. 1864, Paris–d. 1927)

    The Talisman, 1888
    Oil on canvas, 10¾ × 8½″ (27.3 × 21.5 cm)
    Musée d'Orsay, Paris

VINCENT VAN GOGH

The Starry Night, 1889
Oil on canvas, 29 × 36¼″ (73.6 × 92 cm)
The Museum of Modern Art, New York
Acquired through the Lillie P. Bliss Bequest

VINCENT VAN GOGH

Sunflowers, 1888
Oil on canvas, 36¼ × 28¾"
(92 × 73 cm)
Reproduced by courtesy of the
Trustees,
The National Gallery, London

VINCENT VAN GOGH

The Night Café, 1888
Oil on canvas, 28½ × 36¼"
(72.3 × 92 cm)
Yale University Art Gallery,
New Haven
Bequest of Stephen Carlton Clark

VINCENT VAN GOGH

Bedroom in Arles, 1888
Oil on canvas, 28⅜ × 35⅛"
(72 × 89.8 cm)
The Vincent van Gogh
Foundation
Rijksmuseum Vincent van Gogh,
Amsterdam

XVIII.
Art as Escape from Urban Life

ALTHOUGH A NUMBER OF PAINTERS BASED IN PARIS — RENOIR, BERNARD, GAUGUIN, AND Edvard Munch among them — included heads looming up close in the foregrounds of their modern life paintings, none used the startling feature with more success than Lautrec did in *At the Moulin Rouge*. Her shape distorted in insectlike fashion by the extreme fashions of her hat and dress and her skin bathed in blue-green gaslight, entertainer May Milton adds a frightening dimension to this intoxicated nocturnal world with its jaded clientele, including the diminutive artist, whose self-portrait is in the background. Pushing modern life realism to an extreme, Lautrec actually moved into a brothel to record candid observations of the lassitudes and degradations of vice. *Interior on the Rue des Moulins* is the culmination of a group of extraordinary behind-the-scenes pictures blending male fantasy and female fact. While her blank-faced fellow prostitutes await their turns in the garish, theatrically furnished parlor, the woman on the right hikes up her chemise to submit to a medical examination.

Gauguin, fed up with the depressing signs of moral collapse that appealed to Lautrec, became intrigued with the Javanese pavilion at the 1889 World's Fair in Paris (the centerpiece of which was the Eiffel Tower, a symbol of the future of industrial Western societies). Thus with mixed motives, partly sincere, partly self-promotional, Gauguin left European civilization behind in 1891 to observe a more pure and innocent way of life in the South Pacific. Gauguin's journey to a preindustrial society demonstrated to following generations of artists that one can go forward in art by going backward to search for universal meaning in ancient ways of life and forms of expression.

For his very first Tahitian paintings Gauguin synthesized the poses and attributes familiar from Buddhist temple sculpture and Christian icons, transforming native models into angels and members of the Holy Family blessed with the richly colored bounty of a tropical paradise. Before very long, however, the painter realized that his art could become reinvigorated only if he shed his cultivated Christian European mentality and observed the mysterious world of the Tahitians on its own terms.

He inscribed titles on these works, but in a strange language unknown to any viewers in Paris: *Manao Tupapau* (which means "the specter watches over her") purports to show a native girl lying awake in fear of evil spirits. In his extensive written comments on this work, Gauguin claimed that he wanted the complementary colors and undulating lines to evoke an ambiguous mood of sex, fear, and death, and they do just that. Utterly fantastical by Western standards, the dark-faced ghost and the little bursts of phosphorescent light are palpably real to the Tahitian woman, and it was this alternative sense of reality that Gauguin found so compelling. With its intense pink sands and the liquid reflections in the adjacent lagoon, *Aha Oe Feii?* seems more like a "fairytalelike" reverie than a truthful record of everyday life for Tahitian women unashamed to strip naked and unobliged to work. Translated "Are You Jealous?" the title is evidently addressed to the work's eventual European spectators. His enviable situation notwithstanding, Gauguin could hardly wait to return to France and overwhelm the art world with his sensuous new pictures of noble savages in paradise.

Despite Gauguin's physical absence from 1891 to 1893, French painting developed during

PAUL GAUGUIN

  Aha oe feii? (Are You Jealous?), 1892
  Oil on canvas, 26 × 35″
  (66 × 89 cm)
  Pushkin Museum of Fine Arts,
  Moscow

those years in keeping with his ideas about the power of abstraction and the desirability of escape into fantasy. A group of precocious students, reacting to his paintings from Brittany, had formed themselves into a sort of secular brotherhood, calling themselves Nabis (meaning "prophet" in Hebrew). Maurice Denis's (1870–1943) *Procession under the Trees* gives us an excellent idea of how far beyond Seurat these young artists had gone. Not everyday figures familiar from real life but virgins in bridal gowns accompanied by nuns in black enact a ritualistic procession in a park. The incredibly bright daylight suggests that these silhouetted figures are apparitions sleepwalking in a world where trees cast filigree pattern shadows and human behavior is apparently guided by customs and superstitions. Writing under a pen name, Denis in 1890 published the most concise explanation of these stylistic liberties: "Remember that a painting — before it is a battlehorse, a nude woman, or some anecdote — is essentially a flat surface covered with colors arranged in a certain order." This emphasis on a flat pattern was carried to an influential extreme by fellow Nabi Edouard Vuillard (1868–1940), whose interior genre paintings amount to "fairytalelike" transformations of a dressmaker's world (his mother's), suffused with textiles and garments of every color and stripe — these observed against patterned wallpapers and rugs. Extending the homogeneous, textilelike dotting that Seurat and Signac had initiated to suggest a sense of spatial envelope, Vuillard juxtaposed and overlapped patterns until foreground and background melted together, and his so-called decorative pictures thus heralded a new stage of generalized abstraction in French painting. Using color and pattern to transform ordinary scenes into opulent fantasies, Vuillard advocated the art-for-art's-sake faith that images should provide a psychic escape from prosaic real life.

Monet's Tahiti was only slightly outside of Paris, in a village on the Seine named Giverny, where he had moved with his large family in 1883 and had begun to create magnificent gardens

PAUL CÉZANNE

The Basket of Apples, ca. 1895
Oil on canvas, 24⅛ × 31″
(65.5 × 81.3 cm)
The Art Institute of Chicago,
Chicago
Helen Birch Bartlett Memorial
Collection, 1926

that many considered his greatest works of art. With motifs to paint in his own neighborhood, Monet was able to modify impressionist methods in an extraordinary way. Before, he had lugged two or three canvases to some remote site hours away from home and shifted from one to another when the atmospheric light changed, protecting himself against many weather-related delays in output. In Giverny he could have dozens of canvases at hand while he worked and could return to a site in minutes. Instead of relying on breakneck speed of execution, Monet could return with ease to elaborate a painting on consecutive days when he needed to. In this way he was able to make time stop for the painter, to record increasingly instantaneous light effects, lasting perhaps only minutes each, and yet transcribe them in greater detail than ever before.

Starting with his *Haystacks*, Monet recorded the immediacy of the visual act with an unprecedented fullness, and his surface changed dramatically as he added layer after layer of subtle innuendo, resulting in crusts of paint with ridges to catch the ambient light and sparkle even more than was the case in his early impressionist paintings. Throughout the 1890s he exhibited ensembles of paintings at the gallery of Durand-Ruel with similar or identical compositions but with distinct colorations, addressing the flux of time as no painter before had been able to do. Taken as groups, these series amounted to decorative ensembles in the spirit of Vuillard. Taken separately, the paintings provided analyses of the texture of light more thorough, if less systematic, than even Seurat had attempted. In none of them is Monet's basic goal more explicitly stated than in the *Rouen Cathedral* series; in most of these paintings a round form over the central Gothic portal represents a modern clock whose visible identity has been eradicated by the flooding majesty of colored light that creates a more valid and meaningful time.

Cézanne, who once visited Monet in Giverny and envied his speed at work, also preferred to paint in isolation outside Paris. Tahiti for Cézanne was the town of Aix, where he had grown up. Acting the recluse there, he labored over every sort of painting: landscapes, still lifes, portraits, and decorative golden age scenes in the spirit of Poussin or Puvis de Chavannes. It was only in 1895, when the courageous dealer Ambroise Vollard (1868–1939) sought out Cézanne and arranged an exhibition of his works in Paris, that his achievements became known to a new generation of painters. Cézanne had opted to leave considerable areas of blank, untouched canvas in some of these works, and this exhibition initiated a cult for partially finished (and honestly unresolved) paintings. This corresponded to the cult for the fragment already initiated by Rodin in sculpture.

Cézanne's awareness of time as an essential factor in visual experience was no less profound than Monet's and more influential for subsequent generations of painters. In his paintings, perspective seems to crack and space seems to twist. That is to say, Cézanne might record one side of a tabletop according to a certain perspective, but then he would record the opposite side according to a slightly different perspective. The resulting inconsistency (which led many admirers to consider Cézanne a modern primitive unschooled in Renaissance perspective) apparently accounts for the way the eyes shift from one specific detail to another as they examine a scene.

Observing the opposite sides of a single object in this manner, Cézanne developed a unique sensitivity to three-dimensional volume as it is manifested in visual, two-dimensional terms. In one of his landscapes, *The House with Cracked Walls*, the sides of the object, a rural building, literally split asunder as if cleft by a seismic unsettling. Exaggerated by a younger generation, Cézanne's analytic approach to the visual act would result in Cubism. For himself, the transcription of planes perceived with his shifting visual focus suggested new, precariously balanced visual harmonies. Piling patterned textiles on tabletops as opulent backgrounds for his compositions, Cézanne, like Vuillard, advocated decorative abstraction as the essence of art.

HENRI DE TOULOUSE-LAUTREC

Interior on the Rue des Moulins, 1894
Oil on canvas, 44 × 52¼″ (111.7 × 132.7 cm)
Musée Toulouse-Lautrec, Albi

HENRI DE TOULOUSE-LAUTREC

At the Moulin Rouge, 1892–1895
Oil on canvas, 48½ × 55⅛" (123 × 141 cm)
The Art Institute of Chicago, Chicago
Helen Birch Bartlett Memorial Collection, 1928

CLAUDE MONET

Haystacks: Snow Effect, 1891
Oil on canvas, 25⅝ × 36¼″ (65 × 92 cm)
National Gallery of Scotland, Edinburgh

CLAUDE MONET

Rouen Cathedral — Harmony in Blue and Gold, 1894
Oil on canvas, 42⅛ × 28¾″ (107 × 73 cm)
Musée d'Orsay, Paris

197

XIX.
The Close of an Era

PAUL CÉZANNE

Still Life with Plaster Cupid, 1895
Oil on canvas, 27½ × 22½"
(70 × 57 cm)
The Courtauld Institute Galleries,
London
The Courtauld Collection

NOT A SCULPTOR HIMSELF, CÉZANNE NEVERTHELESS SOUGHT TO SUGGEST SCULPTURAL volume in his paintings, as he made rather explicit in *Still Life with Plaster Cupid*. A record of his studio, including paintings propped against the walls at angles, this work qualifies as what Courbet had called a "real allegory." Its arms broken off during the course of time, the statue of Cupid cannot play with the love apples scattered randomly at his feet, where they are colorful rivals for Cézanne's attention. The little god's handicap was one the painter could sympathize with, given his own strictly visual means of observing a tactile world. Analyzed with the eyes instead of the hands, this world is illusory and illogical, its problems exacerbated in an artist's studio. In the background Cézanne included a painting of another statue, thus forcing on the viewer an awareness of multiplying illusions that can enchant sight in *Arabian Nights* fashion.

Understood this way, Cézanne's late works share a mood of mystery with the decorative fantasy visions of Odilon Redon (1840–1916), whose fascination with dream apparitions anticipated the more systematic investigations of the surrealists in the 1920s. In a painting such as *The Cyclops* Redon imagined the weirdly flattened and diminutive appearance that our earthly world might have for the one-eyed giant of Greek mythology. Addressing the looking-at-looking theme in fantastical terms, Redon observed in his mind's eye a monster who stares at a sleeping woman. She is embedded in a textilelike field of little brushstrokes that appear like out-of-focus flowers or like the abstract molten colored glazes on the Oriental ceramics prized by late nineteenth-century collectors.

Paintings like this are apparently a response to the Tahitian works of Gauguin, themselves in part responses to the symbolist lithographs with which Redon first made his reputation as a modern master in the 1880s. Gauguin's ultimate masterpiece, painted after his return to Tahiti in 1895, was a prelude to his failed suicide attempt three years later. Over twelve feet wide, *Where Do We Come From? What Are We? Where Are We Going?* was conceived to look like an ancient fresco, its corners weathered away, recording a golden age civilization where a blue goddess presided over the mysteries of birth and death. In the middle of this once-upon-a-time paradise Gauguin posed a man reaching up to pluck a fruit, thus alluding to the fruit of knowledge associated with the end of innocence and the appearance of sin and evil in the world. Staring out of the picture to where the painter can be imagined to be at work, the relaxing female figures in the mural seem unconcerned by the philosophical implications of the moment. The questions, as far as Gauguin was concerned, are modern questions, and modern painting can progress only if painters look backward to the ancient instincts from which civilization evolved.

With its earnest allusions to the history of culture, Gauguin's "primitivism" sometimes seems insincere or posed. His works, however, appealed enormously to Henri Rousseau, whose genuinely naive temperament had been so exciting to Redon when he had first begun to exhibit in the mid-1880s. Continuing to present his "fairytalelike" visions painted with childlike simplicity at the jury-free independent Salons, Rousseau demonstrated the considerable power of art unconcerned with the subtleties of perspective, proportion, and logical narrative. *The Sleeping Gypsy* describes an imaginary world as far away as the one Gauguin had traveled around the world to find. The full moon casts a strange light over a barren mountainous landscape guarded by a lion that was probably painted from a stuffed animal. This beast hardly seems threatening to the dreaming wanderer, whose odd proportions, not to mention her misshapen mandolin, would make Rousseau a hero to the young Picasso and later to the surrealists. The same twentieth-century artists would venerate the spirit of Rousseau's friend Alfred Jarry, the inventor of the theater of the absurd.

Theater was the preferred idiom of very late nineteenth-century French painting. Challenged by the innovations of newcomers such as Seurat, Gauguin, and Vuillard and those of old colleagues such as Monet and Cézanne, Degas, who had been the most stylistically conservative member of the original impressionist group, became the most radical and modern in the 1890s. The exact chronology of his late works is unknown, since he very seldom chose to exhibit, preferring to keep reworking the same idea or even the same painting over and over. Mimicking Seurat's dots, Degas now would use his fingertips to apply spot patterns in his remarkable interior scenes of nudes drying themselves. These hybrid works, with oils used like pastels and vice versa, are characterized by extremes of color and paint handling that van Gogh seldom had equaled. Degas's figures disappear into floods of colored light just as Rouen Cathedral had dissolved into iridescent pigeon-throat-colored mists in Monet's series variations.

Using his own method, developed in the 1870s, to transpose the same drawing of a figure into several paintings with differing compositions, Degas in his ballet scenes advocated seriality in art in a different way than Monet did. The extent of their rivalry is perhaps hinted at by the haystacks that Degas incorporated as a theater set background in his last great ballet painting. In the foreground a group of his own figure variations, dancers fixing the shoulder straps on their costumes, seem to upstage the Monet motif and assert Degas's variety of instantaneity and realism as well as his figure painter's mentality in contrast to the mere landscapes of the Giverny master.

Pierre Bonnard (1867–1947), a member of the Nabis whose decorative images with overlapping patterns of foliage and textile rival those of Vuillard for delicacy, extended Degas's series of "keyhole" nudes into a frank portrait of domestic sexuality with *Man and Woman*. Judging from the flood of light streaming across the bed where the woman sits beckoning two cats to play, the painting represents morning, with the man at right dressing for the day. The odd detail of the folded screen at the center of the composition can be understood as an exaggeration of the sort of idiosyncratic furnishings common in Degas's works — who would never have included a male figure, the artist or the viewer by implication playing the Adam to every one of his modern Eves.

Taking a bird's-eye view in an abruptly flattened perspective reminiscent of Japanese prints, Pissarro began in the late 1890s to work from upper-story hotel rooms. His *La Place du Théâtre Français* is less a record of movement than a recognition of the decorative patterns inherent in urban traffic. Even so, for Pissarro, who briefly adopted the dot style of Seurat and Signac, the composition seems like a nostalgic reprise of 1870s impressionist compositions by Renoir, Monet, and Caillebotte. It may be that the aging painter was reminded of those early works by the installation of part of Caillebotte's collection at the Luxembourg Palace Museum in 1897. Caillebotte's bequest to the state aroused bitter debate, and thanks to the rancor of archconservatives such as Gérôme, part of the collection was refused. For example, only two of the five works by Cézanne were considered acceptable, and only eight of the sixteen paintings by Caillebotte's fellow gardener, Monet.

His battles with hostile critics otherwise long over, Monet had persevered to become one of the world's most successful artists in the marketplace. In 1893 he was able to buy property adjoining his own in Giverny and make a water garden, across which he constructed a Japanese profile wooden bridge from which he could meditate on water lilies. Eventually he had six gardeners working to keep what became an out-of-doors studio in immaculate order. Related to the sacred lotuses prevalent in ancient art from Egypt to India, China, and Mexico, the water lilies had symbolic overtones that would not have been lost on Gauguin. Moreover, as photosensitive plants, opening and closing with the coming and going of sunlight, the flowers embodied the impressionist creed. Apparently painted from a boat in Daubigny fashion, Monet's first, ultrarealistically rendered pictures of the congested surface of the pond suggest magic carpets embroidered with delicately colored blossoms that beckon the viewer into a world more fantasy than fact.

Called *nymphéas* in French, Monet's water lilies must also be understood as a landscape painter's response to the classical figure paintings with nude female bathers that so preoccupied close colleagues such as Renoir and Cézanne in the 1880s and 1890s. Indeed, the largest of all Cézanne's paintings, apparently worked and reworked for nearly a decade at the end of his life, shows more than a dozen young women gathered under a grove of trees as if they had

reconstituted a pagan sisterhood. Their strangely swollen and elongated anatomies and their crudely indicated facial features make them as savage as the Tahitians used as models by Gauguin. Most unsettling, however, is the way Cézanne rendered their flesh in luminous watercolorlike washes of speckled color that hardly mask his nervous outlines for their forms. Painted this way, the bathers' skins become an extension of the landscape's trembling atmospheric spatial envelope. Although he painted these women from imagination, Cézanne managed to integrate their images into a landscape and thus fulfill the original realist goal of capturing the appearance of a nude in real sunlight. His mysterious assembly of women, more than any other figures in previous French painting, are so closely integrated into the setting, their gestures distended into structure and rhythm, that they herald most of the new pictorial languages that were already becoming art lingo on the streets of Paris's international art colony in the twentieth century.

PAUL CÉZANNE

The Large Bathers, 1906
Oil on canvas, 82 × 99″
(208 × 251.4 cm)
Philadelphia Museum of Art,
Philadelphia
W. P. Wilstach Collection

PAUL GAUGUIN

Where Do We Come From? What Are We? Where Are We Going?, 1897
Oil on canvas, 54¼ × 147½" (139.1 × 374.6 cm)
Museum of Fine Arts, Boston
Purchase, Arthur Gordon Tompkins Fund, 1936

HENRI ROUSSEAU (b. 1844, Laval–d. 1910)

The Sleeping Gypsy, 1897
Oil on canvas, 51 × 79″ (129.5 × 200.7 cm)
The Museum of Modern Art, New York
Gift of Mrs. Simon Guggenheim

ODILON REDON (b. 1840, Bordeaux–d. 1916)

Cyclops, ca. 1898
Oil on panel, 25¼ × 20″ (64 × 50.8 cm)
Rijksmuseum Kröller-Müller, Otterlo

EDGAR DEGAS

> *Four Dancers*, ca. 1899
> Oil on canvas, 59½ × 71″ (151.1 × 180.2 cm)
> National Gallery of Art, Washington, D.C.
> Chester Dale Collection

PIERRE BONNARD (b. 1867, Fontenay-aux-Roses–d. 1947)

> *Man and Woman*, 1900
> Oil on canvas, 45¼ × 24½″ (115 × 72 cm)
> Musée d'Orsay, Paris

CAMILLE PISSARRO

Place du Théâtre Français, Rain, 1898
Oil on canvas, 29 × 36″ (73.6 × 91.4 cm)
The Minneapolis Institute of Arts, Minneapolis
The William Hood Dunwoody Fund

XX.
The Wild Beasts

EARLY TWENTIETH-CENTURY PAINTING IN FRANCE WAS A MATTER OF EXTREMES IN STYLE, EVEN for aging impressionist masters such as Degas, Monet, and Renoir. Large retrospective exhibitions organized to survey the careers of Seurat, van Gogh, Gauguin, and Cézanne familiarized younger artists with four distinct avenues toward individualistic modes of expression based on exaggeration as well as simplification of color and drawing. These abstract options had all developed as alternatives to Impressionism (by now the most popular mode of painting worldwide), with its commitment to unedited reality.

At a van Gogh retrospective organized by the Bernheim-Jeune Gallery in Paris in 1901, André Derain (1880–1954) introduced Henri Matisse (1869–1954) to Maurice Vlaminck (1876–1958), initiating an exchange of ideas that would lead to so-called Fauvism (a derisive term based on the French word *fauve*, which means "wild beast"). Matisse had studied with the Symbolist Moreau, who bequeathed to France his studio and all its contents, including hundreds of preliminary sketches, as a monument to himself. Nearly as controversial as the Caillebotte bequest of impressionist works to the Louvre, Moreau's museum opened in 1903, foreshadowing the retrospective mentality of much twentieth-century art, which would stress analysis of the creative process and, by extension, of artists' biographies.

Matisse got his real education outside the classroom at the gallery of Vollard, where he saw works by van Gogh and Cézanne and began a small collection of his own. From the first he sought ways to fuse space and color. Falling under the spell of Seurat's divisionism (the analysis of color in dotlike units), Matisse emerged with a distinct style of his own in the summer of 1905, which he spent at the Mediterranean village of Collioure, not far from the Spanish border, in the company of Derain, who had just returned from London. With its shrill color and emphasis on decorative arrangements of form, Matisse's *Open Window, Collioure* provoked a critic to coin the term "Fauvism" when it was exhibited along with similar works at the third annual Salon d'Automne in November. Limited to the description of the exterior world as seen through a parted window overlooking a harbor (a picture within a picture), Matisse's more freehanded version of the uniform texture of brushwork developed by Seurat and Signac rendered space in a rather conventional way, albeit in intense tones of pink and red.

What shocked viewers at first was the abrupt contrast between the central part of the painting and the surrounding areas, which represent the foreground, painted in broad zones of only slightly modulated color, indicating the wall of the room from which the painter observed the picturesque scene of bobbing boats. Blue-green to the left and reddish-violet to the right, this blank wall registers a sudden shift from shadow to light as high, discordant visual drama. Suspended planes of color in space, the glass panes of the window opening into the room (each another small picture within the picture) reflect fragments of what is visible in the distance as well as at the sides of the scene, fusing near, far, right, and left. Interlocked in this way, the overlapping, interpenetrating rectangular zones of colored light reveal the plastic excitement of space as a new abstract theme for painting.

Views from open windows were a hallmark of Impressionism, and Monet's stunning exhibition of the opalescent, light-refracting atmosphere viewed from a room in London's Savoy Hotel overlooking the foggy, smoky Thames was among the highlights of the 1904 art season in Paris. As if to capitalize on the popularity of these new paintings and as if to parody Monet's fastidious observation of nuance, Derain did his own views of similar Thames motifs in 1905, using hypercharged colors that were construed as a sign of lunacy by most viewers. With their red-streaked skies above green buildings, Derain's views of London made a travesty of impressionist realism, liberating color from its role in representation and casting it as an abstract, decorative means of expressing the excitement of vision. Self-taught as a painter, Vlaminck understood Fauvism as an extension of van Gogh's liberties and boasted that he used colors as they came, squeezed directly from the tube. Raw and intense, Vlaminck's landscapes painted around Chatou (the site of Courbet's *Young Women on the Banks of the Seine* and Renoir's *Luncheon of the Boating Party*), where he and Derain shared a studio, make his colleagues' works seem delicate and sophisticated. By early 1906 Matisse had decided to attempt monumental paintings in the new style, and Derain quickly followed his lead when he summered in L'Estaque, just outside Marseilles. Orchestrating the dissonant fauve palette in keeping with Gauguin's Tahitian works (which would be showcased at the 1906 Salon d'Automne), Derain transformed his motifs with fruit colors such as banana, mango, and peach. The trees all seem to dance, their trunks and branches undulating to a supernatural rhythm.

Modjesko, Soprano Singer by the Dutch-born Kees van Dongen (1877–1968) evokes sound with more explicit means: The buxom singer seems to exhale an aura of vermilion so intense that its space begins to ripple. During the teens and twenties van Dongen modified Fauvism into a style for high-fashion portraiture while he presided as one of the lions of Montparnasse, the neighborhood that attracted models, collectors, and would-be artists from all over the world. No work more fully embodies the international flavor of Left Bank Fauvism than the primitive-looking portrait of a model, *The Young Finnish Woman*, painted by Russian-born Sonia Terk (1885–1979), who arrived in Paris in 1905 and married the German dealer Wilhelm Uhde, who was among the fauves' most important supporters. Of course, Sonia Terk would leave Uhde to marry Frenchman Robert Delaunay in 1910, initiating a more potent form of international art collaboration.

While the fauves were generally dedicated to painting in the spirit of pagan revels, the group had a conscience in the person of Georges Rouault (1871–1958), a fervent Catholic for whom the graphic social satire of Daumier provided the foundation for exaggeration in modern art. While his colleagues preferred reds and oranges, Rouault's predilection was for the range of blues associated with depression and sadness, moods in keeping with his favorite subjects of prostitutes and clowns, the flotsam of twentieth-century urban life awaiting salvation. Outlined with gracelessly proportioned, contorted outlines into zones washed with shadowy colors, Rouault's figures are the reincarnation of the martyrs recorded in medieval stained-glass windows. His Gothicized, nearly subhuman *Head of Christ*, ruptured with sorrow and dripping with sweat and blood, makes it easy to understand why this style seemed so "bestial" at first.

HENRI MATISSE (b. 1869,
Cateau-Cambrésis–d. 1954)

Open Window, Collioure, 1905
Oil on canvas, 21¼ × 18⅛″
(54 × 46 cm)
From the Collection of
Mrs. John Hay Whitney,
New York

ANDRÉ DERAIN (b. 1880,
Chatou–d. 1954)

Effect of Sunlight on Water, 1905
Oil on canvas, 30¾ × 39⅛″
(80.5 × 100 cm)
Musée d'l'Annonciade,
St. Tropez

MAURICE DE VLAMINCK
(b. 1876, Paris–d. 1958)

Houses at Chatou, 1905–1906
Oil on canvas, 32 × 39⅝″
(81.9 x 100.3 cm)
The Art Institute of Chicago,
Chicago
Gift of Mr. Maurice E. Culburg,
1951

GEORGES ROUAULT (b. 1871, Paris–d. 1958)

Head of Christ, 1905
Oil on paper mounted on canvas,
39 × 25¼″ (99 × 64 cm)
The Chrysler Museum, Norfolk, Virginia

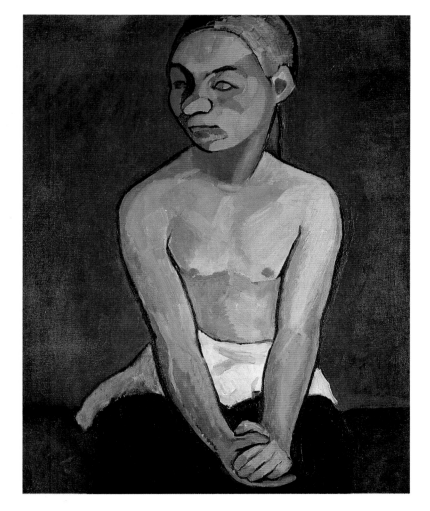

KEES VAN DONGEN (b. 1877, Voorhaven–d. 1968)

Modjesko, Soprano Singer, 1908
Oil on canvas, 39⅛ × 32″ (100 × 81.2 cm)
The Museum of Modern Art, New York
Gift of Mr. and Mrs. Peter A. Rubel

SONIA TERK DELAUNAY (b. 1885, Ukraine–d. 1979)

Young Finnish Woman, 1907
Oil on canvas, 31½ × 24¼″ (80 × 61.5 cm)
Musée National d'Art Moderne, Centre Georges
Pompidou, Paris

XXI.
Picasso and Early Cubism

THE MOST IMPORTANT FRENCH PAINTER OF THE TWENTIETH CENTURY WAS SPANISH. PABLO Picasso (1881–1973) settled in the Montmartre quarter of Paris in 1904, having begun an association with the dealer Vollard by 1901. Resignation was his subject of predilection, and outcasts such as street performers, whores, and drinkers were his usual models. Capturing a mood of pervasive depression with melancholy blue costumes and settings, Picasso invented stock characters for the modern world of tragicomedy. Tired, undernourished, and stoically silent, these characters seem to look at their world as a wasteland. The most impressive of all his early works, *The Family of Saltimbanques*, portrays nomadic acrobats pausing in a desert landscape as if to decide which way to go to find the next audience. The harlequin figure at the far left appears to be a self-portrait of Picasso, who had begun to attend circus performances on a regular basis, often in the company of the brilliant poet and critic Guillaume Apollinaire (1880–1918). On the basis of Marie Laurencin's (1885–1956) group portrait of Picasso, Apollinaire, and their girlfriends gathered on a sort of double date a few years later, the fat clown in Picasso's *Family of Saltimbanques* has been identified as a likeness of this writer. In the painting, Picasso, sitting at Apollinaire's feet to hear him read, appears in rigid profile, as if cut out of an ancient Egyptian mural. Dedicated to childlike simplification in art, Laurencin showed herself in front of a bright bouquet so that the flowers seem to grow from her head. Picasso had introduced her to Apollinaire in 1907 at the gallery of Clovis Sagot (d. 1913), an art dealer who had formerly been a circus clown. Picasso's epic canvas was bought in 1909 by a group of art speculators for eventual resale, and it made headlines when it was placed at auction in 1914, selling for nearly three times what a work by van Gogh or Gauguin would have brought.

At first, however, Picasso's works appealed to only a handful of collectors, the most important of whom were two American writers, a brother and sister named Leo and Gertrude Stein. Around the same time they "discovered" Matisse at the fauve room in the Salon d'Automne in 1905, the Steins bought their first work by Picasso for next to nothing from the little-known dealer Sagot. Immediately these two artists became regular visitors to the Steins' Saturday evening "at homes," which attracted a galaxy of international visitors, converting many of them to modern mindedness in the arts. It was to one of these dinners that Matisse brought the wooden fetish made in the Belgian Congo that he had just purchased in a curio shop. This piece amazed Picasso, who promptly got on the primitive art bandwagon that had begun to roll in response to Gauguin's enthusiasm for the anonymous, timeless shamanistic art of so-called primitive cultures.

The following year, 1907, Picasso began a large canvas that changed the course of twentieth-century painting, *Les Demoiselles d'Avignon (Avignon Prostitutes)*, ostensibly a group portrait in the tradition of Lautrec, with five whores displaying themselves to a spectator-artist outside the picture. Odd rhythms charged this brothel scene with animal energies. Grotesquely distorted by Western standards and more savage than any work of the fauves, the darkened faces of the figures at the left and right have splayed noses and lips, decorative scars, and staring eyes that Picasso had adapted from African sculpture displayed in ethnographic museums. In graphic terms, the jagged shapes in the breasts prefigured the geometric units that Georges Braque (1882–1963) and Picasso himself developed into Cubism in the coming years. In terms of subject matter, the nightmare vision here goes beyond cubist experiment and may be understood as a prelude to the surrealists' anthropological and psychological investigations of primal emotional states.

Although Picasso did not exhibit at Salons, this work became the talk of the Paris art world. Uhde brought Daniel Kahnweiler to see it at Picasso's studio, introducing the painter to

his future dealer. Kahnweiler recalled that for Braque, *Les Demoiselles* was the equivalent of seeing someone drinking gasoline and spitting fire. Apollinaire had introduced Braque and Picasso that same year. Presumably referring to the stylized figures in *Les Demoiselles*, Rousseau boasted that there were two leaders in the Paris art world: himself in the modern style and Picasso in the Egyptian. Rousseau's last great work, *The Dream*, captured the same hothouse atmosphere, with a nude reclined like a whore on a sofa, albeit transposed into a dreamland jungle with a snake charmer serenading what look like toy beasts and overgrown houseplants.

Braque spent the summer of 1908 at L'Estaque, perhaps to be close to the memory of Cézanne, who had died nearby less than two years before. The works Braque painted there extended the simplification of form to its planar essentials and the multifocal perspective Cézanne had invented. Exaggerating these principles, Braque used adjacent or overlapping rectangular units to construct a stylized pictorial order divorced from the appearances of the real world revered by Cézanne. Hoping to exhibit these highly original works at the 1908 Salon d'Automne but refused by the jury (of which Matisse was a member), Braque instead showed them at Kahnweiler's gallery. A concurrent exhibition of the Wright brothers' airplane at the

PABLO PICASSO (b. 1881, Málaga–d. 1973)

Family of Saltimbanques, 1905
Oil on canvas, 83¼ × 90⅜″
(212.8 × 229.6 cm)
The National Gallery of Art, Washington, D.C.
Chester Dale Collection

Grand Palais was the only comparably modern manifestation in town, and Braque received the nickname of Wilbur after one of the aviators. Picasso was the copilot on the flight into what Matisse called Cubism. Hoping to avoid misunderstanding, both men boycotted large public exhibitions and special artist groups.

Works by Picasso painted during the following years are sometimes nearly impossible to distinguish from those by Braque, with each painter fracturing objects into rectangular bits of different sizes, alternatively lightened or darkened to indicate shading. Rendered part by part with these units, once-familiar objects appear to merge dynamically into the now-fractured space surrounding them. It is as if the transformative process of painting images of three-dimensional realities on a two-dimensional flat canvas surface broke and displaced the skin of physical fact into facets that had to be pressed back into sequence, just as parts of the globe must be flattened into mathematically ordered grids by mapmakers. In a cubist still life painted around the end of 1909, Braque included a nail painted in a conventional illusionistic way. It seems to project out from the otherwise spatially neutral surface that contains the cubistically shattered images of a pitcher and a violin. But if the painted nail's painted shadow is a measure of what most viewers would call flat, by comparison the cubist elements in Braque's picture are not flat in any conventional way. During the next few years, Braque and Picasso challenged one another to invent playful ways to stress the paradoxical relationships between fiction and fact.

Cubism spread throughout Europe almost overnight. With its disregard for form as a finite quality, the new style offered a way for scores of mavericks to consolidate their thinking about the role of art in modern life. By February 1909 a group of Italian artists had organized their ideas under the rubric of Futurism and proclaimed them in the French newspaper *Le Figaro*. Advocating the same sort of small jagged units of form, repeated over and over to suggest the quaking of mechanical movement, these artists called for an art that broke entirely with the past. "Time and Space died yesterday," wrote Filippo Tommaso Marinetti (1876–1944) in a controversial manifesto. "We already live in the absolute, since we have already created eternal, omnipresent speed." The futurists' response to the mechanization of the modern world inspired a group of French painters who studied mathematical theories, including the hypothetical structure of the fourth dimension, in relationship to the disregard for conventional illusionistic space and time seen in cubist painting. Supported in the press by Apollinaire, these artists demanded to show their works together at the Salons, and in 1911 they began to meet together to discuss common theoretical interests. The suburb of Puteaux, where a group of brothers named Duchamp lived near the unorthodox Czech painter Frantisek Kupka (1871–1957), became an important gathering place for these artists, who chose to call their effort *La Section d'Or* ("The Golden Section," an ancient mathematical ratio reputed to express a perfect proportion).

The most important member of this group was Marcel Duchamp (1887–1968), who eventually would invent conceptual art. Duchamp went beyond Cubism by following the implications of the new style in an absolutely literal way. His *Coffee Mill* can be understood as a Cubism machine, since its function is to take whole beans and grind them into irregular little bits, brownish in color like the facets in so many paintings by Picasso and Braque, liberating an invisible quality or aroma. To show this coffee mill cubistically, Duchamp turned to the elementary conventions of mechanical drawing, indicating in a single diagram different positions of the same object as well as its appearance in profile, elevation, cross section, and so on.

Duchamp's humor irked his colleagues, who refused to accept *Nude Descending a Staircase* for the Salon des Independants in early 1912. Close in concept to some of the futurist works brought to Paris for a gallery exhibition that year, this painting represents the progressive stages of a single action in diagrammatic fashion. Nudity, the symbol for truth in art, in effect disappears as a result of Duchamp's overlapping step-by-step cubist analyses of the sequential positions of a body in motion. The seemingly absurd discrepancy between the shattered forms and the title of the work promoted futile attempts at understanding, initiating an important new role for titles in twentieth-century art as what Duchamp called "an invisible color."

"Robert should not have broken the Eiffel Tower," explained Rousseau on his deathbed in 1910. He was referring to the son of a woman who was one of his patrons, Robert Delaunay (1885–1941). For Delaunay, the broken forms of Picasso and Braque's Cubism had been anticipated by Gustave Eiffel's ultramodern engineering marvel unveiled as a symbol of modern Paris at the 1889 World's Fair. Observed through the tower's lattices of girders, the city was in a sense compartmentalized into cubist visual bits, as Delaunay stressed in a series of paintings. For

MARIE LAURENCIN (b. 1883, Paris–d. 1956)

Group of Artists, 1908
Oil on canvas, 25½ × 31⅞″ (64.8 × 81 cm)
The Baltimore Museum of Art, Baltimore
The Cone Collection,
formed by Dr. Claribel Cone
and Miss Etta Cone of Baltimore, Maryland

each of them he observed the landmark from a variety of different points of view — from below, from above, and so on. It was as if, as Rousseau put it, he had broken it the way a bad child might break a toy. Whereas the impressionists and even the fauves showed how light can distort or even appear to shatter the physical shapes and colors of objects, in Delaunay's paintings light is subjected to the abstract regimentation of cubism. Thanks in large part to the popularity of Delaunay's paintings, exhibited not only in Paris but throughout Europe, modernistic architecture became one of the most important themes in twentieth-century painting.

HENRI ROUSSEAU

The Dream, 1910
Oil on canvas, 80½ × 116½″
(204.4 × 296 cm)
The Museum of Modern Art, New York
Gift of Nelson A. Rockefeller

Georges Braque

Still Life with Violin and Pitcher, 1909–1910
Oil on canvas, 46½ × 28¾″ (118 × 73 cm)
Kunstmuseum, Basel

Pablo Picasso

Les Demoiselles d'Avignon, 1907
Oil on canvas, 96 × 92″ (238.8 × 233.6 cm)
The Museum of Modern Art, New York
Acquired through the Lillie P. Bliss Bequest

NU DESCENDANT UN ESCALIER

MARCEL DUCHAMP

> *Nude Descending a Staircase, No. 2*, 1912
> Oil on canvas, 58 × 35″ (147 × 89 cm)
> Philadelphia Museum of Art, Philadelphia
> The Louise and Walter Arensberg Collection

ROBERT DELAUNAY (b. 1885, Paris–d. 1941)

> *La Champ de Mars (The Red Tower)*, 1911, revised before 1923
> Oil on canvas, 64 × 51½″ (162.6 × 130.8 cm)
> The Art Institute of Chicago, Chicago
> The Joseph Winterbotham Collection

MARCEL DUCHAMP (b. 1887, Blainville–d. 1968)

> *Coffee Mill*, 1911
> Oil on cardboard, 13 × 15″ (33 × 12.5 cm)
> Tate Gallery, London

XXII.
Pure Abstraction and Pure Fantasy

DELAUNAY'S MOST IMPORTANT ROLE IN THE HISTORY OF FRENCH PAINTING, HOWEVER, WAS TO extend abstraction to a point where color and shape function independently, the way sound functions in music. Like Seurat before him, Delaunay was a student of color theory, including the principle that juxtaposed complementary colors (such as green and red or blue and yellow) intensify one another, and sought to evoke movement and space through color relationships that were considered apart from the appearance of objects. In 1913 he undertook a series of paintings depicting the interaction of circular forms, sometimes even employing a circular canvas format. Using cubist bits of color to form the arcs of these revolving circular forms, Delaunay alluded to the ancient notion of the harmony of the celestial spheres. Apollinaire dubbed these works "Orphic" Cubism, referring to the ancient Greek musician Orpheus.

In one of the most remarkable works in this series, Delaunay simplified his composition along the lines of seven concentric circles of nearly equal width, with each ring divided into four equal arcs of pure color. The flat bands obey a geometric logic that has a hypnotic visual interest, instigating one of the most widespread phenomena in twentieth-century art: the investigation of totally abstract formal relationships. Superimposing several of these disks, each representing in a poetic way the prismatic auras of city night lights, Sonia Terk Delaunay brought her husband's theoretical investigations down to earth, adopting the abstract forms to one of the most radically decorative forms of Cubism.

In France, the Delaunays' major rival as a pioneer in total abstraction was Frantisek Kupka, who claimed to have undertaken a series of his own color theory paintings around 1911–1912. Entitled *Disks of Newton*, these works also celebrate cosmic forms made of concentric bands of color. Among his exhibited works, *Amphora, Fugue in Two Colors*, included at the Salon d'Automne in 1912, best exemplifies Kupka's essential role in the development of abstraction, and the title makes it clear how important it was to express musical equivalents in terms of painting. Of course, *Concerning the Spiritual in Art*, the influential treatise on musical abstraction as the essence of art published in 1912 by the Russian-born painter Vassily Kandinsky (1866–1944), quickly gained an enormous following for ideas in keeping with those advocated by Kupka and the Delaunays.

The logical organization of the arcs and bands of color in these paintings marks an important new stage in the development of Cubism as a way to suggest mental concepts that could not previously be visualized except in allegorical terms. A similar interest in Cubism as a mode of depicting thought is evident in one of the major works of the Golden Section artist Roger de La Fresnaye (1885–1925), *The Conquest of Air*, which was exhibited at the Salon d'Automne of 1913. Adopting Delaunay's morphology, La Fresnaye depicted himself in conversation with his brother Henri, who directed a factory that manufactured airplanes. The black shadows around the table at which they sit seem to indicate that their conversation is taking place indoors. Their thoughts apparently surround them. Below, beyond, and above and represented in brighter colors and at a different scale is a landscape, or rather several landscapes, one with rooftops in the style of Braque's early Cubism, another with a sailboat turned to catch the wind, and another with a hot-air balloon drifting aloft on wind currents that ripple a sort of color chart in the form of the French flag.

Robert Delaunay

Simultaneous Contrasts: Sun and Moon, 1913
Oil on canvas, 53″ diameter (135 cm diameter)
The Museum of Modern Art, New York
Mrs. Simon Guggenheim Fund

The first painters to use Cubism to represent simultaneously the superimposition of figures in exterior physical space and their thoughts in interior mental space were probably Duchamp and Marc Chagall (1887–1985). Newly arrived from Russia in 1910, Chagall settled in an international artist colony in Montparnasse and immediately invented a unique and influential style by blending Matisse's liberated use of color with the cubists' geometrical patterns generated with fractured forms. Adding nonsensical elements from children's art and folk art, including levitating hats, green faces, and upside-down little people and things, Chagall carried on the spirit of fun that Rousseau had nurtured. Not until the advent of Surrealism in the 1920s was the power of Chagall's innovations recognized in full; when it was painted in 1913, a work like *Paris Through the Window* was too anarchic for most viewers. Although Chagall's studio was nowhere near the Eiffel Tower, the image must have been on his mind because of Delaunay's paintings, and the same artist's theories appear to have guided the decoration of the window frame in primary colors. But Chagall, perhaps the man in the room with two faces (one of them blue) on his head, a flower in one of his mouths, and a gold heart in his hand, treated theories lightly. Along with his pet cat (which has a human face), the protagonist in this painting observes a parachuting man, an upside-down train, and a Russian Jewish couple floating head to head in the mists of his memory. In Chagall's hands the cubist pictorial structure became a kaleidoscopic mindscape where times and places could be shown as the the mixture of fantasy and fact that most modern viewers recognize as the true nature of experience.

Francis Picabia (1879–1953), an impressionist painter who converted to Cubism around 1909 and met Duchamp the following year, was also obsessed with the potential of Cubism to evoke the internalized visual experiences of memories and mysteries. At the Salon d'Automne of 1913 Picabia exhibited two huge pictures, the ostensible subjects of which could be inferred only from the titles he stenciled on them. In Duchamp fashion, however, these titles were designed to be intentionally irritating. One of them, *Edtaonisl*, amounts to a sort of cubist word: it was obtained by dividing the French words *etoile* ("star") and *danseuse* ("dancer") into their constituent letters and then shuffling the two words into something incomprehensible. According to Picabia, the painting showed an exotic dancer who was rehearsing on board a ship on which he had been a passenger en route to New York to attend the so-called Armory Show. A fellow passenger who was a Dominican priest loved to watch these rehearsals, and *Edtaonisl* represents what Picabia imagined to be the priest's aroused experience of the gymnastic star observed while waves rocked the ship. The forms in the painting have apparently been cut into segments like the letters in the title and shuffled back together into an abstract pattern with a primitive intensity in the spirit of Picasso's *Demoiselles d'Avignon*.

Relatively much larger than the atomized forms in early, so-called analytical cubist paintings, the abstract shapes in *Edtaonisl* epitomize the so-called Synthetic Cubism developed in pre–World War I Paris. Picasso was the ultimate master of this mode, which evolved from collage; his insertion, around 1912, of cut pieces of printed paper or cloth into analytic cubist works contrasted his unique handiwork with mechanically produced, readymade substitutes for art. Picasso's best work of Synthetic Cubism, carefully premeditated in numerous studies, is *Woman in an Armchair*. Identifiable from its position as much as from its shape, each part of the half-nude woman's anatomy is rendered in a different witty way: her right hand, holding a newspaper (as if models read from boredom with posing), and her feet are claws; her knees are circular knobs; her stomach is a series of arcs to show folds of limp flesh; her raised left arm reveals rows of short black lines for underarm hair; and, most extraordinary of all, her breasts are tipped oval forms that appear to be attached to the body with tacks like the cut paper used in a children's game of pin-the-tail-on-the-donkey. This new vocabulary for the body, as the synthetic sum of parts observed in different ways, had a potential for unlimited variations and soon became one of the main vehicles for surrealist fantasy.

Modern dance of a more serious nature than what Picabia had celebrated in *Edtaonisl* had instigated a riot in Paris in May 1913, when the Russian Ballet first performed Igor Stravinsky's *Rite of Spring*. With its harmonic dissonances and savage rhythms, this work transformed the conventions of musical composition just as the cubists had transformed the conventions of painting. Albert Gleizes (1881–1953), who had been an active Golden Section cubist since 1911 and coauthor of the 1912 book *On Cubism*, which attempted to provide a rationale for the innovative style, painted a portrait of the controversial Russian composer in 1914. Indebted to

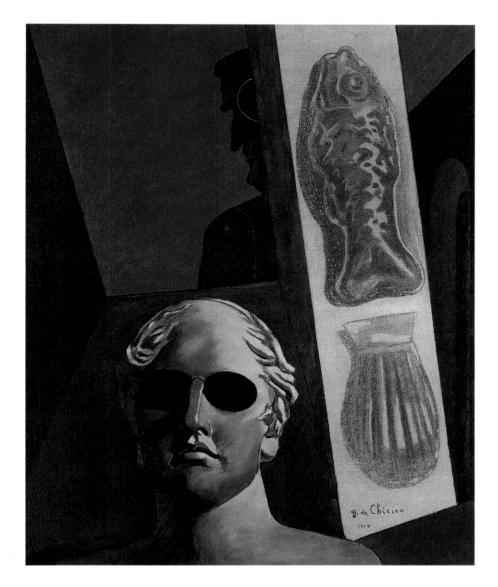

GIORGIO DE CHIRICO (b. 1888, Volo–d. 1978)

Portrait of Guillaume Apollinaire, 1914
Oil on canvas, 31⅞ × 25½″ (81 × 65 cm)
Musée National d'Art Moderne, Centre Georges
Pompidou, Paris

Picasso's Synthetic Cubism, with its bias toward large areas of unmodulated color in interlocking jigsaw-puzzle patterns, Gleizes's portrait includes easily recognizable fragments of reality such as lips, a white shirt with buttons, black lapels, and sheet music, all immersed in a matrix of geometric rhythms that appear to explode from the area of the composer's head. According to *On Cubism*, written with Jean Metzinger (1883–1956), Picasso and Braque had extended the realist movement in art initiated by Courbet. The authors distinguished, however, between conventional reality and true reality, which exists in the mind of the beholder, who projects idiosyncratic forms onto the physical world as part of the act of observation. Looking at his own way of looking when he recorded Stravinsky's likeness, Gleizes expressed his modernistic belief in form as the common denominator of all experience, visual, musical, and logical.

A painter who projected his unique inner vision with incomparable authority, Giorgio de Chirico (1888–1978), arrived in Paris in 1911 and by 1913 had converted a small band of admirers to his strange world of long shadows and vast spaces with ancient colonnades and towers, an antique statue of the dreaming Cretan princess Ariadne, and a steaming locomotive. Almost all his works were entitled *Enigma* or *Melancholy,* and they conformed to what Apollinaire considered the ultimate modern means for art — surprise. As a poet, Apollinaire traded on a contempt for time and place, an obsession with far-fetched associations, and a talent for proposing unexpected juxtapositions of unrelated things to provoke new meanings. De Chirico's portrait of Apollinaire includes a menacing shadow of the poet's profile in the background. Two odd white circles like targets mark the shadowy likeness, who seems to peer into a crypt that contains a plaster statue of a balding man wearing a blind person's dark glasses. The splayed angles of the black walls create an irrational mindscape that has influenced almost every subsequent image of the subconscious. When Apollinaire was wounded in combat in 1916, the odd targets seemed in retrospect to have been premonitions and thus justified the high regard for this visionary painter. Since it was Apollinaire who coined the term "Surrealism," this portrait became an icon after World War I as that poetic movement got under full sail.

SONIA TERK DELAUNAY

Electric Prisms, 1914
Oil on canvas, 9⅞ × 9⅞″ (25 × 25 cm)
Musée National d'Art Moderne, Centre Georges
Pompidou, Paris

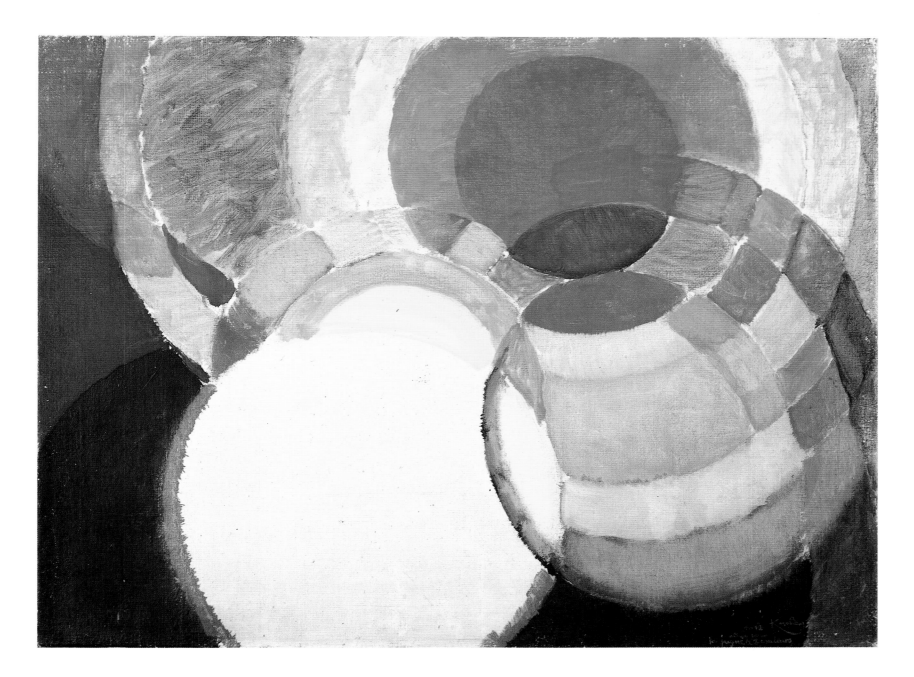

FRANTISEK KUPKA (b. Opocno, Bohemia–d. 1957)

Disks of Newton in Two Colors, 1911–1912
Gouache and watercolor on paper,
9⅞ × 12¼″ (25.2 cm × 32.6 cm)
Musée National d'Art Moderne, Centre Georges
Pompidou, Paris

ROGER DE LA FRESNAYE (b. 1885, Le Mans–d. 1925)

The Conquest of Air, 1913
Oil on canvas, 92⅞ × 77″ (236 × 196 cm)
The Museum of Modern Art, New York
Mrs. Simon Guggenheim Fund

FRANCIS PICABIA (b. 1878, Paris–d. 1953)

Edtaonisl, 1913
Oil on canvas, 118¼ × 118⅜″ (301.6 × 300.4 cm)
The Art Institute of Chicago, Chicago
Gift of Mr. and Mrs. Armand Phillip Bartos

Marc Chagall (b. 1887, Vitebsk, Russia–d. 1985)

Paris Through the Window, 1913
Oil on canvas, 52⅜ × 54¾″ (133 × 139 cm)
Solomon R. Guggenheim Museum, New York
Gift, Solomon R. Guggenheim, 1937

234

ALBERT GLEIZES (b. 1881, Paris–d. 1953)

Portrait of Igor Stravinsky, 1914
Oil on canvas, 51¾6 × 44⅞″ (130 × 114 cm)
Richard S. Zeisler Collection, New York

PABLO PICASSO

Woman in an Armchair, 1913
Oil on canvas, 58¼ × 39″ (148 × 99 cm)
Collection of Mrs. Victor W. Ganz, New York

XXIII.
Matisse's Alternative to Cubism

ALTHOUGH MANY MODERN-MINDED PAINTERS HELD CONVENTIONAL ART TRAINING IN LOW regard and promoted intuition as a more effective approach to originality, Matisse opened an art school in 1908, welcoming dozens of students, many of whom were foreigners. Whereas Picasso, Braque, and their disciples in Cubism generally worked on small or easel-scale canvases and used inexpensive pigments for grays and earth colors, Matisse painted ever larger canvases, insisting on lavish, expensive colors, which he worked and reworked to luminous perfection. His ability to indulge himself this way was bolstered by generous patrons including not only the Steins but two Russian merchants with business in Paris, Sergei Shchukin (1854–1936) and Ivan Morozov (1871–1921). Shchukin, who began by collecting Cézannes and Gauguins in quantity, wanted to open a gallery of modern art in Moscow so that Russian artists could keep up with innovations in Paris. In 1909 Shchukin, who would eventually acquire more than three dozen paintings by Matisse, commissioned murals on the themes of dance and music for the stair hall in his home.

Exhibited at the Salon d'Automne in 1910 before being shipped off, *The Dance*, with its five nudes, amounts to Matisse's answer to *Demoiselles d'Avignon*. In every way this remarkable painting is the antithesis of Cubism. Instead of multiplying each form into hundreds of fragments, Matisse simplified the background into two zones formed by a single curving line. Similarly, he used line with unprecedented economy and expressive effect for the figures in motion, each little more than a single silhouette with a minimum of internal drawing. Using the most saturated colors, Matisse created abstract spatial relationships that pulsate to accompany the rhythm of the dancers, their vermilion bodies in vibrant contrast to the blue and green. As a group, the five figures form an ellipse, and their feet, backs, and heads touch the rectangular painting's edges so that the space in the landscape and the space in the dance are coextensive and perfectly balanced.

What Matisse dreamed of, he wrote, was "an art of equilibrium, purity and tranquillity" that could provide the modern viewer with "a calmative for the intellect, something analogous to a good armchair that relieves him from physical fatigue." In this sense, the closest parallel to Matisse's art was Monet's decorative series of water lily paintings, which were exhibited with his dealer in Paris in 1909. On a more literal level, Matisse's Apollonian spirit has counterparts in Golden Age landscapes such as the *Joy of Life* by Suzanne Valadon (1865–1938), which represents a forest glade with a male figure standing to one side and staring at a quartet of female bathers, all rendered with simplified silhouettes. More than twenty years earlier, Valadon had begun an art career as a model for Renoir, Puvis, and Lautrec. In her subsequent painter's role, she developed a unique sensitivity for poses and gestures full of humor and mystery, evidently influencing the figure paintings of Duchamp and Balthus, among others. Valadon's son, Maurice Utrillo (1883–1955), became a fixture of both the Montmartre and Montparnasse art scenes, repeating the same postcard view scores of times with mechanical dispassion and drinking up the profits. Despite the limited use to which he put his natural gift for painting, Utrillo captured a genuinely modern mood of urban solitude, and works such as *Le Lapin Agile*, which portrays one of Picasso's favorite Montmartre hangouts, are precious records of one of the greatest periods in the history of French painting.

As if in response to Matisse's *Dance* at the 1910 Salon, Bonnard exhibited at the 1911 Salon

MAURICE UTRILLO (b. 1883, Paris–d. 1955)

Le Lapin Agile, ca. 1912
Oil on canvas, 50 × 61″ (127 × 155 cm)
Musée National d'Art Moderne,
Centre Georges Pompidou, Paris

RAOUL DUFY (b. 1877, Le Havre–d. 1953)

Abandoned Garden, 1913
Oil on canvas, 59 × 67″ (150 × 170 cm)
Musée d'Art Moderne, Ville de Paris,
Paris

CLAUDE MONET

Water Lilies: Morning, 1916–1926
Oil on canvas, 77½ × 502½″
(197 × 1276 cm)
Galeries de l'Orangerie,
Musée du Louvre, Paris

d'Automne a monumental triptych that had been commissioned for the home of Shchukin's rival, Morozov. The panels represent the perfect relaxation of life in St. Tropez, including women and children playing with cats and a parrot in a shaded garden. Suffused with gold and lilac and dotted with white, Bonnard's resplendent vision, tailored for the fantasies of a deep Russian winter, at first seems like a late form of Impressionism. However, time does not appear to be frozen in Bonnard's works as much as it seems to be extended, and parts of his dense pictures can be understood to gradually come forward or recede in space like details in a carefully detailed narrative drawing on memory to enhance the significance of immediate experience. Marcel Proust's convoluted verbal style in his epic novel series, *The Remembrance of Things Past*, which began to appear in 1913, is perhaps the best counterpart to the slow, self-indulgent, and relaxing form of painting that Bonnard developed as an idiom for mural decorations.

Matisse wanted to invent explicit signs to express the experience of space as a succession of interlinking sensations. Used in strictly illogical ways, color and space function as such abstract signs in a large painting that Matisse made of his studio at the end of 1911. Although the walls of the studio were in fact white, in this painting Matisse represented them as a saturated vermilion, undifferentiated from the red of the floor and the room's furniture. This was probably not a concession to the red velvet walls that were standard in the most prestigious art galleries; rather, it was an abstract way to describe his studio as a red-hot contemplative forge and make the space in the studio appear special in an allegorical way, free from three-dimensional logic and thus suitable for the creation and display of art. Not just the figures in the paintings on the studio's back wall but the objects in the room twist effortlessly as if in a liquid, from the trailing ivy to the peculiar chair back with its rungs out of alignment. This daring monochromatic painting was a controversial centerpiece of two of the most important exhibitions to showcase new French art outside of France: in 1912 at the Second Post-Impressionist show in London and the following year in the famous Armory show in New York, Chicago, and Boston. In Chicago they hanged Matisse in effigy and burned copies of two of his paintings before a crowd on Michigan Avenue.

Matisse's sense of visual space having distinctly more freedom than physical space is graphically rendered in a painting of a bowl of goldfish executed around the same time and acquired by Shchukin. The four fish cluster at the glass to stare back at the viewer, who also can see the displaced backward images of the fish reflected through the water's surface. Thus, thanks to optics (rather than Cubism), the painter could present viewers with the same objects in two places in the same space at once. The Rousseaulike jungle of plants in various sizes around the bowl make scale nearly impossible to apprehend. Without the near and far logic of scale, the space in the room represented in the painting is as fluid to the eyes and imagination as is the space contained by the fishbowl represented in the room. One of Matisse's ultimate metaphors for space, like the dance, the motif of goldfish in an aquarium appears in more than a dozen different paintings.

No other French painter understood Matisse's sense of liquid space as well as Raoul Dufy (1877–1953), who was with Braque in L'Estaque when he painted his first cubist paintings in 1908. The following year, however, Dufy developed a totally naive and childlike style that had great decorative appeal and led eventually to his success as a fabric designer. *The Abandoned Garden*

(1913) combines all these disparate visual experiments into an enchanted space observed in imagination from several different bird's-eye views. Indeed, every object in this strange picture seems to flutter, since Dufy applied color with parallel hatchings like a schoolchild's scribbles. Moreover, the mysterious coexistence of black nighttime and blue daytime zones provides a new pictorial freedom that even Matisse had not contemplated.

In paintings done during the following years, however, Matisse responded to Dufy's bold innovation, inserting black zones of shadow into otherwise colorful still lifes and even outdoors scenes. A similar motive guided Matisse to divide the background view out of a window in the *Piano Lesson* into contrasting rectangular areas of outdoor green and indoor dark gray. This window view used as a transition between near and far was one of Matisse's many reprises of the fauve *Open Window, Collioure*, and in the *Piano Lesson* the grillwork of the window's balcony is a large-scale version of a similar decorative motif on the music stand at the nearby piano. The explicit relationship between these forms suggests a visual connection between here and there analogous to the free flow of sound through space. The metronome visible in the foreground, its blade poised between rhythmic sweeps, seems to have measured space for the painter while it measured time for his son seated at the piano. Matisse used the shape of the little device to construct an image of the right side of the boy's face, as if his concentration on the music had literally begun to transform the boy into an extension of its metronomic law.

The most remarkable aspect of Matisse's paintings of these years is the absence of any reference to the savage war that had suddenly turned the Paris art world topsy-turvy, sending some painters, including Braque, into battle and others, such as the Delaunays, Picabia, and Duchamp, into exile. For a foreign artist such as Amedeo Modigliani (1884–1920), who had come to Paris from Italy in 1906, the war made it still harder to sell enough works to subsist. Perhaps in response to the diminished market, Modigliani put the cubist idiom aside to undertake a series of nudes with extremely simplified features in the spirit of Valadon and Matisse. A small exhibition of these paintings in Paris caused a scandal in early December 1917 because Modigliani had represented the models' pubic hair. Police censorship only added to the alcoholic Bohemian artist's mystique and encouraged other artists to be more explicit when they treated nudes.

At the very end of 1917 Matisse went to visit Renoir, the master of the modern nude, at his Mediterranean villa in Cagnes. Crippled by rheumatism since the turn of the century, the old impressionist had continued to paint courageously from a wheelchair, with brushes strapped to his wrists. Perhaps as a result of his deteriorating eyesight or his manual handicaps, Renoir's late works depart from the virtuoso realism of classical Impressionism. Merged in quasi-organic fashion into their settings, Renoir's last nudes are strangely proportioned giantesses with enormous hips and feet. The liberties taken by Renoir with the female anatomy in these works must have provided some of the justification needed for Matisse, Picasso, and the surrealists to reconsider the body as a fluid sensual field observed subjectively in accordance with the wishful thinking of desire.

Renoir's close friend Monet remained isolated for the war in Giverny. Fighting the sporadic deterioration of his eyesight as a result of cataracts, Monet was determined to carry out

SUZANNE VALADON (b. 1867, Bessines–d. 1938)

The Joy of Life, 1911
Oil on canvas, 48⅜ × 81″ (123 × 206 cm)
The Metropolitan Museum of Art, New York
Bequest of Miss Adelaide Milton de Groot, 1967

HENRI MATISSE

The Dance, 1910
Oil on canvas, 101¼ × 153½″ (258 × 390 cm)
Hermitage Museum, Leningrad

AMEDEO MODIGLIANI (b. 1884, Livorno, Italy–d. 1920)

Reclining Nude with Coral Necklace, 1917
Oil on canvas, 25¼ × 39¼″ (64 × 99 cm)
Allen Memorial Art Museum, Oberlin College,
Oberlin
Gift of Joseph and Enid Bissett, 1955

a decorative ensemble of interlocking murals that were begun in 1914 and were based on his earlier paintings of the water lilies in his luxurious garden. Observed with the artist's head bowed as if in prayer, the watery surface extends from top to bottom of the canvases without including either bank or horizon. Clouds reflected in the water before and below the spectator evoke the space behind and above, with the result that the meditative visual act encompasses the fullness of physical space. With the outbreak of hostilities and the departure of his son to the front, Monet and his old friend Georges Clemenceau, head of the Senate's armed forces committee, began to understand these murals as symbols of national victory (the lily had been a symbol of the French monarchy) and of the powers of light and peace to prevail over aggression. After long negotiations, it was decided to install the best of these huge works as a national monument at the Orangerie in rooms with specially curved walls so that the spectator is literally surrounded by Monet's fantasy vision. The opening of the rooms in May 1926, just days after the arrival of Lindbergh on his solo transatlantic airship flight, marked the first time in the history of Western art that rooms of paintings had been designed exclusively for nonutilitarian, nonceremonial visual meditation. Comparing Monet's achievement with that of Michelangelo, the surrealist André Masson (1896–1987) would call these rooms the Sistine Chapel of Impressionism.

PIERRE BONNARD

Mediterranean Triptych, 1911
Oil on canvas
Left: 160¼ × 58⅝″ (407 × 149 cm); center:
160¼ × 59⅞″ (407 × 152 cm); right: 160¼ × 58⅝″
(407 × 149 cm)
Hermitage Museum, Leningrad

HENRI MATISSE

The Red Studio, 1911
Oil on canvas, 71¼ × 86¼″ (181 × 219 cm)
The Museum of Modern Art, New York
Mrs. Simon Guggenheim Fund

HENRI MATISSE

Piano Lesson, 1916
Oil on canvas, 96½ × 83¼″ (245 × 213 cm)
The Museum of Modern Art, New York
Mrs. Simon Guggenheim Fund

XXIV.
Cubism and the Machine Style

MARCEL DUCHAMP

The Large Glass, or *The Bride Stripped Bare by Her Bachelors, Even*, 1915–1923
Oil and lead wire on glass,
109¼ × 69⅛" (226 × 176 cm)
The Philadelphia Museum of Art,
Philadelphia
Bequest of Katherine S. Dreier

BY 1915 GLEIZES, PICABIA, DUCHAMP, AND HIS FUTURE BROTHER-IN-LAW, THE SWISS-BORN JEAN Crotti (1878–1958), had established a French wartime colony in New York. They saw New York as the most modern city, reckoning that such daring plastic gestures as the Brooklyn Bridge, the Woolworth Building, and even modern plumbing fixtures went beyond most modern European art. Their irreverent attitude quickly found support among American artists such as Man Ray (1890–1976), who would move to Paris after the war, and collectors such as Walter and Louise Arensberg, John Quinn, and Katherine Dreier, who acquired many of the greatest masterpieces of French modern art that are now in American museums. The Arensbergs gave Duchamp a place to live and work and decided to collect all his works as if each were a fragment of a greater whole. Eventually, when their collection was donated to the Philadelphia Museum of Art in the early 1950s and put on public view, it became a focus for interest in biographical art appreciation and interpretation.

By the time the Arensbergs decided to resettle in California in 1921, the whole of Duchamp's activity was synthesized in a large work consisting of two roughly four- by five-foot glass panes. Duchamp eventually inscribed the work (which Dreier bought from the Arensbergs) with the date 1915–1923, noting that it was "unfinished." He likewise inscribed a wacky French title: *The Bride Stripped Bare by Her Bachelors, Even*. Painting on glass freed Duchamp from the figure-ground dilemma that dictated how conventional painters, including cubists, were obliged to consider space. Attempting, or at least fantasizing about, sexual interpenetration, Duchamp's figures in this work float in an indeterminate space for which the literal surroundings of the room observed through the glass serve as a background. The "figure" in the upper sheet, concocted out of assorted funnel, gear, and piston shapes, is the bride, copied from one of Duchamp's early mechanical cubist paintings. The lower glass sheet is the realm of the bachelors, whose complex behavior Duchamp had carefully studied in around a half dozen smaller works, all of them copied here as an incomplete nonsensical diagram of the machinations (expanding, gliding, filtering, grinding, shooting) of male sexual desire prompted by sight. The work shattered during shipment for an exhibition, but in 1936 Duchamp traveled to Dreier's Connecticut home to piece the work back together sliver by sliver. He expressed pleasure in the beauty of the cracks, the work of chance (perhaps Duchamp's favorite "medium" as a conceptual artist), which gave the so-called *The Large Glass* a cubist look.

Still Life Before an Open Window (*La Place Ravignon*) also was part of the Arensbergs' collection. This work by the Spanish-born cubist Juan Gris (1887–1927), whom Apollinaire had called the most demonically logical of the Golden Section artists in 1912, epitomizes the theme of spatial interpenetration that obsessed cubist painters just as it obsessed Matisse. Bathed in blue light, the tree seems to spread forward over the balcony into the shadowy foreground room, where a wooden table acts as alter ego for the tree's trunk. (It is worth noting that Duchamp described his abstract *Bride* as treelike.) Atop this table are a newspaper and a variety of dishes, including a wineglass and a glass decanter. As already mentioned, such glass objects are favorite props in cubist still lifes, since transparency allows for observation of an object in space simultaneously with observation of space in, around, and through that object. Moreover, curved glass shapes

refract, reflect, and distort what is observed through them in cubist fashion, and in Gris's painting the letters "JO" and then "NAL" on the masthead of the newspaper read through the wineglass are magnified twice and threefold.

Duchamp's *The Bride Stripped Bare* sparked a revolutionary new form of picture making among his closest colleagues. For example, Crotti began to use glass as a support in works containing mechanically stylized juggling figures with springs for spines, such as *The Clown*, which incorporated three glass eyes to underline his parody of the looking-at-looking, or retinal, theme. As Duchamp was fond of pointing out, impressionist painting was devoted to sense impressions registered on the retina, but this new art would go beyond the retina to analyze the thought processes that anticipate and react to such retinal stimuli. Leonardo da Vinci, for whom the eye was the window to the soul, had defined painting as a mental thing, and for Duchamp, Leonardo was the archetypal genius.

Picabia, who was a gifted poet, created mechanomorphic portraits and genre scenes of unforgettable insight and humor. For example, he did a caricature of the photographer and art dealer Alfred Stieglitz as a broken camera and represented "an American girl in the state of nudity" with a drawing of a Forever brand spark plug. When such images were dispersed through his magazine, *391*, Picabia helped initiate the international Dada movement, which was predicated on absurdity as the most effective antidote to modern regimentation. Drawing on de Chirico's illogical perspective systems and robotlike figures made up of bric-a-brac as well as Duchamp's Leonardoesque passion for futuristic mechanical inventions, Picabia in exile created some of the most influential paintings of World War I. *Parade Amoureuse* (*Loving Parade*) was probably conceived as a response to news about the Paris premiere of Jean Cocteau's (1889–1963) *Parade*, a realist ballet with music by Erik Satie and cubist costumes designed by Picasso. Pinned together like contraptions that perform an assembly-line variety of tasks, the mechanical elements in Picabia's picture seem to be involved with one another in a more explicitly emotional way than even Duchamp's "bride" and "bachelors." The pistons, coils, gears, and levers assume humanoid roles as torsos, arms, and eyes doing God knows what to one another in the name of love.

Duchamp did his last painting in 1918, afterward making objects that defy the conventional categories of painting, sculpture, and drawing but nevertheless allude to art ideas in conceptual terms. Like *The Bride Stripped Bare*, this last painting is a compilation of motifs that Duchamp had developed in smaller works, and its verbless title, *Tu M'* ("*You Me*"), is as puzzling as the painting's contents. An extension of the collages invented by Braque and Picasso, *Tu M'* is about different levels of reality and illusion in painting. Its playful spirit is evidenced by the tear at the center of the canvas held together by safety pins. The tear is not real but painted illusionistically, yet the pins *are* real. A real bottle-cleaning brush projects from the canvas perpendicularly, as if it had been jabbed through from the other side. Just below, the image of a hand is signed by A. Klang, a commercial artist whom Duchamp hired as a collaborator, thus debunking the sanctity of an artist's unique manual virtuosity as an essential criterion for art. The shadows painted on *Tu M'* are tracings of the real projected images of three of the iconoclastic sculptures Duchamp called "readymades," since he had not made them with his own hands but had chosen them from everyday life. Recorded in *Tu M'*, the *Bicycle Wheel* at the left and the *Hatrack* at the right stress Duchamp's conviction that the artist's primary responsibility is to decide what form to use; the execution of that form is secondary to the original creative conception.

The decision made in 1848 to admit photographs into the Salons as a form of art was taken as an omen of the demise of painting, and Duchamp's decision in 1918 to stop painting was taken as another signal that conventional painting had run its course. From then on, new materials, hybrid media, and collaborations would begin to encroach on the domain that had once been the prerogative of painting and photography. As if to announce his maverick antipainting decision, Duchamp obtained a postcard reproduction of Leonardo da Vinci's *Mona Lisa* and scribbled a mustache onto the face of the image the way a vandal might. Picabia published a reproduction of Duchamp's conceptual work as a Dada icon in *391*. Another example of the maverick's liberated attitude toward materials is preserved in a painting, by his sister Suzanne Duchamp (1889–1963), depicting a geometry book he sent to her when she married Crotti, instructing them to hang it from their balcony so that the wind would choose problems by turning and tearing out pages. Duchamp's indifference to the work of art's survival heralded a new freedom for artists from the requirements and limitations of history-minded institutions.

If any French painter managed to extend painting after the war in the face of Duchamp's skepticism, it was Fernand Léger (1881–1955), one of the Golden Section cubists supported by Apollinaire. Drafted as a medic and trench digger and sent to the front in 1914, Léger captured the Dada horrors of mechanized warfare better than did any other French painter. Several crude works made from the tops of ammunition cases with scraps of his uniform glued on to make the forms are all that survive from his firsthand experiences, but while he was recuperating in a hospital from gas poisoning Léger undertook a monumental canvas showing soldiers playing cards. Stylized as robots with segmented limbs, these modern warriors seem to wear medieval armored suits like the combatants in paintings by Léger's favorite Italian Renaissance master, Paolo Uccello. Smoking pipes and wearing medals, they seem anything but thoughtful and heroic, suggesting on the contrary that war has no more purpose than a game does.

The civilian world after the war was enormously different in one respect, thanks to the proliferation of billboards with advertisements. "We live in a geometric world," Léger explained, and he dedicated an enormous painting to capture the complex geometric hustle and bustle of modern urban life that had obsessed the Delaunays before the war. Indeed, something like one of their disks is prominent in the lower left of Léger's painting. Everything is flat, simplified, and bright to draw attention like a poster or sign, and everything is fragmentary as if to suggest a rapid environment where observations are made on the fly. In Léger's hands the cubist breaking and flattening of forms came to symbolize the modern urban experience. The only figures, who descend a staircase leading out of the painting in the center, are dark robots, apparently lost in the noisy visual excitement. For Léger, however, the modern environment was not depressing or hostile. Instead, the contrasting forms of contemporary advertising expressed a new visual order that was addressed to the masses. The sense of movement in *The City* anticipates Léger's enthusiasm for film as the most powerful art medium of the future, and in 1924 he would direct one of the classics of the experimental silent cinema, the *Mechanical Ballet*, photographed by Man Ray. Gathering filmstrips as a bank of images to be repeated like accents in a painting, Léger celebrated the aesthetic value of modern objects in this film, just as Duchamp had celebrated these objects with his readymades. Léger's interest in art of or for the streets, in step with populist art movements from Russia to Mexico in the postwar years, heralded a new tradition in French painting that extended well into the 1960s, as can be seen in works by Daniel Buren, Jacques de La Villéglé, and Raymond Hains.

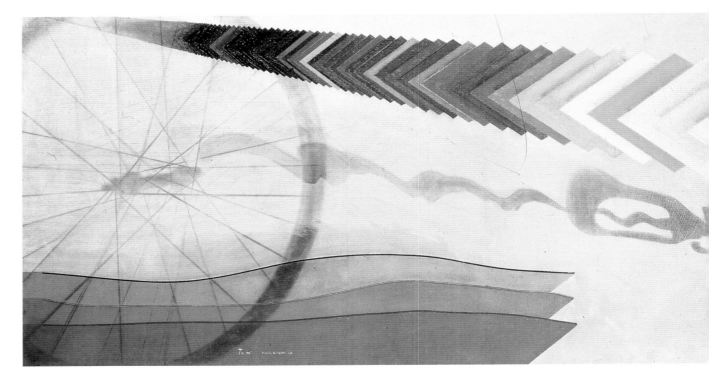

JUAN GRIS (b. 1887, Madrid–d. 1927)

Still Life Before an Open Window
(La Place Ravignon), 1915
Oil on canvas, 45⅞ × 35⅛″ (116.5 × 89 cm)
Philadelphia Museum of Art, Philadelphia
The Louise and Walter Arensberg Collection

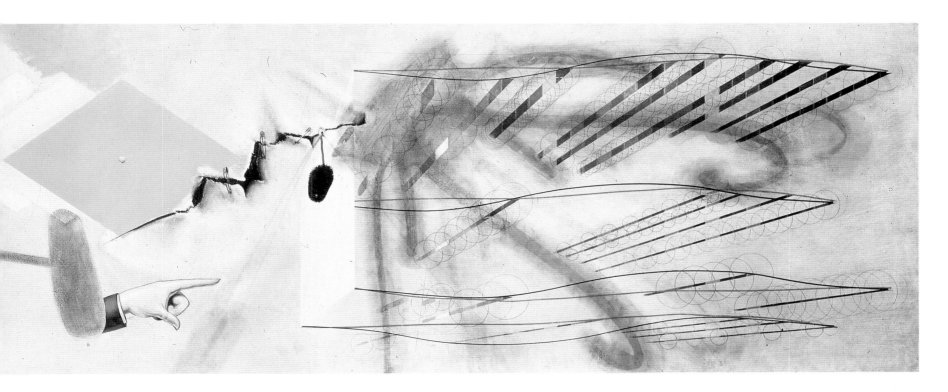

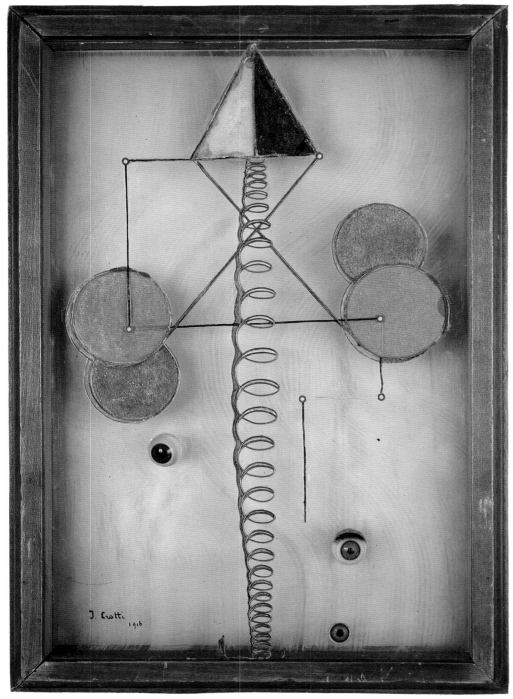

MARCEL DUCHAMP

Tu M', 1918
Oil on canvas with long brush attached, 27½ × 133¼"
(69 × 339.7 cm)
Yale University Art Gallery, New Haven
Gift of the Estate of Katherine S. Dreier

JEAN CROTTI (b. 1878, Bulle–d. 1958)

The Clown, 1916
Mixed media, 37 × 25" (94 × 63.5 cm)
Musée d'Art Moderne de la Ville de Paris, Paris

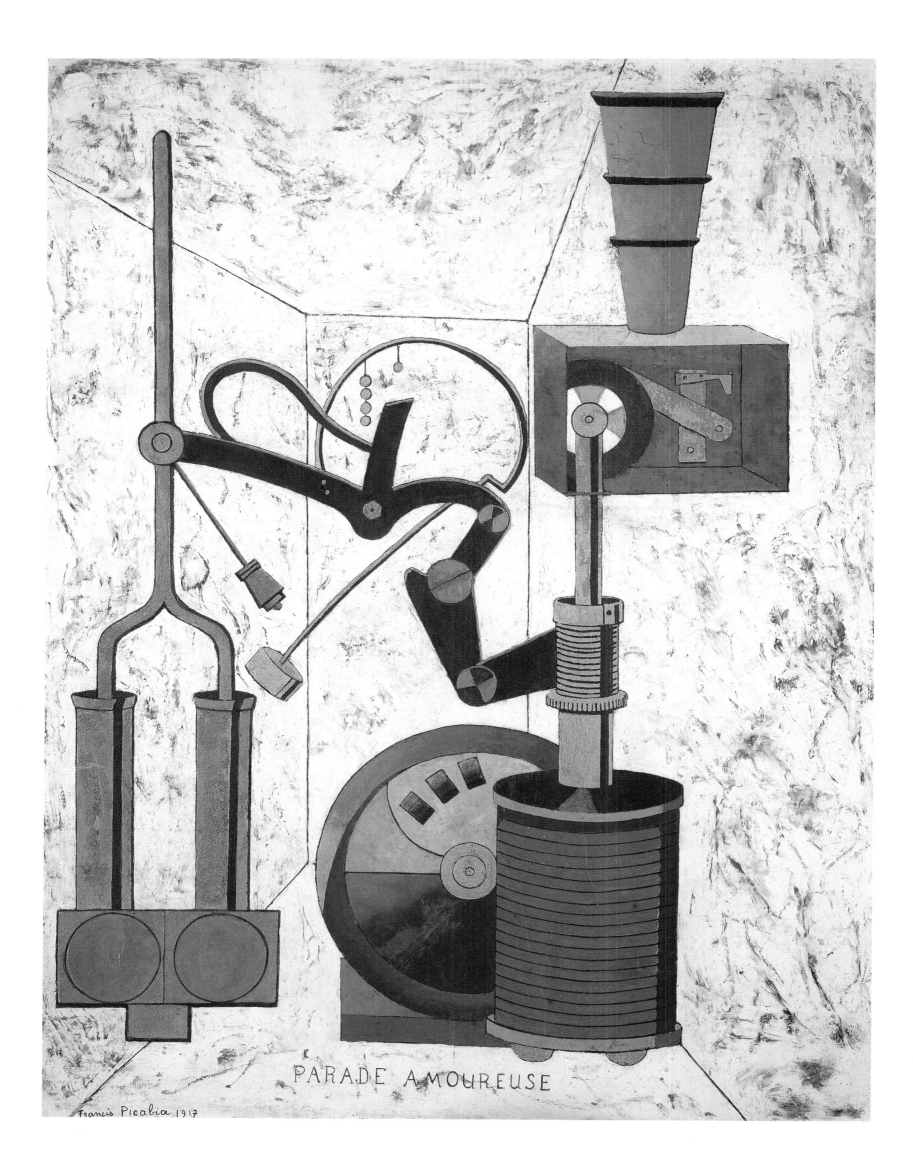

PARADE AMOUREUSE

Francis Picabia 1917

XXV.
World War I, Dada, and Purism

GEORGES ROUAULT

Christ of the Outskirts, 1920
Oil on paper mounted on canvas,
36¼ × 29⅛″ (92 × 74 cm)
Bridgestone Museum of Art,
Ishibashi Foundation, Tokyo

ROUAULT'S *CHRIST OF THE OUTSKIRTS* OFFERED THE SHARPEST POSSIBLE CONTRAST TO Léger's upbeat attitude about an urban future. Drawing on the bleak, nocturnal city vistas introduced into art by de Chirico, Rouault responded to the war and the desolation it left behind as symptoms of a lost world in search of salvation. Although his Catholic piety was anathema to many modern-minded art theorists, especially the surrealists (who would hold the Church, along with other institutions, responsible for nurturing the values that had led to the wanton violence of world conflict), Rouault's paintings share a mystical mood sustained by imprecise outlines, muddy colors, and otherworldly lighting that would characterize much surrealist painting. Rouault's outsider mentality, however, would remain an undercurrent until the end of the next world war, when painters such as Dubuffet and Fautrier would recognize the full potential of his crude vision.

Like religion, Cubism fell into disregard among many painters after the war, when the government auctioned off hundreds of paintings acquired by the German-born Kahnweiler. Flooding the market with works by Picasso, Braque, Gris, and Léger, these sales gave a new generation a chance to evaluate the major prewar modern movement, and many theoretical-minded artists responded skeptically to what they considered to be self-indulgent distortions of objects to suit individualistic decorative schemes. For Amédée Ozenfant (1886–1966) and for Swiss-born Charles Edouard Jeanneret (1887–1965), better known by his architect's trade name, Le Corbusier, the original cubists had correctly recognized the geometric, mechanical fabric of modern industrial life but had failed to absorb the fundamental doctrines of modern existence and make works that emulated and functioned like machine-manufactured objects. Active theorists who spread their so-called purist principles in a periodical and in books, these artists advocated an integration of life and art on the basis of design, as did the de Stijl artists in Holland and the Bauhaus artists in Germany. Le Corbusier's famous definition of a house as "a machine for living" seems only slightly extreme in the context of the government-sponsored 1925 World's Fair of Modern Decorative and Industrial Arts held in Paris to celebrate recovery from the war and the dawn of a better future founded on a cultural-industrial alliance.

As painters, Jeanneret and Ozenfant were specialists in the still life, developing a sober variety of Synthetic Cubism close to Léger's hallmark style. Out of respect for the aesthetic value of objects in themselves, they did not fragment or distort shapes in classic cubist fashion. Contrary to early cubist dogma, guitars in purist still lifes appear whole, as symbols for painters' responsibility to follow a mathematical rationale analogous to musical harmonics. To stress their advocacy of underlying structural design principles in a still more explicit fashion, both painters emphasized perfect geometrical shapes as modules prevalent in a variety of everyday objects. In Jeanneret's *Still Life*, the geometrical profile of mass-produced objects and the geometrical shadows they cast create an orchestrated dialogue of pure forms overlapping and extending one another. The mass-produced tabletop objects interlocked profile to profile in Ozenfant's compositions seem to hover in perfect balance, each streamlined to escape gravity or friction.

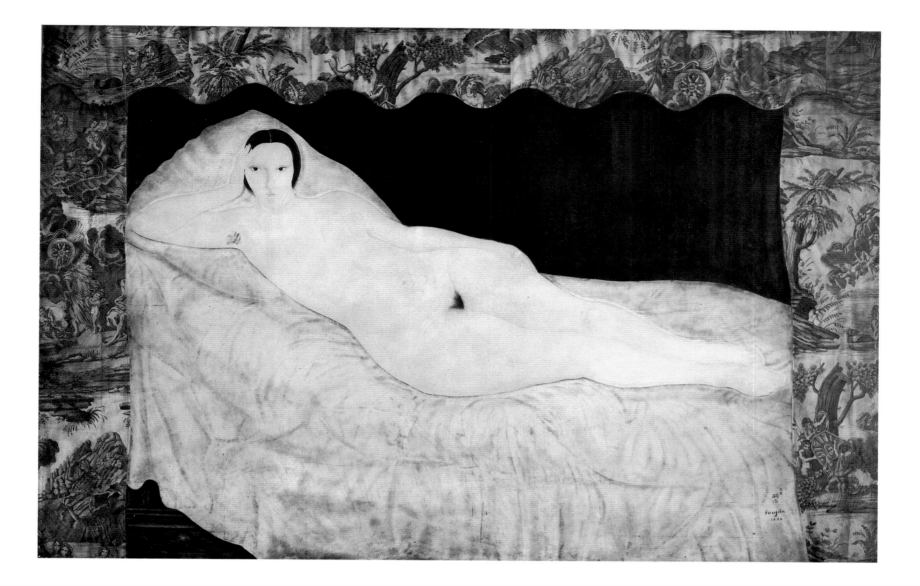

With an exquisite sensitivity for color, Ozenfant superimposed empty and transparent as well as half-full and semitransparent vessels, establishing color shifts from plane to plane with intervals as measured as the tones of a musical scale.

Reproduced around the time it was exhibited at the Salon d'Automne of 1921 in *The New Spirit*, Jeanneret and Ozenfant's periodical, Léger's *Three Women* exemplifies the postwar impulse to consider the world in terms of the geometric perfection of mass-produced objects such as vases, bowls, and pillows. Juxtaposing and overlapping whole objects with related shapes and patterns, Léger created jazzy rhythms as complex as any to be found in classic cubist compositions with shattered fragments as modules. With their molded body parts, stuffed and round, the three naked women installed in Léger's painting like humanoids in an Art Deco harem have physically evolved in keeping with the objects in their environment. Their spherical heads and breasts and their cylindrical necks, arms, and fingers seem like demonstrations in a solid geometry textbook, and their sex appeal hardly goes beyond that of robots. Man-made decor in clear shapes and colors like semaphores for a new consumer's language has more appeal than does man himself (or woman). Even so, Léger's obvious allusion in this large painting to the classical tradition of Ingres's nudes suggests how purist theory was predicated on traditional values as the enduring basis for modern art. Of course, given Léger's sense of humor — witness the black cat nested on the reclining woman's legs — he always escaped the regimentation of theory that sometimes restricted his fellow purists, Jeanneret and Ozenfant.

With equal humor, the Japanese-born Tsuguharu Foujita (1886–1968), who arrived in Montparnasse in 1913, presented a painting of a nude in the context of decor at the following year's Salon d'Automne. As was the case with Léger, Foujita's starting-off point for the simplified rendering of a nude was probably Modigliani's controversial paintings of a few years before. Unlike Léger, Foujita, for the sake of contrast, posed his purist female body under a canopy made from an ultrabourgeois fabric based on Renaissance allegorical designs. With his bangs and accent, Foujita was a willing art celebrity for the international press and exemplified the

TSUGUHARU FOUJITA (b. 1886, Japan–d. 1968)

Nude with Jouy Fabric, 1922
Oil and crayon on canvas, 51⅛ × 76¼″
(130 × 195 cm)
Musée d'Art Moderne de la Ville
de Paris, Paris

party-loving, commercially successful society artist of 1920s Paris. He even managed to win the Legion of Honor in 1925! This excessive success raised doubts about his sincerity and his priorities as a serious artist, and only recently has it been possible to reevaluate his idiosyncratic talent more objectively.

It was a German-born artist, however, who set a completely new direction for French painting after the war. Max Ernst (1891–1976) settled in Paris in 1922 with help from the poet Paul Eluard (1895–1952), who had squared off as the painter's adversary in trench warfare only six years before. Immediately after the Armistice, Ernst plunged into the subversive Dada activities in Cologne, creating scandal after scandal when he managed to exhibit his unorthodox works with their absurd images. These works were inspired by Ernst's exposure at commercial galleries and in magazines to new works by leading Paris artists. Chagall and de Chirico gave Ernst license to invent fantastical creatures and settings; Picasso and Braque in their collages gave him license to incorporate images displaced from nonart contexts, such as newspapers, into drawings and paintings and so to disregard the borders between art and life. Ernst's unique talent for collage — inserting an image of angels into the cockpit in a photograph of an airplane, for example — reminded the French Dada advocate André Breton (1896–1966) of the provocative absurd images invented by a forgotten nineteenth-century poet who called himself the Count of Lautréamont, like "the chance encounter of a sewing machine and an umbrella on a dissecting table."

Chance was crucial to Dada, an aggravated art-focused reaction to the war that began in the neutral cities of New York and Zurich in 1915 but took root throughout Germany and in Paris as soon as hostilities subsided. "Dada signifies nothing," explained its chief spokesperson in Paris, the poet Tristan Tzara (1896–1963). Staging events designed to debunk established values and spotlight blatant hypocrisies, these artists resorted to insult and riot to get attention. One of their favorite targets was art itself, and there is no better example than Duchamp's defaced version of the *Mona Lisa* of Dada strategies designed to challenge sacred cows. As Duchamp's work suggests, Dada artists accepted certain vandalous liberties associated with childhood or mental incapacity as states of escape from corrupt societal values.

Publicizing the potential of incongruous, illogical propositions to awaken viewers and readers to the sort of subconscious and dream states studied by Freud, Breton arranged for an exhibition of Ernst's works ("beyond painting," according to the poster) in 1921. Ernst's complex group portrait of the major figures in the movement in Paris speaks volumes about the mentality of Dada's proponents, most of whom were writers or wrote in addition to creating visual art. Advocates of an overt literary bias for visual art, who had been ostracized in the name of art for art's sake since the days of Courbet and the realists, argued that painting no longer could shirk the responsibility to address thought and intuition, which guide and limit sight as much as the rods and cones on the retina do.

With this painting Ernst fulfilled a dreamlike fantasy, gathering together such new associates as Eluard and Breton, along with his former colleague in Germany, Jean Arp (1887–1966). At their side are such diverse kindred spirits as de Chirico, the Italian Renaissance painter Raphael Sanzio (1483–1520), and the nineteenth-century Russian novelist Feodor Dostoevski (1821–1881), on whose lap Ernst is seated while gesturing in the language used by deaf mutes to communicate a verbal idea in a visual way. The setting is not Paris but the remote, barren, and pure white cutting edge of an otherworldly-appearing alpine glacier. Illuminated in theatrical fashion, the swelling crowd of freethinkers must be understood as an apparition, since the sky is the pitch-black scene of an eclipse. This fantastical eclipse generates concentric radiating circles, a diagrammatic event that apparently refers to the abstract disk paintings of the Delaunays. In the foreground a still life with an elaborately cut apple that looks like the model for an avant-garde building probably alludes with disrespect to paintings by the purists.

When Breton published the first *Surrealist Manifesto* in 1924, this Dada group underwent a radical change of strategy, modifying their cult of individual freedom in order to function along collective theoretical lines like the purist. Surrealist theory called for a systematic investigation of instinct, rather than (purist) logic, even though systematic thought was a contradiction of its own principles.

Max Ernst (b. 1891, Brühl, Prussia–d. 1976)

At the Rendezvous of Friends, 1922
Oil on canvas, 51¼ × 76″ (130 × 193 cm)
Museum Ludwig, Cologne

Fernand Léger

Three Women, 1921
Oil on canvas, 72¼ × 99″
(183.4 × 251.5 cm)
The Museum of Modern Art,
New York
Mrs. Simon Guggenheim Fund

Le Corbusier, born Charles Edouard Jeanneret (b. 1887,
  Chant-de-Fonds, Switzerland–d. 1965)

Composition with Lantern and Guitar, 1920
Oil on canvas, 31⅞ × 39⅜″ (81 × 100 cm)
Öeffentliche Kunstsammlung Kunstmuseum, Basel

Amédée Ozenfant (b. 1886, Saint-Quentin–d. 1966)

Accords, 1922
Oil on canvas, 51⅛ × 38¼″ (130 × 97 cm)
Honolulu Academy of Arts, Honolulu
Gift of John Gregg Allerton, Commemorating
the 40th Anniversary of the Academy, 1967

XXVI.
Surrealism and Its Affinities

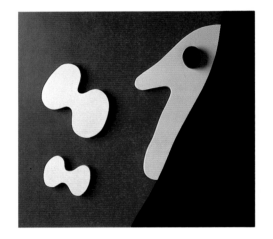

BRETON DEFINED SURREALISM IN 1924 AS "PURE PSYCHIC AUTOMATISM, BY WHICH WE PROPOSE to express [by any means] the real process of thought . . . in the absence of any control exercised by reason and outside any aesthetic or moral preoccupations." Automatic writing, which Breton and his colleagues had advocated since 1920, involved assuming a trance state and logging the stream of consciousness as a specimen of repressed desires and truths. For visual artists, there were any number of analogous techniques for investigating similar mental territory.

Beginning around 1916, Arp had extended cubist collage by dropping torn-up pieces of paper and pasting them where they fell. The resulting chance-generated patterns suggested strange associations that were possible only in an illogical fantasy world. Arp, who developed this process to make hybrid objects (they could as easily be considered paintings as low relief sculptures) from scraps of painted wood, would only later give titles to these compositions of toylike forms arrived at in this mediumistic fashion: for example, *Bow Ties and Head* and *Birds in an Aquarium*. Preferring irregular, rounded ("biomorphic") shapes to perfect geometrical ones, Arp was an antipurist but nevertheless advocated simple forms and simple colors for the sake of clarity and impact. For Arp, art could enhance awareness of elemental natural forces in flux, and he relished the forms' suggestive powers, addressing his works to viewers capable of childlike fascination with clouds that could one minute look like camels and the next moment look like whales.

Using assemblage (pasting three-dimensional objects onto the painting's surface) in a similar fashion, Picabia favored more specific associations, substituting one thing for another the way a poet uses similes and metaphors. For example, starting with a canvas scumbled with blue paint to evoke a sky with clouds, he added well-defined, albeit irregular biomorphic shapes to define a woman's head in the most elementary way, as if she were conjured during a child's daydream. Substituting matchsticks, hairpins, and coins for conventional "lines" as graphic equivalents for hair, facial features, and a necklace, Picabia endowed his image with signs to represent greed and explosive passion, effectively going beyond painting to a more poetic realm of expression.

André Masson, an emerging cubist painter, met Breton in 1924 and immediately developed a form of automatic drawing, allowing his hand to track the pen across a sheet of paper without asserting control. Recognizing preconscious images in the resulting scrawl, Masson then heightened and refined their contours, rendering these hallucinating automatic pictures more explicit. Within a few years he was able to work in this uncontrolled way on canvas, dripping threads of paint as lines to meander through surfaces that he often had coated irregularly with sand (another "beyond-painting" mutation of the collage principle of hybridizing media). These lines on the sand suggested magical prehistoric hieroglyphs, and Masson added highlights of color, often blood red, as in *Fish Drawn on the Sand*, to enhance the suggestion of violence resulting from his abstract linear delirium.

Masson's studio was next door to one used by a versatile Catalan-born artist named Joan Miró (1893–1983), whose poet's imagination tended to associate a cast of folkloric characters and their menagerie with the resulting arabesques and biomorphic shapes of his automatic

FRANCIS PICABIA

Match Woman II, 1924–1925
Oil, etc., on canvas, 35½ × 28⅛"
(90 × 72 cm)
Collection of Mrs. Edwin A. Bergman,
Chicago

painting practices. Most often in the mid-1920s, Miró would begin a painting by saturating the canvas with coats of one or more very liquid paints, cultivating irregular stains to evoke forms, just as stains in a damp wall had suggested grotesque figures to Leonardo da Vinci centuries before. Miró, however, tended to see the same sort of shapes over and over, some sprouting five little buds to act as fingers or toes and others extruding curves to suggest torsos or mouths not far removed from Arp's morphology. With graffitilike dots and squiggles added to these "heads" to make eyes and mustaches, Mirós shapes come to life in a liquid space as animated amoeboid cartoons for birds, horses, hunters, policemen, or lovers.

Of course, Picasso had anticipated the free and suggestive transformations of shape that the younger surrealist artists began to develop as a visual vocabulary in the 1920s. "We claim him as one of ours," Breton wrote in 1925 in his periodical, *The Surrealist Revolution*, admitting that the surrealists "have but to pass where Picasso has already passed, and where he will pass in the future." However, as he had kept apart from organized cubist movements before the war, Picasso again preferred to remain independent. Even so, he became good friends with several of the surrealists, whose works acted as catalysts and challenges to his protean genius. In *The Embrace*

(1925), for example, Picasso addressed the unleashed libidinal energy that the surrealists were committed to explore, and the furious result is like a purist Léger painting gone berserk. Recognizable in the interlocked patterns of bright colors are biomorphic signs for lovers engulfing and penetrating one another with swelling, opening, pulsing body parts: a hairy male arm registered as a vermilion centipede, a mouth that could belong as easily to her figure as to his and that looks more like a vagina than like any facial part, eyes and noses pushed all over the face by the squeezing and merging of flesh during a passionate kiss. With their garish clothing, Picasso's nightmarish figures are the humanoid kin of the creatures conjured up in carnival paintings by Miró and Picabia.

Meanwhile, with no endorsement from the surrealists, the Lithuanian-born Chaim Soutine (1894–1944) was that same year acting out a nightmare in the name of art in his Montparnasse studio. Obsessed by a painting by Rembrandt in the Louvre that shows a carcass hung up for disembowelment by butchers, Soutine brought a side of beef from the slaughterhouse back to his studio and painted it with expressionist gusto while it decomposed, excreting vibrant putrid colors. When the meat dried out, Soutine threw fresh blood on it so that his painstaking confrontation with gore could continue no matter how his neighbors or the police might try to intervene. Although Soutine claimed to hold van Gogh in low regard, his own paintings executed with nearly insane intensity transcend what most people would categorize as reality for the sake of a more demented or spiritualized realm of meditation.

Picasso's friend Picabia, who was among the most active proponents of this mid-1920s "monster" phase of Surrealism, also developed an especially elegant hieroglyphic mode to represent the mixed emotions of passion with superimposed images of loveliness and violence. In *Salome*, for example, a tracing of the salient features of a head like that of Botticelli's Venus, with its undulating hair, here crowned with thorns in martyrdom, overlays the image of a palatial hall with the naked Salome dancing astride a platter with the decapitated head of John the Baptist. Mysterious unfolding lotus blossoms float within the same pictorial web, intertwining between the other images to evoke the liquid realm of fantasy.

Picabia, Ernst, and de Chirico all inspired the development of Yves Tanguy (1900–1955) into a painter of expansive landscapes executed with the minute delicacy associated with the non-Western spaces charted in Chinese scrolls. As barren as a desert or the ocean floor, Tanguy's imaginary realms nonetheless support a wealth of arcane biomorphic forms that cast sharp shadows while they float and crawl through an otherworldly atmosphere. Each carefully shaped little protoplasmic creature seems endowed with awareness of its role in a farfetched drama observed by a biologist using a microscope. The mists and the undulating fauna that characterize these dreamscapes resulted from ingenious rubbing, scratching, and even fingerprinting. In tandem with Tanguy's fluid brushwork, this sort of expanded graphic vocabulary might suggest gassy oil pits attended by primeval derricks and dirigibles, as in the eight-panel screen that is Tanguy's epic masterpiece.

In turn, Tanguy's morphology became grist for the mill of the Spanish-born Salvador Dali (1904–1989). A virtuoso stylist capable of translating the most fantastical ideas into either abstract or photographically realistic pictorial terms, Dali exploded onto the Paris art scene in 1929 as the coauthor of *Le Chien Andalou (The Andalusian Dog)*, an outrageous surrealist film that begins when a girl's eye is slit open with a razor to reveal her innermost psychological being. Yet Dali always dismissed admiration for craftsmanship, stressing that for him technical perfection was simply a means to an expressive end. Breton loved the new recruit, writing in the introduction to the catalog for Dali's first exhibition of paintings in Paris that "with Dali perhaps all the great mental windows are opening up." Sometimes cosigning his works with his lifelong companion, Gala (Eluard's ex-wife and Ernst's ex-mistress), Dali sought to represent his own recurring obsessions, formulating what he called the "paranoiac-critical method" to explain how the mind's eye can develop the capacity to perceive overlapping images automatically.

A painting such as *Eggs on a Plate Without the Plate* incorporates no fewer than three overlapping images suggested by the appearance of the most banal meal. (For Dali, perception could often be understood as a sort of ingestion or cannibalism.) In addition to its literal meaning as food, the yellow hemisphere of the cooked yolk evidently suggested the sun breaking through clouds, and so Dali decided to juxtapose an image of eggs on a plate with the altogether imaginary image of an egg hung and silhouetted against the sky from a cord like a light bulb.

Sagging from gravity and thus biomorphic in shape, the suspended yolk also suggests the emergence of a baby's head from the uterus at birth. Although it reflects the panes of a window on its curved surface, the yolk-sun-baby form actually confronts a hanging gold pocket watch that appears to melt, apparently symbolizing the persistence of time from day to day and generation to generation. These strange apparitions are set on the terrace of a starkly modern house overlooking the sea, and through its upper window an adult and a child can be observed as observers, a surrealist embodiment of the looking-at-looking theme so crucial to earlier generations of French painters. With shameless paintings like this one, full of sexual associations, Dali would become a household word, and he actively courted publicity with Dada-style gestures designed to outrage everyone, his fellow artists included. His ultraindividualistic behavior and openly mercenary attitude to the art market temporarily discredited Surrealism for many collectors and critics, but today the achievements of Dali and his colleagues can hardly be underestimated.

The paintings of Balthus (b. 1908), short for Balthasar Klossowski de Rola, were first presented in an exhibition in Paris in 1934 that delighted the surrealists and shocked the public. Depicting young girls in everyday situations with an awareness of their roles as sexual creatures, Balthus's paintings addressed the hypocrisy of a fundamental taboo against child molestation. Perhaps the most unforgettable of these images depicts a street in Paris with pedestrians and shoppers going about their business, oblivious to the plight of a schoolgirl trying to escape a sexual assailant. Rendered with the stiff gestures associated with the murals of the Renaissance painter Piero della Francesca, who had also been one of Seurat's favorite masters, the figures in *The Street* are all observed from below, as if from a child's point of view. None seems to notice what is going on, and the collective disregard or denial of these wooden characters underlines the horror of the attack with fierce irony. Even though the artist modified the offensive gesture of the man grasping the girl by repainting his hand moved slightly away from her sex, this painting is still a haunting evocation of the seemingly inescapable and therefore horrifying character of the dream experience.

The Embrace, 1925
Oil on canvas, 51¼ × 38⅛″ (130 × 97 cm)
Musée Picasso, Paris

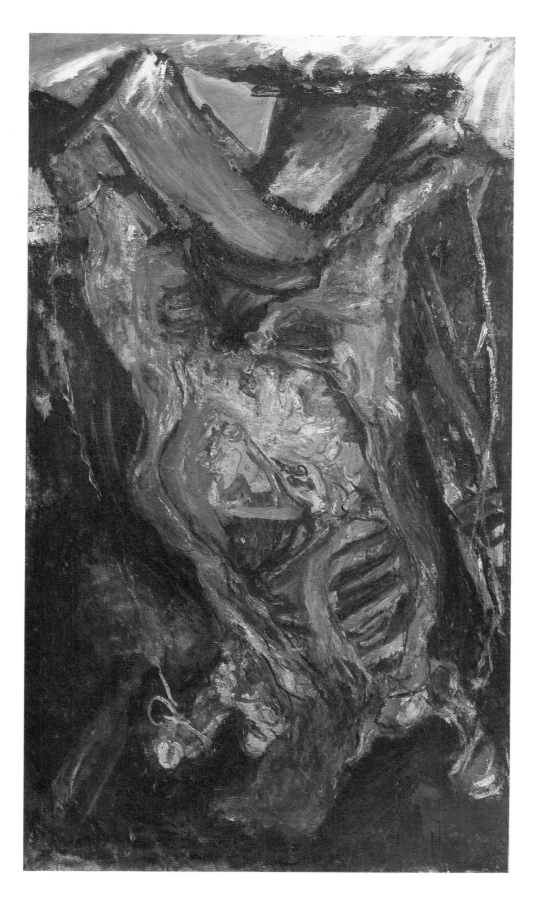

CHAIM SOUTINE (b. 1894, Smilovitchy,
Lithuania–d. 1943)

Side of Beef, 1925
Oil on canvas, 78¼ × 44⅞″ (200 × 114 cm)
Musée de Peinture et de Sculpture, Grenoble

YVES TANGUY (b. 1900, Paris–d. 1955)

Four-Panel Screen, 1928
Oil on wood, each panel 31 × 37¼″ (78.8 × 94.5 cm)
The Art Institute of Chicago, Chicago
The Joseph Winterbotham Collection

ANDRÉ MASSON (b. 1896, Balagny–d. 1987)

Fish Drawn on the Sand, 1927
Oil and sand, 39⅜ × 28¼″ (100 × 73 cm)
Kunstmuseum, Bern

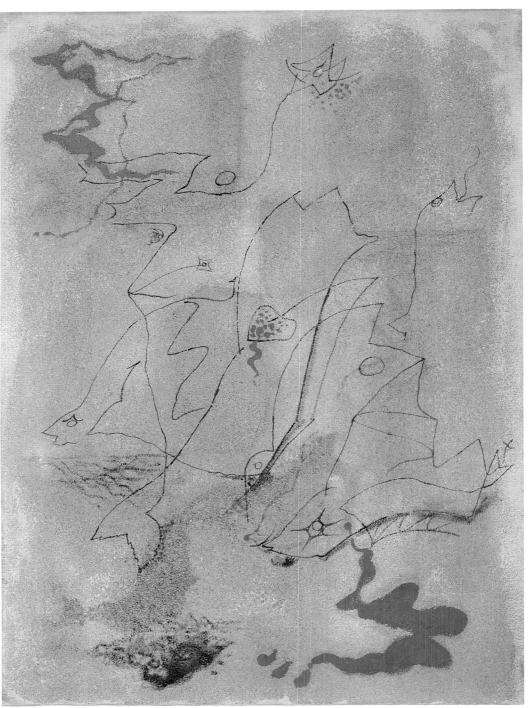

Joan Miró (b. 1893, Montroig–d. 1983)

The Gendarme, 1925
Oil on canvas, 97¼ × 76⅞″ (248 × 195 cm)
Claire B. Zeisler Collection, Chicago

Balthus, born Balthasar Klossowski de Rola (b. 1908, Paris)

The Street, 1933
Oil on canvas, 76¾ × 94½″ (195 × 240 cm)
The Museum of Modern Art, New York
James Thrall Soby Bequest

SALVADOR DALI (b. 1904, Figueras–d. 1989)

Eggs on a Plate Without the Plate, 1932
Oil on canvas, 23¼ × 16½" (60 × 42 cm)
Salvador Dali Museum, St. Petersburg, Florida

XXVII.
Old Values and New Threats

PIERRE BONNARD

Terrace at Vernon, ca. 1928
Oil on canvas, 95½ × 121⅝″
(242.5 × 309 cm)
Kunstsammlung
Nordrhein-Westfalen, Dusseldorf

PIERRE BONNARD

Nude in Bathtub,
Oil on canvas, 95½ × 121⅝″
(242.5 × 309 cm)
Musée d'Art Moderne de
la Ville de Paris, Paris

UNCONCERNED WITH PEDANTIC THEORIES ABOUT THE ESSENCE OF MODERN CONSCIOUSNESS, some of the greatest French painters between the world wars, including Matisse, Braque, Vuillard, and Bonnard, clung to the enduring values of the French tradition, creating masterpieces that celebrated the French way of life with ever greater opulence and sophistication. Bonnard, who bought a small house at Veronnet, not far from Monet's home and garden at Giverny, was the obvious heir to the great impressonists, having transformed their stenographic brushwork into a vehicle for timeless decorative reveries, sometimes on a monumental scale. Considering Monet's ultimate fulfillment as a decorative painter with his ensemble of *Water Lilies* murals, inaugurated only months after his death in 1927, Bonnard's great late 1920s landscapes perhaps should be understood as responses to the passing of the last of his lifelong heroes. Orchestrated with consummate richness, the irregular strokes in different shades of green and shadowy blue-green used to depict the dense screen of foliage in *Terrace at Vernon* are a eulogy to Monet's technique. The parakeet perched on the railing hardly seems out of place in such a paradisical setting infused with the glow of light. Included as an accent of color no different from the blond woman at the left and the lemons visible on an adjacent tabletop, the bird nevertheless suggests a musical frame of reference for the treatment of space and color throughout this composition. In a similar way, the print dress worn by the woman visible at the lower right as she climbs up to the balcony provides a decorative frame of reference for Bonnard's abiding sensitivity to textile patterns, a heritage from his early Nabi years alongside Vuillard.

Bonnard's great paintings of nudes in their bathrooms are, of course, a personal extension of the extraordinary variations on this theme that were introduced by Degas when Bonnard was still in art school. Using the subject as a pretext for odd poses, skewed viewpoints, and the light-splashed play of soft pastel colors, Bonnard painted some of the most sophisticated images of sensuous relaxation in the history of art. The sexually tense young women in the paintings of Balthus are like an unsettling retort to the bourgeois goddesses depicted by Bonnard. With his art-for-art's-sake temperament, unconcerned with superficial originality or titillation, Bonnard put color and line at the service of old-fashioned Renoiresque reverie, conjuring up interior worlds in which the body melts away.

Only Matisse and Dufy approached Bonnard's mastery of decorative art. A cycle of four murals by Dufy, executed in 1928 and 1929 for a villa in Antibes, conjures up a "fairytalelike" world of sailing ships, nasturtiums, and parrots. Undoubtedly encouraged by his experiences as an haute couture textile designer for Poiret, Dufy had come to accept color and form as independent entities that he could "print" separately. The resulting interplay of splashes of local color only more or less overlapping with outlined forms such as the silhouettes of feathers or fronds is an exaggerated version of the incomplete alignment in watercolors with pencil guidelines by Cézanne, among others. In Dufy's hands, the misalignment seems to indicate a mutual freedom of form and space; the color areas indicate where a form has just been in a world animated with both physical and luminous flutter. Dufy's personal hallmark, this childlike disconcern for restraining boundaries eventually had counterparts in the work of painters committed to automatism, such as Miró, and those committed to abstraction, such as Léger and

RAOUL DUFY

*Mural Decoration for Villa Atlanta,
Antibes,* 1928
Oil on canvas, 107 × 122⅞″
(272 × 312 cm)
Private Collection, France

Hartung. But only Dufy understood the endless innuendo of this technique, and his works, whether at easel or mural scale, are rich variations on the most simple premise. "You have to really love what it is to have pleasure," wrote Gertrude Stein in 1946, "and Dufy does really love what it is and we have the pleasure."

Mobilized at the very outset of World War I, Braque fought at the front and received such a serious head wound that it was feared that he might lose his sight. After his discharge in 1916, the cofounder of Cubism became more introverted and introspective. Continuing to paint in nearly complete independence of trends in the art world, Braque worked predominantly in the still-life genre, extending Cubism to its fulfillment as an abstract decorative mode. *The Round Table* (1928–1929) is perhaps the greatest of his art-for-art's-sake variations of the synthetic cubist still life. Rendered within a space under dramatic pictorial compression, the forms in this paintings are flat silhouettes without mass. A knife represented in the middle of the still life is particularly appropriate, since the hard outlines seem to have been whittled (as in a woodcut print) rather than drawn. Spatial depth is registered by shifts in red, browns, and tans, all carefully modulated. The sheet music on the tabletop, including the piece entitled "Etude" ("Study"), encourages the viewer to think of form and color in terms of pitch, rhythm, harmony, and other abstract musical relationships.

Totally nonfigurative abstraction, with color and shape used exclusively to convey an ultimate structural logic or intuitive rhythm, had advocates in Paris since around 1910, when the Delaunays and Kupka exploited the so-called Orphic variety of Cubism, creating visual harmonies with disk-shaped spectra of colors. The most extreme of all abstract painters, Dutch-born Piet Mondrian (1872–1944) limited himself to primary colors, straight lines, and flat rectangular shapes as fundamentals. Mondrian made Paris his home, but, even so, it was outside France, in Germany, Holland, and Russia, that pure plastic abstract art took precedence as the most modern form of expression. Only with the influx of foreign painters to the postwar Paris art scene did abstract painting take root, most notably in the work of a group organized in

1931 by the Belgian-born Georges Vantangerloo (1886–1965) and the French colleagues Jean Hélion (b. 1904) and Auguste Herbin (1882–1960). Coordinating exhibitions and publications during the next five years, their Abstraction-Création association, which Dali referred to as a "degrading example of mental debility," provided an extraordinary arena for new plastic ideas. Associated with the group from the outset was the American Alexander Calder, who developed his mobile sculptures in response to Mondrian's abstract paintings.

Hélion, who had been a figure painter in the late 1920s and would return to that mode in the 1940s, developed in the mid-1930s a manner of abstract composition predicated on interlocked flat shapes with slightly irregular silhouettes that suggested simplified architectural forms rendered in odd perspectives. In its use of long linear forms for linkage, Hélion's morphology of complex equilibrium closely resembles Calder's, with its monochrome pads delicately balanced on rodlike armatures. The modulated monochrome backgrounds in Hélion's paintings resemble the similarly monochromatic spatial matrices in biomorphic paintings by Miró and Kandinsky, who emigrated to Paris from National Socialist Germany in 1933. Given his credentials as a pioneering advocate of abstraction and his leading role at the Bauhaus school during the 1920s, Kandinsky was in demand for Abstraction-Création activities. But like Arp and even Hélion (who resigned in 1934), Kandinsky shunned group-sponsored theories. Indeed, his work in Paris during the final eleven years of his life might be described as less abstract and more surrealistic. Even though he never used specific images in his compositions, he invented an elaborate cast of Miróesque biomorphic characters, apparent cousins to the microscopic organisms illustrated in science textbooks. Teeming with such forms, paintings such as *Blue Sky* can be viewed as the incomprehensible hieroglyphics of a lost ancient or extraterrestrial civilization in which abstract geometric order did not restrain the exuberance of thought.

Rigorous geometric order was, however, essential for the theoretical-minded Herbin, who had been affiliated with the cubists both before and after the war. Around 1927 he had begun to develop a totally abstract pictorial language limited to regular planar shapes such as triangles, squares, and circles and carefully contrasted colors in order to communicate spiritual truths. Indebted to Herbin's obsession with the romantic color theories of Goethe, paintings such as *Air, Fire* were attempts to create an abstract visual "Esperanto" that would strongly influence the next generation of geometrically minded, hard-edge artists led by Vasarely.

In regard to intensity of color, no painter surpassed Rouault in the 1930s. His crusted surfaces resulted from the use of layer upon layer of paint to obtain jewellike, phosphorescent, and dull incandescent glows that resembled Gothic stained glass. Evidently, Rouault's passion for the complexities of printmaking led him in later works to add glaze upon glaze to the enameled surfaces of his oils. *The Old King*, an imperious profile image of a quasi-biblical ruler (Jarry's absurd King Ubu was one of Rouault's favorite characters), was begun during World War I in 1916 but was not finished until 1937. By that date, it could serve as an omen for the impending second world conflict: The little white flower in the king's hand seems like an awkward gesture of peace.

An upsetting mood of imminent conflict and death seems apparent in the works of many painters in Paris in the late 1930s as atrocities tolerated in the name of fascism continued to make headlines. The destruction of Guernica forced Picasso to react to warfare as he had never felt compelled to do from 1914 to 1918. Characteristically, Braque was unwilling to use explicitly political symbols in his art, yet the wounded veteran painted increasingly somber still lifes starting around 1937. In several of these paintings he included a human skull as a prop and abstracted the shape of his painter's palette until the thumb hole became an eye socket and the grip became a death's-head mouth. Braque denied the presence of any symbolism in the skulls, but in 1939 he wrote that "like everyone else . . . the painter is . . . influenced, upset or perhaps worse, by the march of history. . . . But we must insist on a categorical distinction between art and actuality."

No painting more poignantly or explicitly counters such art-for-art's-sake thinking than Chagall's *White Crucifixion*. At the time widely considered the leading painter of the School of Paris, Chagall became a target of Nazi hatred. Beginning in 1933, his work was presented in propaganda exhibitions designed to discredit "abominable" or "degenerate" artists. Chagall took French citizenship in 1937, while Nazi persecution of Jews in Germany escalated, leading to the infamous Kristallnacht in November 1938. In this painting, exhibited in 1940, Chagall portrayed the dying Christ as a Jew, as a reminder that Nazi atrocities represented an assault on Christian values no less than on Jewish ones. Around this apparition of the suffering Christ, Chagall painted people fleeing from a world turned topsy-turvy amid the billowing smoke from a burning synagogue. Although he later painted out several explicit details, evidently hoping to make his image more timeless, it has recently been shown that for its initial public showing Chagall had included swastikas on the armband of the soldier and on a flag and that another figure had worn the sort of sign mandated by the Nazis that read: "I am a Jew."

With the occupation of Paris by Nazi troops in June 1940, the history of French painting went underground and abroad. While symbols of free culture such as Matisse, Picasso, Braque, and Kandinsky remained in France, the majority of artists in Paris emigrated, mostly to New York. Indeed, the Museum of Modern Art in New York extended invitations to welcome Chagall, Matisse, Picasso, Dufy, Rouault, Masson, and Ernst. Needless to say, the Jews and German-born among them were obliged to accept the invitation. In the opinion of many jingoistic American observers, New York from this point on had replaced Paris as the world's art center.

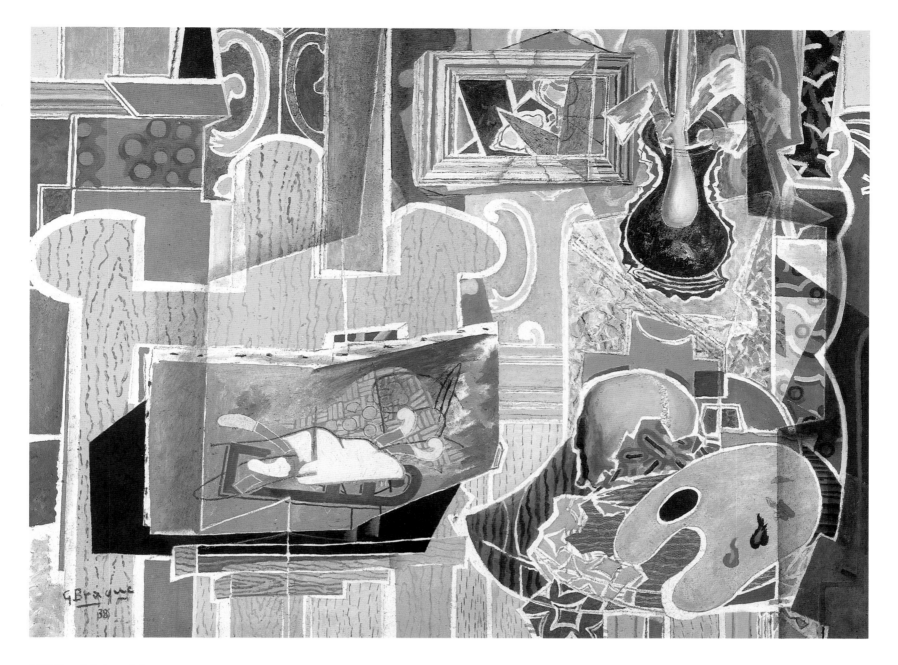

GEORGES BRAQUE

> *Vase, Palette, and Skull*, 1939
> Oil on canvas, 38⅛ × 51⅛″ (97 × 130 cm)
> Collection of Mr. and Mrs. David Lloyd Kreeger,
> Washington, D.C.

GEORGES BRAQUE

> *The Round Table*, 1929
> Oil on canvas, 57¼ × 44¾″ (145.4 × 113.6 cm)
> The Phillips Collection, Washington, D.C.

Jean Hélion (b. 1904, Couternes–d. 1987)

Composition, 1934
Oil on canvas, 56¼ × 78¼″ (144.3 × 199.8 cm)
Solomon R. Guggenheim Museum, New York

Vassily Kandinsky (b. 1866, Moscow–d. 1944)

Blue Sky, 1940
Oil on canvas, 39⅜ × 28¾″ (100 × 73 cm)
Musée National d'Art Moderne,
Centre Georges Pompidou, Paris

Auguste Herbin (b. 1882, Quièvy–d. 1960)

Air, Fire, 1944
Oil on canvas, 25⅝ × 36¼″ (60 × 92 cm)
Musée National d'Art Moderne, Centre Georges
Pompidou, Paris

MARC CHAGALL

White Crucifixion, 1938
Oil on canvas, 60¾ × 55″ (154.3 × 139.7 cm)
The Art Institute of Chicago, Chicago
Gift of Alfred S. Alschuler, 1946

GEORGES ROUAULT

The Old King, 1916–1936
Oil on canvas, 30¼ × 21¼" (76.8 × 54 cm)
The Carnegie Museum of Art, Pittsburgh
Patrons Art Fund

XXVIII.

World War II Art

THE FIRST FRENCH PAINTER TO ARRIVE IN NEW YORK TO AVOID THE WAR WAS THE CHILEAN-born Matta (b. 1912), who had come to Paris to study architecture with Le Corbusier and then drifted under the influence of Dali and Breton. In an important article published in 1938 in the lavish surrealist magazine *Minotaure*, Matta called for a surrealist architecture "in touch with other suns, [including] utterly liberated objects that would act as psychoanalytical mirrors of plasticity." His astounding paintings amount to renditions of such fantastical architectural projects. Very much indebted to Tanguy's realistic paintings of imaginary wasteland spaces, Matta rendered exploding landscapes, ripped apart on seismic fault lines, with particles hurtling through measureless space. *The Earth Is a Man*, among the grandest of his meditations on the internal-external spatial matrices interconnecting body systems with the forces of the universe, can be understood as the image of a modern battleground. The shattered cosmic spaces in Matta's paintings were a particularly graphic demonstration of automatism as an intellectual means of liberating the artistic imagination, and young American painters such as Jackson Pollock were quick to adapt this graphic mode for dramatic self-analysis, transforming Surrealism into something rough, raw, and intensely personal.

Ernst and Masson were even more important as models for Pollock and other young Americans. As a German citizen, Ernst had been interred by the French when war had broken out, and he finally escaped Europe with the help of the American heiress Peggy Guggenheim, whom he would later marry. Her gallery in New York became a center for European art in exile. Always inventing new ways to construct images, Ernst experimented in America with a technique he called oscillation, an automatic method of applying leaking paint from a hole punched in a can suspended and swung above a canvas from a string. The results of these experiments, designed to chart the flight of a non-Euclidean fly, are visible in an ambitious work showing the artist in his studio. Portraying himself, as always, in the guise of a bird monster, Ernst painted a picture within a picture. The abstract canvas included on the bird's easel shows the traces of the oscillation technique, which has been cited as an important source for the famous quasi-automatic drip technique invented by Pollock, who got his start at Guggenheim's gallery.

Pollock's works of the early 1940s, prior to his invention of drip painting, more closely resemble the nightmarish paintings of ancient myths by Masson, who used a variety of primitive art motifs. Like Breton, Masson escaped Europe on a ship sailing for Martinique, reaching the United States from there two months later. *Antille* records a dream from Masson's passage. Automatic images suggesting birds, strange flowers, and phosphorescent lights all coalesce around and within the apparition of a naked black woman writhing in a hot Caribbean night of the painter's subconscious.

A photograph taken in March 1942 at a gallery in New York owned by Matisse's son, Pierre, includes not only Matta, Ernst, and Masson but Tanguy, Chagall, Léger, Mondrian, Ozenfant, Lipschitz, and others. Man Ray was in California by then, and Duchamp had not yet reached New York. By June these artists were publishing a magazine, *VVV* (for "Victory"), and by October they had organized an exhibition to raise funds for French children and prisoners. Both Ernst's *Surrealism and Painting* and Matta's *The Earth Is a Man* were included in the exhibition, which was entitled "The First Papers of Surrealism" (for the artists' immigration papers) and installed by Duchamp.

In Paris, in the spring of 1941 a group of brave abstract painters led by Jean Bazaine (b. 1904) put on an exhibition entitled "Twenty Young Painters in the French Tradition" to demonstrate that French art would disregard the occupation. The following year, the Museum of

Modern Art opened in Paris, housed in the Palais de Tokyo constructed for the 1937 World's Fair. While officials realized that this important museum, planned for more than a decade, was still far from ready, they preferred for national pride to open it immediately rather than wait. No one showed more courage than Picasso, who attended the funeral at Montparnasse Cemetery for the Jewish painter Soutine on August 11, 1943.

Perhaps the most moving group of war paintings was begun that year by Jean Fautrier (1898–1964), a reclusive veteran of World War I who was hidden from the Gestapo by colleagues in the Resistance. Working on small pieces of paper in a little garden building at a medical clinic in the countryside, Fautrier spread a thick paintlike substance with a palette knife to create the distorted faces of dozens of anonymous "hostages." Against the powdery off-key colors of the backgrounds, these faces with crusty textures evocative of sores, wounds, and decomposing flesh are as moving as the gauntest prewar works of Rouault and those created just after the war by Alberto Giacometti (1901–1966). Among the three most significant art events in the months immediately after the liberation of Paris, the exhibition of Fautrier's hostage series in 1945 helped set an important new postwar direction for French painting.

The other two crucial events were the Salon d'Automne of 1944, which included a group of nearly eighty works Picasso had painted during the war as a gesture of freedom and resistance, and an exhibition in October 1944 at the René Drouin gallery that introduced a scandalous new artist named Jean Dubuffet (1901–1985). Although Dubuffet had gone to art school just after World War I, he had decided against an art career; only twenty years later, after World War II, did he return to art, reacting to the general intellectual upheaval. Sharing Fautrier's sensitivity to crude materials and graffitilike drawing, Dubuffet would become the greatest French artist of the second half of the century. Dissatisfied with the results of conventional art schooling, he sought to duplicate the unique instinctive expressive power in the art of children and the mentally disturbed and incorporated the crude mannerisms of graffiti into his paintings, "enriched" with such materials as tar, gravel, and shards of glass. In 1946 he published an essay for art collectors, explaining that his works would not be addressed to "the mere gratification of a handful of specialists, but instead would entertain and interest the man in the street.... It is the man in the street that I want to reach, to whom I feel closest, with whom I want to make friends and enter into confidence and connivance...."

A portrait of Fautrier by Dubuffet epitomizes the irreverence at the heart of the latter's vision. Using a chalky white, he fashioned a grotesquely misproportioned image, the head the same size as the body with its stubby little legs. Like a naive caricaturist, he scratched and scrawled the exaggerated facial features as if to ridicule his fellow artist. For all the stylized naiveté, however, the resulting image is both tender and sophisticated, presenting Fautrier as a pale nocturnal owl with wide staring eyes and a wrinkled mind, the sort of creature who could have painted the "hostages."

Having learned Arabic, in 1947 Dubuffet was ready to make a pilgrimage to north Africa, following in the footsteps of Delacroix and Matisse. Leaving behind the dilapidated postwar urban wasteland, he attempted to develop a timeless barbaric and nomadic sensibility. Everything in these desert pictures is drawn with childlike awkwardness: The sun is a yellow circle with yellow spokes; the desert is a flat backdrop that extends across nearly the entire composition, leaving only a strip of blue for sky at the top; and the figures and camels are cartoonlike, as if the artist had no grasp of perspective or proportion. These figures seem to be scratched out of the sand background, foreshadowing Dubuffet's subsequent works devoted exclusively to earth textures, throbbing with misshapen images and irregular abstract patterns. To bolster his case for an art unspoiled by Western intellectual culture, Dubuffet began to collect what he referred to as "raw" art (l'art brut), organizing exhibitions in the late 1940s (actually conceiving a museum, which would open in 1976 in Lausanne) of fantasy works done in a variety of materials by inmates of institutions, craftspeople, and artists outside the professional mainstream. Among the latter was Gaston Chaissac (1910–1964), whose figures rendered from flat shapes like pieces of a puzzle would have a considerable influence on Dubuffet's works.

While Dubuffet's spirit extended across the Atlantic, receiving a sympathetic reaction from the Dutch-born Willem de Kooning, his greatest immediate impact was on a group of foreign painters and poets who had gathered in postwar Paris. Meeting informally at a café on the Quai Saint-Michel, in 1948 these young radicals formed a group called COBRA, an acronym for their

JEAN DUBUFFET

Fautrier araignée au front, 1947
Oil on canvas, 45⅝ × 35″ (116 × 89 cm)
Collection Dorothea and Natasha Elkon, New York

GASTON CHAISSAC (b. 1910, Avallon–d. 1964)

Totem, 1950
Oil on Pole, 65″ Height (165 cm)
Galerie Louis Carre, Paris

native cities: Copenhagen, Brussels, and Amsterdam. The Dutch member Karel Appel (b. 1921) and the Dane Asger Jorn (b. 1914) shared Dubuffet's faith in raw art made impulsively in response to the universal human need for self-projection. Their ideas about a "new figuration" were founded on their admiration for the direct expressive force of children's art and its freedom from conventions regarding materials and styles. The first group exhibition in Paris did not take place until 1951, by which time COBRA was about to dissolve. The loud colors, crude forms, and sticky surfaces of COBRA paintings, however, established a vital counterbalance in postwar French painting, bridging romantic attitudes about primitive figure painting to more mainstream attitudes favoring gestural abstraction.

The open-mindedness and humor of Dubuffet and the COBRA artists notwithstanding, in the immediate postwar period the prevailing mood among French artists was intensely earnest. Returning to Paris after the war, the Swiss-born surrealist sculptor Alberto Giacometti exemplified the spirit of the times, inventing a new way to represent a figure as an elongated armature, the flesh pared away until scarcely more than a vulnerable, nervous skeletal presence remained. His output as a painter began to keep pace with his output as a sculptor. Since Giacometti often used the same models for both techniques or made paintings of his sculptures, these postwar works seem to be about the interrelationships between two- and three-dimensional images. The artist's shadowy, dusty studio is always the nearly colorless setting for these paintings, which owe a considerable debt to Daumier. Like Daumier, Giacometti so emphasized webs of nervous lines that his oils seem less like images of reality than like images of drawings or of the artist's searching act of observation. The gray figures in his paintings of the 1940s and 1950s seem ready to crumble under the pressure of the space around them. The artist's close friendship with Jean-Paul Sartre (1905–1980), the leading advocate of existentialism, may explain the empty moods in such works, which can be understood as a drama of the individual's uneasy relationship to a purposeless universe.

Perhaps the most remarkable individual phenomenon of the postwar era was the skyrocketing career of Bernard Buffet (b. 1928). His first exhibition in 1947 led to his receiving the Critics' Prize the following year, and before long his works were showcased in galleries around the world. By 1973 a museum devoted to his works was inaugurated in Japan. Buffet's appeal was predicated on his simple, clear approach to representation and his obsessive mood of destitution, like an updated version of Picasso's blue period. Although uninterested in the sort of Old Master approach to drawing so important to Giacometti, in whose works no shape is ever explicit, the unpretentious Buffet likewise specialized in bleak settings and undernourished figures. Working year after year in a hallmark style based on spiky black outlines, however, Buffet came to exemplify the worst sort of commercialism, trading more and more on decorative still lifes and pretentious or hackneyed themes such as the horrors of war and the circus. However, in the postwar generation Buffet was hardly alone in his tendency to repeat himself for the sake of consistency.

Buffet's inclination to overproduce and to exhibit too often is in diametric contrast to Balthus's tendency toward secrecy and a strictly limited production. As a result, Balthus has maintained his reputation as a modern French figure painter. His consistently conventional style, however, serving as a vehicle for unconventional subject matter about the sexual fantasies of girls, has made his art every bit as predictable as Buffet's. With its domestic props of simple geometrical shapes, *Nude Playing with a Cat* exemplifies Balthus's art at its best, an extension of Ingres's and Degas's variations on the languid female body transformed by light into an abstract sign for voyeuristic desire.

Hélion's postwar figure paintings are generally more interesting, both because his simplified style anticipates 1960s pop painting and because his representational works so closely relate to the great abstract paintings of the 1930s. *The Wrong Way* (1947), with its red, white, and blue color scheme suggesting the French flag, makes the abstract-representational interrelationship explicit. One of the "balance" compositions of the prewar period is included on an easel to the left as a painting within this painting. The male figure in the middle is presumably Hélion, and the upside-down nude on the right is presumably a model in his studio. Given the surprising similarity between the binary forms in the "balance" painting and the model's arms and legs, she could have posed for it; conversely, the painter could have attempted to present his credentials as a strictly abstract-minded figure painter of the future.

Both Hélion's abstract-representational premise and his simplified comic-book figure style derive directly from the works of Léger, who returned to Paris in 1945 and, like Picasso, joined the Communist party. While large public murals for churches, universities, and even the United Nations took up much of Léger's energies, he nevertheless developed a new body of late easel paintings. The most unforgettable of these works are variations of the theme of construction workers interconnecting girders for a modern skyscraper. Angling off against the sky at right angles to one another, the brightly colored girders can be understood as a three-dimensional projection of Mondrian's abstract grid, transposing it into what Léger's architect friend Le Corbusier had called a "machine for living." Silhouetted against the sky, the girder skeletons are like symbols for logic, contrasting with the rounded shapes of passing clouds in the background. Progressing with such simple tools as ropes and ladders, the worker-heroes in these paintings straddle past and future, rebuilding France as a mass culture. Stressing these aspects of the postwar construction boom, Léger apparently wanted to draw a parallel between his own times and France's great Gothic age of communal culture.

The greatest postwar figure paintings of all, however, were made with painted pieces of paper, by Matisse. Having decided to remain in France for the duration of the war, Matisse sought peace and security in Nice, eventually moving inland to Vence when Nice became a potential target for attack. Explaining that using scissors to cut paper allowed him "to draw in color," Matisse became increasingly obsessed with inventing abstract shapes in this manner, using what he called "signs" for the objects in his compositions. Biomorphic entities in the spirit of Arp's Dada shapes, these cutout paper "signs" provided Matisse with the stylized vocabulary for a new sort of abstract art dealing with bursting life, sparkling light, and undulating bodies. Whether carried out as little abstract studies or orchestrated into great decorative symphonies, Matisse's cut paper "paintings" are his final great legacy. The stained-glass windows he designed for the little chapel in Vence were conceived as cut paper works; translated by craftspeople into shapes of colored glass, Matisse's leaves and flowers for the "Tree of Life" windows installed at the chapel in 1951 are no less a reminder than is Léger's *Builders* of the glorious Gothic French art heritage.

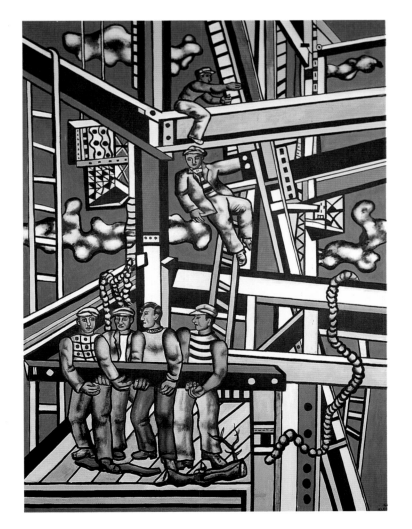

FERNAND LÉGER

The Builders, 1950
Oil on canvas, 118⅛ × 78¼″ (300 × 200 cm)
Musée National Fernand Léger, Biot

ABOVE:

MATTA, born Roberto Antonio Sebastian
Matta Echaurren (b. 1911, Santiago, Chile)

The Earth Is a Man, 1942
Oil on canvas, 72 × 95⅝″ (182.9 × 243 cm)
Private Collection, Chicago

RIGHT:

KAREL APPEL (b. 1921, Amsterdam)

Sleeping City, 1952
Oil on canvas, 38½ × 51³/₁₆″ (98 × 130 cm)
Galerie Nova Spectra, The Hague

OPPOSITE:

ANDRÉ MASSON

Antille, 1943
Oil and tempera on canvas, 49⅝ × 33½″
(126 × 85 cm)
Musee Cantini, Marseille

284

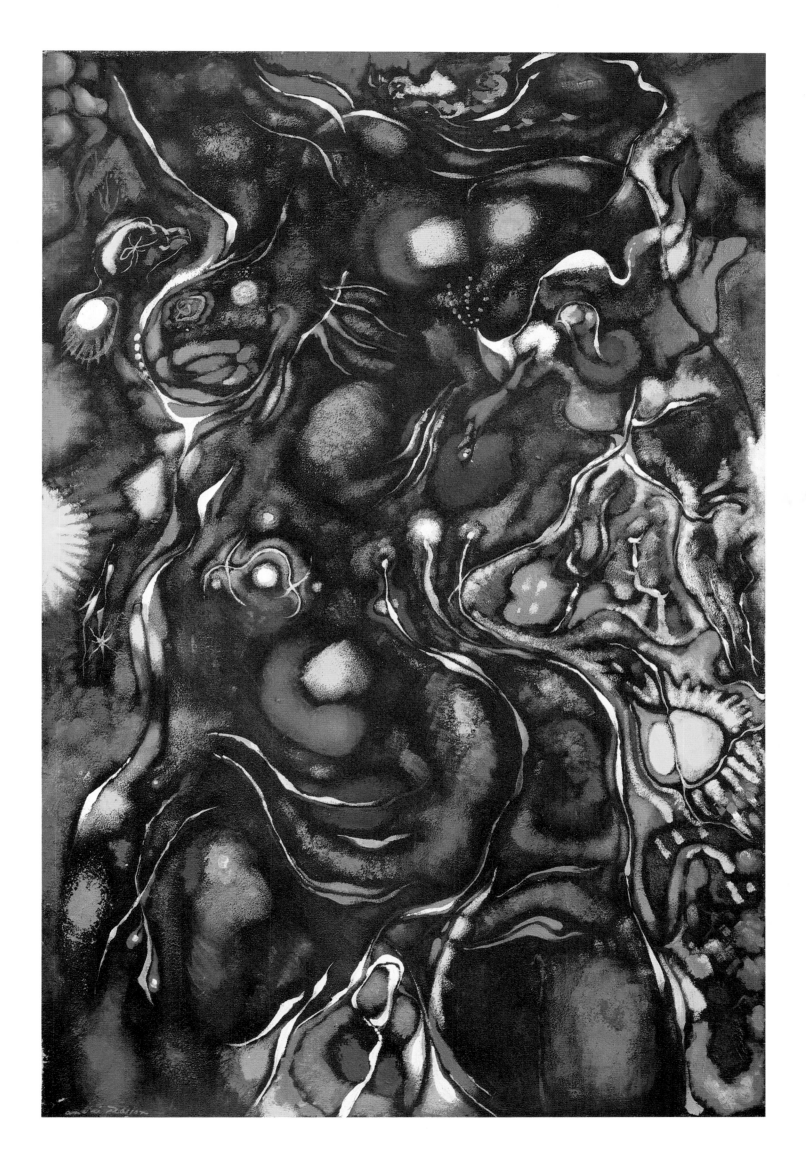

MAX ERNST

Surrealism and Painting, 1942
Oil on canvas, 77 × 92″ (195.5 × 233.6 cm)
The Menil Collection, Houston

JEAN FAUTRIER (b. 1898, Paris–d. 1964)

Oradour-sur-Glâne, 1945
Oil, water-based paint, and dry
pigment on paper mounted on canvas,
57⅛ × 44⅛″ (145 × 112.7 cm)
Private Collection, U. S. A.

ALBERTO GIACOMETTI (b. 1901, Stampa,
    Switzerland–d. 1966)

3 Plaster Heads, 1947
Oil on canvas, 28¾ × 23⁷⁄₁₆″
(73 × 59.5 cm)
Alberto Giacometti Stiftung, Zurich

Nude Playing with a Cat, 1949
Oil on canvas, 25⅝ × 31¹¹⁄₁₆″ (65.1 × 80.5 cm)
National Gallery of Victoria, Melbourne
Felton Bequest 1952

BERNARD BUFFET (b. 1928)

Nude Man Next to Fireplace, 1947
Oil on canvas, 72¼ × 84″ (160 × 178 cm)
Musée Bernard Buffet, Surugadaira, Japan

JEAN HÉLION

The Wrong Way, 1947
Oil on canvas, 44½ × 57″ (113 × 145 cm)
Musée National d'Art Moderne, Centre Georges
Pompidou, Paris

XXIX.
Postwar Abstract Painting

DENISE RENÉ, A FASHION DESIGNER WHO DECIDED TO OPEN A GALLERY AFTER THE WAR, provided essential support for so-called concrete abstraction — art generated from the application of mathematical systems in order to avoid subjectivity. Her first exhibition, in June 1944, showcased one of the most prolific and influential of these artists, the Hungarian-born Victor Vasarely (b. 1908), who had studied Bauhaus principles before settling in Paris in 1930. A master of color interactions and perspective, Vasarely engineered the perspectival structure of his paintings' surfaces into realms of cerebral space with repetitive patterns projecting and receding in the viewer's eyes as geometric optical illusions. While he has been criticized for making impersonal formulaic objects that are not paintings in the conventional sense, Vasarely has welcomed the challenge to go beyond painting with design, extracting his sense of pattern from everyday urban patterns and, since the mid-1950s, applying his ideas to architectural projects, interrelating art and life in a literal way. The case for pure plastic abstraction extended from the works of de Stijl, suprematist, and Bauhaus pioneers such as Mondrian, Lazlo Moholy-Nagy, Paul Klee, and Sophie Taeuber-Arp was bolstered in 1949 by the publication of two important books, one theoretical and the other historical: Herbin's *Non-Figurative Non-Objective Art* and the critic Michel Seuphor's *Abstract Art: Its Beginnings and Its First Masters*. The following year, the pure abstractionists Jean Dewasne (b. 1921) and Edgard Pillet (b. 1912) decided to open the Studio of Abstract Art, a school in Paris dedicated exclusively to the study of pure abstraction and new materials for applying its principles.

Arriving in Paris to study under the provisions of the G.I. Bill, the American Ellsworth Kelly (b. 1923) was befriended by individuals in the camp of pure abstraction, including Seuphor, who provided introductions to some of the old master abstractionists still working in Paris, from the Italian-born Alberto Magnelli (1888–1971) and Vantangerloo to Arp and Rumanian-born Constanin Brancusi (1876–1957). By the beginning of the 1950s, Kelly had become one of the most original abstract artists at work in Paris, experimenting with design by using string and wood as materials for low relief works, shaped supports, and monochrome surfaces.

Kelly's French counterpart was the self-taught François Morellet (b. 1926), for whom the rigorous Swiss abstractionist Max Bill served as a role model. Like Bill, Morellet generated compositions with preconceived mathematical systems, rejecting the intuitive placement of line and color associated with the arch-abstractionist Mondrian. Uninterested in the kinetic color theory that obsessed his supporter Vasarely, Morellet applied his systems in the early 1950s to create works which anticipate not only the so-called op-art rhythms of 1960s English painters such as Bridget Riley but also the minimal compositions of the American Frank Stella. Unlike the reductivist Stella, Morellet began to investigate the role of chance in his application of systems and also to surrender his own role in the choice and execution of systems to the artificial intelligence of computers, anticipating the systemic aesthetic explored in the mid-1960s by the American Sol Lewitt. By the mid-1950s, Vasarely had begun to explore the kinetic potential of geometric abstractions and publish theories about the responsibility of artists to confront a mechanized future at the disposal and service of all humankind rather than a privileged intelligentsia concerned with obsolete conceptions of humanism and individualistic expression. Among his most important colleagues was Israel-born Yaacov Agam (b. 1928), who came to Paris in 1951 and soon took a leading position in the kinetic abstraction movement.

Capitalizing on his enormous success, Vasarely opened his own didactic museum in Gordes in 1970, and in 1976 he opened in Aix-en-Provence, where Cézanne had kept his studio throughout

MARIE-HÉLÈNE VIEIRA DA SILVA
(b. 1908, Lisbon)

The Corridor, 1950
Oil on canvas, 25½ × 35⅞" (64.7 × 91 cm)
Tate Gallery, London

his career, a foundation to support the Bauhauslike study of architectural design and present examples of his own pioneering ideas in this area.

Immediately after World War II, Vasarely's concrete abstract art was referred to as "cold," in contrast to the "hot" gestural abstract art that developed in Paris. The impresario of hot painting was Georges Mathieu (b. 1921), a college student versed in law and literature but devoted to free-form painting. When Mathieu arrived in Paris in 1947, he immediately began to organize like-minded painters, including Jean Atlan (1913–1960), Hans Hartung (1904–1989), Jean-Paul Riopelle (b. 1924), and Wols (Alfred Otto Schulze, 1913–1951). Collectively, their art was designated as "lyric abstraction" (or *art informel* or *tachisme*) and was compared with the similar gestural abstract painting that had emerged in postwar New York. In 1948 Mathieu helped organize an exhibition including both French lyric abstractionists and so-called American abstract expressionists such as Pollock, Rothko, de Kooning, and Tobey. Thus began the jingoistic struggle between Paris and New York for recognition as the art center of the postwar world. While the American abstract painters tended to use gesture as means of individualistic self-expression, the French painters tended to stress jazzlike improvisation as a means of creating decorative signs impervious to any kind of interpretation. Calligraphic at their most delicate and graffitilike at their most brutal, Mathieu's dramatic paintings immediately gained recognition in New York, providing a stimulus to painters such as Cy Twombly. Like Pollock, who was his hero, Mathieu insisted on using paint with the greatest immediacy, sometimes squeezing it directly from the tube to create the equivalent of brushless strokes. Given the painter's goal of realizing a simultaneity between intention and result, speed was the essential theoretical dogma of lyric abstraction as defined by Mathieu, who extended Pollock's method of working with the canvas on the floor into an early version of performance art. By 1957 Mathieu had begun a sort of world tour, executing huge works in front of audiences in Japan, the United States, the Middle East, South America, and Europe. Often he would wear special costumes for these athletic performances that extended Dali's showmanship for the cause of gestural abstract painting.

The German-born Hartung fled Nazism for Paris in 1935, where he developed an improvisational style indebted to the early abstract works of Kandinsky. At the outbreak of World War II, Hartung enlisted in the French Foreign Legion and saw combat in both north Africa and Europe, losing a leg as a result of a bad wound. After the war he began to participate in new exhibition opportunities such as the Salon de mai (May Salon), founded in 1945 by Gaston Diehl for young unknown painters, and this exposure brought his work to the attention of Mathieu. Refined and balanced, Hartung's hallmark abstractions most often consist of strokes scribbled in rhythmic clusters. The initial stroke is a matter of impulse; its rapid repetition, however, is carefully controlled by the artist's intuitive sense of visual weight and emphasis. At first Hartung's compositions tended to include several of these clusters in balanced compositions against a monochrome background, but in the 1950s he increasingly preferred the complicated silhouette of a single network of similar repeated strokes. In 1960 he won the grand prize at the prestigious Venice Biennale.

Wols had the briefest career of any French painter. Born in Berlin, he studied architecture with Ludwig Mies van der Rohe at the Bauhaus before fleeing to France in 1932. He was working mainly as a photographer when he was interned in a camp for German nationals, during the war. He gained recognition as an abstract artist only in the postwar period, beginning with an exhibition of works on paper at the René Drouin gallery in 1945. In these works, ultimately derived from the experiments of Klee and Kandinsky, spots of color are transformed into exploding microcosms with lives of their own. An advocate of the power of accident in experience, Wols, who worked in a tiny hotel room without an easel or much light, was, like Giacometti, admired by Sartre. In 1949, when the new French painting was first presented at a gallery in New York, Wols, Mathieu, and the Belgian-born Henri Michaux (b. 1899) were recognized as the luminaries. Michaux, a writer as much as a painter, extended lyric abstraction in late 1950s in works executed under the influence of drugs.

Riopelle, who shifted his activities from Montreal to Paris in 1946, was attracted by Surrealism before falling in with Mathieu. By 1950 he had developed a dense brand of abstraction, squeezing pure color directly from the tube onto the canvas. After 1952 he developed his signature style of curling patterns of colors by working with a palette knife to shingle mosaiclike patches of paint. Riopelle's heavily worked, complex surfaces relate his paintings to those by the Lisbon-born Marie-Hélène Vieira da Silva (b. 1908), who was established in Paris by 1926, and the Russian-born Nicolas de Staël (1914–1955), who settled in Paris in 1932. Both these painters sought to retain the idea of three-dimensional space in abstract paintings. In the case of Vieira da Silva, who excluded the figure from her art, the results were like vast empty theater sets, the floors and walls rendered in little blocks of color arranged in obsessive rows. Although she claimed to have received inspiration from Bonnard, her paintings bring the finger-imprinted surfaces of Giacometti's sculptures to mind. A love of similarly thick, enamellike surfaces characterizes the best of de Staël's pictures. Like Hartung, de Staël served in the Foreign Legion. Only after the war did abstract painting concern him, and even then his works almost always evoked observed experiences: figures, still lifes, landscapes, and even cityscapes with rooftop skylines. Just as a jazz musician allows a recognizable tune to emerge from otherwise free musical improvisation, de Staël provided traces or suggestions of conventional subject matter in his abstract paintings. Given his intense palette of chrome yellows, vermilions, and cobalt blues, de Staël's paintings recall the luminous daring of Bonnard and the fauves at the outset of the century. Both in France and abroad his paintings won considerable acclaim even before de Staël threw himself to his death out of the window of his studio at Antibes in 1955. His fellow Russian Serge Poliakoff (1900–1969) developed a closely related abstract style without any figurative associations, using large, brightly colored blocklike forms highlighted against dark backgrounds.

After de Staël's career abruptly ended, Pierre Soulages (b. 1919) was recognized throughout the 1950s as the best abstract painter in France. By the time of his first one-artist exhibition in 1949, Soulages had developed a unique style characterized by broad black brushstrokes. Often compared to the American painters Franz Kline and Robert Motherwell, who also limited themselves mostly to black and white, Soulages seldom worked, as they did, from impulse. Instead, his art is one of measure, and it comes as no surprise that since childhood his favorite subjects were trees. The same sense of trunk and branch structure is evident in his use of complex webs of shadow to trap space and light.

TOP:
FRANÇOIS MORELLET (b. 1926, Cholet)

From Yellow to Violet, 1956
Oil on canvas, 43⅜ × 85″ (110.3 × 215.8 cm)
Musée National d'Art Moderne, Centre Georges
Pompidou, Paris

ABOVE:
VICTOR VASARELY (b. 1908, Pecs, Hungary)

Exterior of Foundation Vasarely Building, 1976
Foundation Vasarely, Aix-en-Provence

WOLS, born Alfred Otto Wolfgang Schulze (b. 1913–d. 1951)

The Vowels, 1950
Oil on canvas, 31⅞ × 23⅝″ (81 × 60 cm)
Museum Ludwig, Cologne

GEORGES MATHIEU (b. 1921, Boulogne-sur-Mer)

Les Capétiens Partout, 1954
Oil on canvas, 116⅛ × 236¼″ (295 × 600 cm)
Musée National d'Art Moderne, Centre Georges
Pompidou, Paris

JEAN-PAUL RIOPELLE (b. 1923, Montreal)

Robe of Stars, 1952
Oil on canvas, 78¾ × 59″ (200 × 150 cm)
Museum Ludwig, Cologne

HANS HARTUNG (b. 1904, Leipzig, Germany–d. 1989)

T 1949/6, 1949
Oil on canvas, 44⅞ × 63¼″ (114 × 162.5 cm)
Staatsgalerie, Stuttgart

NICOLAS DE STAËL (b. 1914, St. Petersburg, Leningrad–
d. 1955)

Composition of Roof Tops, 1952
Oil on board, 78¾ × 59″ (200 × 150 cm)
Musée National d'Art Moderne, Centre Georges
Pompidou, Paris

OPPOSITE:

PIERRE SOULAGES (b. 1919, Rodez)

3 April 1954, 1954
Oil on canvas, 76¾ × 51¼″ (195 × 130 cm)
Albright-Knox Art Gallery, Buffalo, New York
Gift of Mr. and Mrs. Samuel M. Kootz, 1958

XXX.
Objections to Abstraction

Jean Dubuffet (b. 1901, Le Havre–
    d. 1985)

Family Life, 1963
Oil on canvas, 59 × 76¾"
(150 × 195 cm)
Musée des Arts Decoratifs, Paris

No French artist had a greater impact on the course of 1950s and 1960s art, both in Paris and outside France, than did the judo specialist Yves Klein (1928–1962), whose mother and father were lyric abstractionists. Klein's brief public career was both an expression of his deep-rooted mysticism and an extended publicity stunt. Although his works are primarily conceptual in nature, conceived as a reaction against the prevailing gestural style of abstraction, Klein created poetic and exquisitely beautiful art objects that give a physical dimension to his concepts. Although he and his close friends, including Arman (b. 1928) have explained how his all-blue paintings developed in tandem with Rosicrucian religious meditations in the late 1940s, it was only in 1955 that Klein publicly exhibited a painting: a three- by seven-foot all-orange canvas.

While precedents for such extreme abstract statements extended back to Malevich's suprematist *White Square on White* composition of 1918, Klein's subsequent output made it clear that his obsession with purity to the point of invisibility was far more than a mere historical revival. Pursuing his idea that painting can provide "absolute unity in perfect serenity," Klein extended his monochrome obsession to a series format, presenting rooms full of all-ultramarine paintings during the next several years. The blue surfaces, which serve as symbol of the sky void, became a hallmark that the artist patented as International Klein Blue in 1960. The monochromes were not hung in a conventional way from the wall but were presented on stalklike stands to stress Klein's assertion that his blue zones heralded an age of levitation. Nothing could be more formal in execution and presentation to an audience accustomed to so-called informal art with its cult of calligraphic brushwork and texture.

As if to address the issue of texture so important to Dubuffet, in 1957 Klein began to make works with sponges soaked in his blue paint. Some of the sponges were presented individually, held up by rods like his monochrome paintings. Others were glued to the surfaces of monochrome paintings, evoking sections of the fantastical floor of an intensely pure ocean. In a conceptual way, the sponges, with their magnetic capacity to absorb, embody maximum blue. Klein's most controversial gesture was an exhibition entitled "The Void," consisting of nothing, which opened on his thirtieth birthday: for two weeks in the spring of 1958, the Iris Clert Gallery, with its white walls, became an artwork by Klein's decree. Challenging the materialistic consumer mechanics of the art world, Klein's hoaxlike immaterial gesture foreshadowed the antics of installation and performance artists in the following decade. After the exhibition, Klein announced that he would sell quanta of nothing as art, calling them "Immaterial Pictorial Sensibility Zones." In characteristic fashion, Klein devised a complex performance-ritual to celebrate such art sales. Extending this conceit, in 1960 he published an extraordinary staged photograph of himself leaping from a rooftop into the void, suggesting that his conceptual powers were superhuman.

Klein staged his most ambitious gesture in March 1960, inviting fellow artists (including Mathieu, whose gestural art performances supplied the precedent for this enterprise), collectors, and critics to a swank gallery for an evening demonstration of his so-called Anthropometries, canvases imprinted in blue with the paint-covered bodies of nude models ("living brushes"). Epitomizing the New Realism movement engineered that year by the critic Pierre Restany, Klein's paintings represented a literal interaction between real life and art. At their best, Klein's blue nudes rival the most sensuous images of the nude in the history of French painting. Placed on canvas in poses with sweeping gestures, the models left imprints symbolic of elemental pressing forces such as gravity and desire. Considered in terms of the fundamental figure-ground relationship of conventional painting, the traces of bodies on Klein's ultimate paintings appear to

swim or fly with spiritual freedom in a sheerly conceptual, sheerly visual void.

A remarkable coincidence relates Klein's works to the 1920s automatic abstract paintings of Miró, some of them near monochromes, all of them images of fantasy spaces. Miró took a new look at these early works, painted in Paris, when he settled into a new home and studio on the island of Mallorca in 1956. This nostalgic experience initiated Miró's greatest late paintings, including a group of three monumental all-blue oils executed in March 1960, when Klein was performing with his living brushes in Paris. The calligraphic placement of a minimum of spots and a single line in each of Miró's paintings rivals the exquisite delicacy of Klein's late works, and taken in tandem, their 1961 works stake an impressive claim for French painting's continued primacy in world art.

Using a variety of unlikely materials for poetic effect, other artists mimicked the look of lyric abstraction to subvert and/or extend the realm of painting. Among the most remarkable were two artists from Brittany, Jacques Mahé de La Villéglé (b. 1926) and Raymond Hains (b. 1926), who decided in 1949 to collaborate on a variety of picture making that became known as *affichisme* ("posterism") when their works were first exhibited in 1957. Challenging the notion that art is the expression of an individual's unique creativity, the decision of the two New Realist artists to collaborate initiated an important trend, and during the 1970s and 1980s such teams of artists became fairly common in the art world. La Villéglé and Hain's concepts about technique were no less challenging. In the tradition of Léger, these artists are connoisseurs of urban street art, especially attracted to the complex, roughly textured surfaces that result when weather and vandalism corrode and tear away parts of posters to reveal layers of former posters underneath. "Readymades," such real, albeit accidental compositions amounted for La Villéglé and Hains to abstract lyric art taken for granted by urban passersby. In effect accepting the anonymous defacers of these posters as well as such impersonal forces as weather as co-collaborators, La Villéglé and Hains carefully removed their favorite dilapidated posters, stealing their art by night, so to speak. Mounted on canvas, these works function as abstract paintings with bits of letters, words, and images still evident here and there in the archaeological strata of modern publicity that they had chosen and preserved as art. An Italian artist, Mimmo Rotella (b. 1918), and another Frenchman, François Dufrêne (1930–1982), also worked with poster surfaces in the 1950s, but whereas they tended to alter what they found, to emphasize particular visual or poetic elements, La Villéglé and Hains were purists, respecting the creativity of the street as a fellow worker.

Dubuffet was hardly less experimental in his choice of materials. While many artists were returning to Europe after the war, he set off for Chicago and New York in 1951 to experience American urbanism. Setting up a studio near New York's Bowery, infamous as a neighborhood for indigents, the irrepressible French artist staked out a new territory of primitive visual culture hardly less exotic than north Africa. Conventional paints did not satisfy the pretentiously unpretentious Dubuffet, who invented a wide range of sticky soups with glues, asphalt, dirt, and anything else he pleased, referring to these materials as "pastes" or "coatings." Fascinated with the way in which these gritty, crusty materials survived when they dried and hardened on his canvases, in 1952 Dubuffet began to tear away at the skins, revealing undersurfaces just as vandals had scraped away at the posters La Villéglé and Hains had salvaged as pictures.

Back in France, Dubuffet went from one remarkable series to the next, incorporating butterfly wings, banana peels, and dried leaves to make fantastical "paintings" that he referred to as, among other things, "assemblage pictures" "*matériologies*," and "*texturologies*." Accompanying his exhibitions with written introductions to promote his novel ideas, Dubuffet explained his partiality for downtrodden beauties such as trampled, fallen leaves disintegrating into soil, in which he might recognize the approximate shape of an animal, seemingly out of place in the fragile texture of decay. "The painter is right," Dubuffet wrote in 1964, referring to the apparitions in his pictures, "only in painting what he does not see but hopes to see."

After major retrospectives in Paris at the Musée des Arts Décoratifs and in New York at the Museum of Modern Art in the early 1960s, Dubuffet developed his ultimate graphic mode, a form of automatic writing or doodling for which he invented the term *hourloupe*. Capricious and meandering to represent flux, Dubuffet's hourloupe line creates a jigsaw-puzzle world of interlocking zones with irregular biomorphic shapes. He filled in some of the zones with stripes, using mostly the French flag colors of red, white, and blue to color the hourloupe world. In this way he suggested all sorts of creatures, with everything reduced by this style to a fanciful common graphic denominator. *Family Life*, for example, includes scores of puppetlike faces and bodies of every scale, all interwoven to the point where they seem hidden in a sacred pictographic texture from Peru or China. The characters in the hourloupes are of course familiar from Dubuffet's earlier series and were adopted by a number of other painters to create "raw art" universes of their own. Early 1960s paintings by Belgian-born Pierre Alechinsky (b. 1927), one of the COBRA artists, both anticipate and echo the teeming, hieroglyphic child-minded realms that Dubuffet perfected in the hourloupes.

In the late 1960s, working with epoxy and cast polyurethane, Dubuffet created three-dimensional hourloupes resembling the piled stone prehistoric markers included in Tanguy's surrealist paintings. In addition to single three-dimensional figures, Dubuffet undertook several architectural fantasies for garden settings. The most complex of these, begun in 1969 but not finished until 1977, is the Villa Fabula, a concrete, steel, and polyester wonderland at Périgny-sur-Yerre, a small village near Paris. Ultimately derived from the fantastical rock gardens created by the turn-of-the-century Spanish architect Antonio Gaudí, Dubuffet's "park" is the setting for a structure with irregular curving cavelike walls that houses his 1967–1969 *Cabinet Logologique*, an enormous wraparound hourloupe mural. With its architectural and sculptural dimensions, the Villa Fabula complex is unique in the history of French painting.

Countering the playful hourloupe irregularity of Villa Fabula, in the late 1960s and 1970s Jean-Pierre Raynaud (b. 1939) created bizarre home environments of exaggerated order, using popular construction materials such as Panolac to cover floors, walls, and ceilings with a uniform grid of small white tiles. In the earliest of these clinical interiors, the artist provided bright red object accents such as fire extinguishers, apples, and flowerpots. However, his obsession with creating an all-white, all-grid world led him to create furnishings covered with the same Panolac material that disappear into the setting. Making his debut in 1965 as a pop artist concerned with so-called psychic everyday objects in the spirit of Magritte, Raynaud extended painting to include walls and architecture. Hardly unique in the 1960s, when artists on both sides of the Atlantic suddenly felt obliged to create ensembles, Raynaud's interest in environmental art should be evaluated within the French tradition of decorative art. His laboratory interiors, for example, are a direct response to Klein's "void" exhibition. Moreover, when Raynaud announced that he would not leave his windowless white bunker for two years, he extended the tradition of Klein, Dali, and Mathieu and added a public dimension to their intensely personal work by performing and manipulating the press. Of course, Raynaud's disregard for paint and brushwork makes his work seem out of place in this survey. However, by the mid-1960s, French painting was at an impasse, and whether or how that art form might or should survive became the essential frame of reference for Raynaud and for most of his generation.

YVES KLEIN (b. 1928, Nice–d. 1962)

Sponge Painting, RE 15, Blue, 1960
42⅛ × 23⅝″ (107 × 60 cm)
Kunstsammlung Nordrhein-Westfalen,
Dusseldorf

OPPOSITE, TOP:
JEAN PIERRE RAYNAUD (b. 1939, Courbevoie)

First-Aid Station, 1988
Ceramic tile, enameled metal
42⅞ × 67½″ (109 × 171.7 cm)
Private Collection, Paris

OPPOSITE, BOTTOM:
YVES KLEIN

People Begin to Fly, 1961
Dry blue pigment in synthetic resin
on paper on fabric,
97 × 156½″ (246.4 × 397.6 cm)
The Menil Collection, Houston

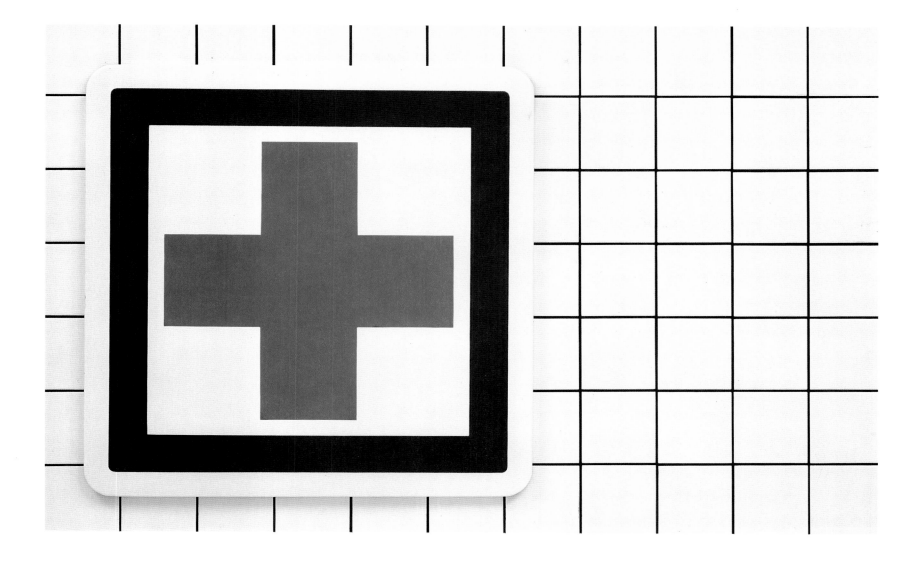

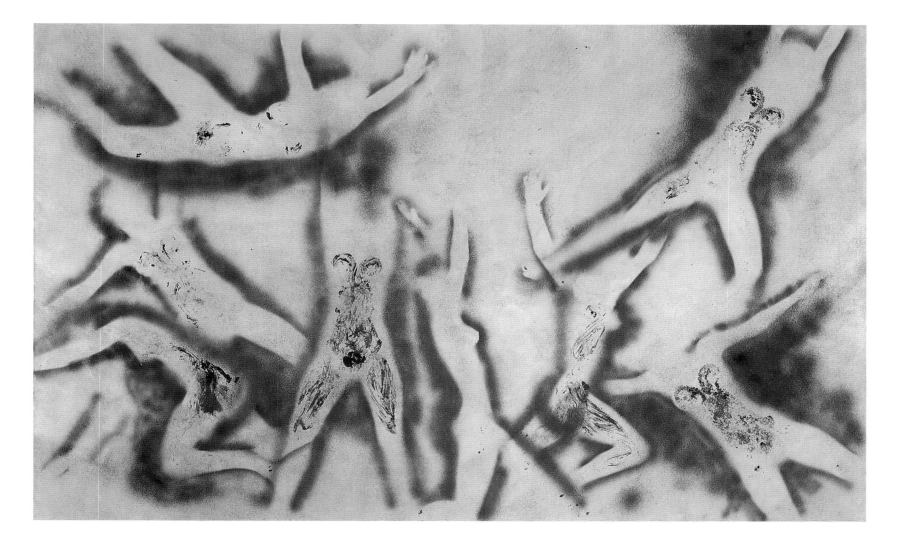

JACQUES MAHÉ DE LA VILLÉGLÉ (b. 1925,
    Brittany) and RAYMOND HAINS
    (b. 1926, Saint-Brieuc)

Ach Alma Manetro, 1949
Collage, 22¹³/₁₆ × 100¾″ (58 × 256 cm)
Musée National d'Art Moderne, Centre
Georges Pompidou, Paris

JOAN MIRÓ

Bleu, II, 1961
Oil on canvas, 106¼ × 131⅞″
(270 × 335 cm)
Musée National d'Art Moderne,
Centre Georges Pompidou, Paris

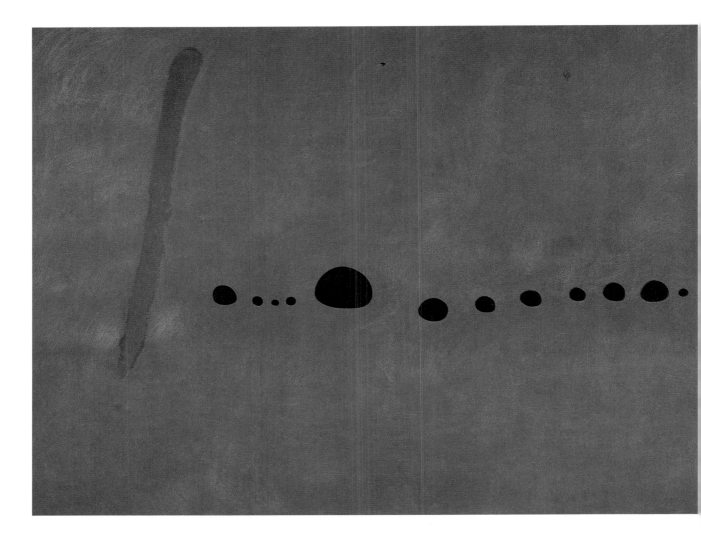

JEAN DUBUFFET

Cabinet Logologique, 8/1967–2/1969
Polyester resin, 137¼ × 275½ × 236¼″
(350 × 700 × 600 cm)
Fondation Jean Dubuffet, Perigny-Sur-Yerres

XXXI.
The End of Painting and Painting Since Then

THE FORMATION OF THE NEW REALIST GROUP IN 1960 BROUGHT ATTENTION TO THE widespread skepticism about art for art's sake and modernism — the notion that advanced painting should be devoted exclusively to the extension of the inherent abstract essentials of painting: surface and shape. Engaged in a transatlantic pop art dialogue, the New Realists, including Klein, La Villéglé and Hains, and Arman, aimed their work at a new media-educated audience in an openly commercial way. Superficially unsophisticated with regard to art traditions, their conceptual works urged a reconsideration of painting in the late twentieth century. Like the other members of the New Realist group, Martial Raysse (b. 1936) was determined to bring literal reality into art and thus relate art directly to modern life. Obsessed, as was his friend Alain Jacquet (b. 1939), with Old Master images of nude or seminude bathing women and with the advertising and film counterparts to these Venuses, Raysse composed works from mass media photographs, transferring them onto canvas with specially fabricated silk screens. The New York artists Robert Rauschenberg and Andy Warhol had used the same technique for their paintings beginning in 1962.

Raysse colored these "readymade" images with lurid acrylic paints. In many works, Raysse would extend his literalist style by adding real consumer objects such as beach balls and umbrellas. Relating these objects to his painted images, Raysse stresses the relative artificiality of real-life colors. For example, he might juxtapose a green painted area with a patch of artificial grass and then add a green neon light.

Arman constructed paintings from real objects in two modes: tantrums and accumulations. In the late 1950s he made a (tantrum) work by throwing a jar of paint against a canvas and in Duchamp fashion patiently gluing the glass pieces where they fell as a result of the impact. Obviously a parody of gestural abstract painting, this work anticipated Arman's interest in recycling cast-off objects. By 1958 he began to collect banal used objects by category (clocks, toy guns, radio tubes), keeping these accumulations in drawerlike boxes. When covered with a sheet of glass to make the accumulation exhibitable, the boxes acted as picture frames. Consequently, these assemblages look and function like pictures, in particular like abstractions based on repetitive brushwork. As if to stress his lack of interest in brushwork or even paint, Arman has created scores of accumulations of squeezed-out paint tubes, sometimes embedding them in polyester resin to create ultramodern monuments. Presenting store-bought paints as technological fossils, these witty works celebrate the end of painting as an up-to-date mode of expression.

Of course, Duchamp had abandoned painting as a form of expression for himself by 1918, and thereafter he pretended to concern himself with chess, wordplay, reproductions of his early works, and installations of exhibitions of his friends' works. In his opinion, artists would go underground in the future. In 1969, a year after the burial of his ashes in the family cemetery in Rouen, Duchamp assumed the role of "underground" artist literally, when a foundation announced the gift of a major "new" work to the Philadelphia Museum, where the majority of his other works were already on view. The enigmatic artist had worked on it in secret for the last twenty years of his life. Titled like a Dada geometry problem, *Given: 1. The Waterfall, 2. The*

Martial Raysse (b. 1936,
Golfe-Juan, Alpes-Maritimes)

Remember Tahiti in September 1961, 1963
Assemblage, 70⅞ × 66⅞ × 17¼″
(180 × 170 × 45 cm)
Louisiana Museum of Modern Art,
Humleback, Denmark

Illuminating Gas has at its core a hyperrealist sculpture of a naked spread-legged woman lying on a bed of twigs in a field. Presumably this was his "Bride" come to earth from her former abstract realm. Viewers can only regard this bizarre sculpture voyeuristically from behind an old door with two eyeholes for peeping. As a result of this limitation, the woman's identity remains a mystery, as does much else. The door barrier delimits Duchamp's three-dimensional work as a two-dimensional experience. Thus Duchamp, in the first artwork ever from beyond the grave, gave an object lesson in the frustrations that accompany the static-viewpoint convention of Western painting.

Duchamp had confessed a horror at repeating himself, but by the 1960s many young artists had come to realize that repetition lies at the heart of modern image-flooded civilization and that the possibility of pictorial originality for all artists has been exhausted. Duchamp was among the visitors in June 1967 to the Museé des Arts Décoratifs, where four young painters were staging a polemical exhibition stressing the possibility of art with minimal imagery. Each showed a square canvas. Daniel Buren (b. 1938) decorated his square with vertical stripes; the Italian-born Niele Toroni (b. 1937) covered his square with equally spaced, equally sized short brushmarks all in the same color.

Determined not to make egocentric one-of-a-kind artworks valued for the purported significance of a unique image, Buren and Toroni always repeat exactly the same motifs. Since

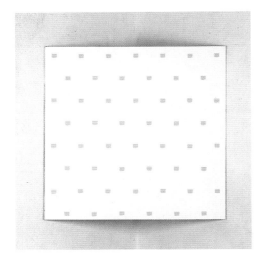

NIELE TORONI (b. ca. 1940, Muralto, Switzerland)

Imprints of Paintbrush No. 50, 1988
Oil on canvas, 78¾ × 78¾" (200 × 200 cm)
Collection Frac Limousin, Limoges

1965, Toroni has limited himself to the single motif of imprints made by a no. 50 paintbrush, spacing the imprints thirty centimeters apart. His apparent contempt for originality and virtuosity in art (in fact, his works are quite original, and he must apply his paint with Zenlike control) is combined with a sincere contempt for commodification. To avoid conventional art responses from viewers and collectors, Toroni does without conventional stretched canvases. Instead, he generally hangs his canvases directly against the wall, extending them onto the floor when the walls are too short. Arranged in an exhibition space, Toroni's hallmark paintings are extremely beautiful decorations in a tradition extending from the Middle Ages to Vuillard, Matisse, and Dubuffet. The repeated little marks measure and define the space they happen to occupy and thus invite the viewer to react to the space in conjunction with the art, to consider the immediate experience of looking at art rather than the unique visual lore associated with a particular art object. Of course, there is also a venerable tradition of repetition in modern art, from Satie's music to Gertrude Stein's prose ("Rose is a rose is a rose"), and Toroni's imprints oblige a viewer to ponder that tradition of regarding nearly identical inflections. Seemingly without other significance, Toroni's brushmarks define nothing less than the essential act of painting and thus urge appreciation for what it means to paint.

A brilliant theorist, Buren epitomizes the 1960s artist committed to exploring the original social dimensions of art, extending painting outside of its traditionally class-oriented private or institutional contexts to heighten public awareness and enjoyment. With obvious reference to La Villéglé and Hains, in 1968 Buren covered two hundred street posters with green and white striped paper. Simultaneously, he exhibited more of the striped panels at the Museum of Modern Art in Paris, stressing the continuity between art (museum) and nonart (street) contexts and audiences. He also hired people to walk through the city with striped panels on their backs to stress the freedom of art to present itself in static or kinetic situations without distortion of its aesthetic value. Although such complex works about painting could be documented with photographs, his work resides in the immediate experience, and that experience could hardly be treated as an art commodity in a conventional sense.

Over the years Buren has applied his stripes to intercity buses, sailboats, and even trains, demonstrating ways that art can intrude on and contribute to everyday life. For *Photo/Souvenir: Watch the Doors, Please*, conceived in 1980 for a specific spot in the Art Institute of Chicago, he covered the doors of railroad cars with his stripes. Visitors to the museum who looked out a window overlooking train tracks could see art outside the museum context. Of course, the striped doors appeared in the viewer's frame of vision only according to the train schedule, which Buren posted next to the museum window. Spectators had to synchronize looking at art with the facts of life. Installed only on a temporary basis, Buren's work nonetheless remains unforgettable for anyone who has experienced it, and in theory the work could be repeated: his idea, not any precious object, is the painting.

The unorthodox theories and projects of artists such as Toroni and Buren have parallels in the discontents with institutional powers that erupted into the May 1968 strikes and riots in France ultimately transformed the educational system and led to the election of a socialist government. In contemporary painting, this spirit of revolutionary change was manifested in the ideas of a group of artists who exhibited together in 1970 under the name Support-Surface. Contemptuous of the status of art in a modern society, these polemical artists devised strategies to subvert the art product and in theory to save art from complicity with the evils of modern life. For example, they agreed not to sign or date their works and to work with images that could be reproduced easily so that their ideas would be circulated freely. To free art from the special interests of investors and historical institutions, Support-Surface theory urged artists to work with impermanent materials and produce works in cumbersome formats with banal images. Moreover, many of these artists decided to give up stretchers and even canvas. Claude Viallat (b. 1936), the most successful member of the group, was an art teacher with a special interest in demonstrating new directions for students. His early works sometimes consisted of strings with knots, a way to organize space without subjugating it. Most frequently, Viallat works on coarse supports such as tarpaulins and awning canvas, using decorative repeat patterns in the spirit of Buren's stripes and Toroni's brush imprints. Regardless of their visual appeal from a 1990 perspective, it hardly seems that Support-Surface works have managed to escape or even subvert art world systems to any significant extent.

Museums in France, as elsewhere, have evolved to manage art movements designed to debunk their authority. Significantly, when the Georges Pompidou Center, a vast museum complex devoted to twentieth-century art, opened in Paris in 1977, its first exhibition was devoted to the career of Duchamp. Since the majority of Duchamp's works are in the Philadelphia Museum of Art, the French public had remained underinformed about one of the greatest modern French masters. Designed to reassert French authority in the modern art field, the Pompidou Center needed to reclaim him and thus make it clear that Paris accepted unconventionality in art as the essential condition for change and growth.

Like other modern museums, the Pompidou has been obliged to commemorate a paradox: Painting is dead, long live painting! Perhaps the West has reached a situation accepted for centuries in the Oriental art world, in which innovation has no special value in art and very traditional modes coexist with more progressive ones as options for modern artists. In 1990 a good deal of the best art in France takes the form of traditional painting. Many of France's best painters are in their sixties or even older, and although their recent works appear old-fashioned, when these painters developed their signature styles only a few decades ago, they were looked upon as radicals. During the twentieth century it has become the norm for artists to outlive their early acclaim. As they refine their unique expressive means, these artists inevitably fall out of the innovative mainstream featured in the topical art press. As a result, despite the unorthodox premises of their art, it is the ongoing commitment to painting as an expressive vehicle and as a sophisticated manual discipline that is most impressive about Eugène Leroy (b. 1910), Martin Barré (b. 1924), and the American-born Joan Mitchell (b. 1926).

Leroy applies paint without restraint, often squeezing it directly from the tube, covering his canvases with impasto layer on top of thick, oozing, crusted impasto layer. Sometimes he will work on a single painting for over a decade, allowing for the drying time between layers and for obsessive scraping out and rebuilding. Embedded in the physical paint, Leroy's figures are all but obscured, seeming to emerge from or to slip into a mineralogical state of nonentity. He prefers the predominantly earthy, autumnal colors used by Dubuffet in the 1950s for his texturologies, but throughout Leroy's paintings are veins of intense color that shimmer when light plays on the pocked surfaces. Whereas Dubuffet, Giacometti, and Rouault are the French painters closest to Leroy, Rembrandt is his hero. Leroy had gallery exhibitions even before World War II, but only in the 1980s did this reclusive painter finally gain a wider audience.

Barré, whose career got going in the late 1950s, is as much an advocate for simplicity of means as Leroy is for complexity. In his early works Barré tended to leave most of the canvas blank and apply short lines of color directly from the tube, often repeating one slight mark on opposite sides of the canvas to activate the sense of pictorial space. Even in his most minimal works there is always the implication of a triangle at odds spatially with the rectangular shape of the canvas. In the 1960s Barré applied diagonal lines to canvas with paint sprayed from a can. Limited by this dumb tool, Barré created works that appear to parody the precise minimal taste of the period with fuzzy, inept stripe patterns. His interest in pattern as one dimension of abstraction gives his easel-scale works of the 1970s and 1980s a very decorative look, but his complex manipulation of geometry as a vestige of perspective-oriented space is both more traditional and more challenging than are the environmental decorations of his contemporaries.

Joan Mitchell had established herself as one of the strongest second-generation New York abstract expressionist by 1955, when she met Riopelle in Paris and began an emotional relationship that would last until 1979. She moved to Paris in 1959, and a decade later she moved to the village of Vétheuil on the Seine, in the heart of Impressionism country. Generally working on the nearly mural scale initiated by New York artists around 1950, Mitchell paints in response to weather and landscape. While her favorite painter is van Gogh, she has inherited the realm of Bonnard. Master of a wide repertoire of brushstrokes, including splatters and drips, she is able to shift the scale and speed and the mood of space without a trace of effort. Each of her strokes has a shape that weaves it into and around the adjacent strokes to invent unique patterns that are like abstract narratives. It is her sense for color, however, that most sets Mitchell apart. Modulating space with flurries of a single color in different values, she fills her broad compositions with compelling light. In her most recent works, master painting survives in France, long after many painters had given up on painting as a lost cause.

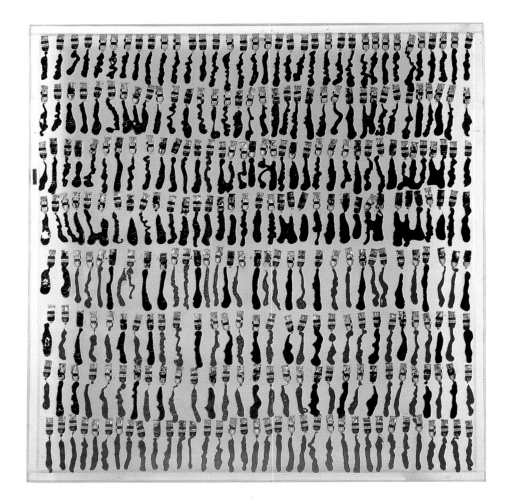

ARMAND FERNANDEZ, called Arman (b. 1928, Nice)

Black Tie, 1967
Accumulation of paint tubes and watercolor
in resin, 47 × 50″ (119 × 127 cm)
Private Collection, New York

MARTIN BARRÉ (b. 1924, Nantes)

Untitled (67–2–14), 1967
Oil on canvas, 27½ × 25½″ (70 × 65 cm)
Foundation Daniel Templon, Paris

EUGÈNE LEROY (b. 1910, Tourcoing)

    Couple, 1968
    Oil on canvas, 77 × 44½″ (195.5 × 113 cm)
    Edward Thorp Gallery, New York

MARCEL DUCHAMP

    Given: 1. The Waterfall 2. The Illuminating Gas,
    1946–1966
    Mixed media assemblage, 95½ × 70″ (242.5 ×
    177.8 cm)
    Philadelphia Museum of Art, Philadelphia
    Gift of the Cassandra Foundation

Daniel Buren (b. 1938, Boulogne-sur-Seine)

Photo/Souvenir: Watch the Doors, Please, Dates of
exhibition: 1980–1982
A work *in situ* and in motion as viewed from the
interior of The Art Institute of Chicago. The Art
Institute of Chicago, with the Permission of the
Regional Transportation Authority, the Illinois Central
Gulf Railroad, and the South Suburban Mass Transit
District

YAACOV AGAM (b. 1928, Rishon Letzion, Israel)

Salon Agam, 1971–1975
Musée National d'Art Moderne, Centre Georges
Pompidou, Paris

JOAN MITCHELL (b. 1926, Chicago)

No Birds, 1987–1988
Oil on canvas,
Diptych: 87½ × 156″ (222 × 396 cm)
Robert Miller Gallery, New York

Index

Credits